Makarand R. Paranjape is a widely published critic, poet, fiction writer and literary columnist. He is currently professor of English at Jawaharlal Nehru University, New Delhi. His latest books include *Another Canon: Indian Texts and Traditions in English*, *Altered Destinations: Self, Society, and Nation in India* and *Making India: Colonialism, National Culture and the Afterlife of Indian English Authority* (forthcoming).

ACTS OF FAITH
Journeys to Sacred India

Makarand R. Paranjape

HAY HOUSE INDIA
Australia • Canada • Hong Kong • India
South Africa • United Kingdom • United States

Hay House Publishers (India) Pvt. Ltd.
Muskaan Complex, Plot No.3, B-2 Vasant Kunj, New Delhi-110 070, India
Hay House Inc., PO Box 5100, Carlsbad, CA 92018-5100, USA
Hay House UK, Ltd., 292-B Kensal Rd., London W10 5BE, UK
Hay House Australia Pty Ltd., 18/36 Ralph St., Alexandria NSW 2015, Australia
Hay House SA (Pty) Ltd., PO Box 990, Witkoppen 2068, South Africa
Hay House Publishing, Ltd., 17/F, One Hysan Ave., Causeway Bay, Hong Kong
Raincoast, 9050 Shaughnessy St., Vancouver, BC V6P 6E5, Canada
Email: contact@hayhouse.co.in
www.hayhouse.co.in

Copyright © Makarand R. Paranjape 2012
who asserts the moral right to be identified
as the author this work

The views and opinions expressed in this book are the author's own and the facts are as reported by him, which have been verified to the extent possible, and the publishers are not in any way liable for the same.

All rights reserved. No part of this book may be reproduced by any mechanical, photographic, or electronic process, or in the form of a phonographic recording; nor may it be stored in a retrieval system, transmitted or otherwise be copied for public or private use – other than for 'fair use' as brief quotations embodied in articles and reviews, without prior written permission of the publisher.

ISBN 978-93-81431-35-1

Designed and typeset at
Hay House India

Printed and bound at
Rajkamal Electric Press, Kundli, Sonipat, Haryana (India)

Om Sri Satgurubhyo Namah

Contents

Acknowledgements	9
Prologue: The Open Door	13
Chapter 1: *Na Hanyate*	23
Chapter 2: Sacred India	33
Chapter 3: India's 'Truths'	58
Chapter 4: Pilgrims and Spiritual Travellers	75
Chapter 5: A Search in Secret India	83
Chapter 6: Travels through Sacred India	95
Chapter 7: A Passage to Tiruvannamalai	105
Chapter 8: Lessons from Svadhyaya	128
Chapter 9: Among the Swaminarayans	153
Chapter 10: 'The Hour of God'	180
Chapter 11: Ten Meditations on the Guru	196
Epilogue: Love Matters	208
Notes and References	223

Acknowledgements

I have incurred many debts in writing this book. The greatest of these is, of course, to the guru. As I say later in this book, the guru is an idea, or I should say, ideal, that transcends individuals. But 'he' is also a person and an institution. I bow to the guru who, owing to his infinite compassion, has taken so many forms ever to lead us from darkness to light. From life to life, not to speak of the several lives lived in one, have I felt this guiding presence in the fortunate encounters with many who helped me in my quest for truth. I offer my salutations, both to those who feature in these pages and to those who don't. Ultimately, the whole universe conspires to liberate you – as, indeed, it once did to bind you. All depends on your perspective and readiness.

Many of these chapters have appeared in earlier versions or portions in edited books and journals; some also began as papers in conferences or as talks. My thanks to the editors and publishers of the former and to the organizers and hosts of the latter for encouraging and nurturing these words. I reserve a special word of gratitude for Ashok Chopra, my publisher, who commissioned this book, and for Raghav Khattar for his painstaking copy-editing. This work, in its present form, owes much to their inputs, but all the errors and shortcoming are my own.

Many years ago when my novel *The Narrator* was published, unlike my usual practice of sending a copy to Yogi Ramsuratkumar, I avoided doing so. The Yogi, the 'mad beggar' of Tiruvannamalai, had established an unbreakable bond with me. When we had met, he said, 'This beggar has been waiting for you for a long time.' I knew, instantly, that it was the other way round: it was I who had been waiting to find him for ages. I am sure that without that meeting and subsequent connection, my life would have been incomplete. It was, by no means, a conventional guru-shishya relationship for I must confess that I could not implicitly obey his commandments.

Yet, he tolerated me, showering his love and grace, overlooking my vanity and stupidity. Now he asked why I had not sent him a copy of my

Acknowledgements

only novel. After some hesitation, I blurted out, 'I was a bit *ashamed*, Bhagawan!' He smiled at me quizzically. I realized instantly how foolish I was to think that I should hide my 'bad' side from him or that I should project myself as better than I was to secure his good opinion. So, taking courage in both hands, I stammered, 'Bhagawan, it has some . . . you know . . . indecent passages . . . !'

The Yogi laughed heartily. 'Did you hear that?' he turned to Devaki Ma, his disciple, eyes sparkling with merriment. 'It appears Makarand Paranjape has tried to write something . . .' he paused for a minute, then added in a higher pitch, '*sensational*, entertaining . . . perhaps, he wants to be *popular* . . .' again he laughed out loud. Ma also smiled. I looked down, mortified. Then, eyes blazing, he looked at me: 'Does not matter . . . It is Father's will. *Nothing* Makarand Paranjape writes will be devoid of spirituality . . . !' Again, he turned to Ma, saying a little more softly, 'It can't be otherwise, isn't it, Devaki?' Ma gave me a very sweet, sidelong look.

A strange kind of relief, tinged with some disbelief, swept through me.

Vijayalakshmi Ma, another of Bhagawan's closest disciples, in another context, once said, 'There is a monster in each one of us, straining to come out. The only question is whether we can tame it or let it take over.' My efforts to come to terms with my monster were often expressed in my writings. Therefore, not everything I wrote made me happy. Sometimes, it was like owning up to Frankensteins that one had inadvertently produced. But what to do? One had to offer up everything, good, bad and ugly to the fire of dispassion, doing one's best and letting go of the rest.

Justice Arunachalam, Yogi's spiritual successor and the present head of the Yogi Ramsuratkumar Ashram, told me: 'Many things are impossible for us, but Bhagawan makes them happen. Even though we are unfit or undeserving, we are made to do Father's work.' In spite of our unworthiness, our energies are harnessed to the greater cause. I would like to believe that this book is an example of such grace. For at every step of its completion, I have seen a hidden hand directing its outcome. In that sense, this book itself in an act of faith.

There should be no confusion about the subject position of its

Acknowledgements

author, though. I have no pretensions to spiritual realization. This is not the work of a person who has attained self-mastery or one who claims to guide the perplexed. Rather, it is a record of my struggles with myself, the help I received, and the path I trod. If it is useful to fellow-seekers or strengthens their faith, I shall consider my labours rewarded.

Makarand R. Paranjape

Prologue

The Open Door

I was reaching up to the box in the loft, groping inside without quite knowing what my hands were touching. On the verge of giving up, I pulled something out inadvertently, which fell to the floor. I stepped down, disappointed that I had not found what I was looking for. But suddenly I noticed what had fallen down. An envelope – and jutting out of it, a photograph. It was of Professor Girdhari Lal Tikku, or Giri as he used to be called, and me. The photo had been shot at the comfortable Tikku residence, 108 W. Mumford Drive, in Urbana, a small mid-Western university town, where I went to graduate school to do my Masters and PhD. Giri, looking very self-assured, had an arm around me. I fit quite snugly next to him, but the body language suggested a certain respect, even diffidence.

Giri was my teacher. Not just a professor whose courses I took but, I was convinced, a real guru. When I knew nothing of pursuing the spiritual life, he put *The Gospel of Sri Ramakrishna* in my hands.[1] That was almost 15 years before the photo and not long after our chance encounter in the huge foyer of the main library of the university. Though it was our very first meeting, he immediately began speaking to me with an unnerving familiarity, as if I were a well-known acquaintance. I, on the other hand, had considerable difficulty figuring out who he was. He said, 'Of course, everyone is here to study, to get a career, and so on, but tell me what is it that you really want?' I decided to take up his opening gambit, to play along: 'I want to know who I am.' He smiled, 'Ah, I may be able to help you there; as to your studies and career, that is a different matter.' Actually, he was very helpful in both, much more so than I had ever imagined at first contact. Yet the bond that developed between us was not professional – it was spiritual; it was a bond of love.

Prologue

Now, several years later, on the morning of the Indian Independence Day, 15 August 1995, I got a call from Professor Braj B. Kachru, another teacher of mine from the University of Illinois. The message was terse, 'I'm sorry to tell you that Giri passed away today.' I was too stunned to respond immediately. Professor Kachru added, 'He went peacefully, in his sleep. Rima (his wife) and the kids are ok.' Professor Kachru informed me that Giri had been diagnosed with 'The Big C' some months ago. I remembered that he had suffered from a variety of ailments in the last few years. In fact, while I was still at Urbana-Champaign, he had already undergone a triple-bypass surgery.

I recalled that time vividly. It was at the Carle Clinic that I went to visit him when he was still under intensive care. I was feeling miserable, but I wasn't sure if I should be sombre or cheery. My confusion must have been evident to him. The moment I sat down he smiled and said, in Hindi, '*Iss tarah muh nahin banatein* (Don't make such a long face).' The atmosphere lightened up immediately. He not only put me at ease, but showed me that commiseration or concern is not the same as passing one's own anxiety on the patient. He was still – and always – showing me the way.

A few years later in 1987, after I had returned to India and was teaching at the University of Hyderabad, Giri came to visit. It was a hectic trip. We also travelled together, taking an overnight train to Gulbarga University in the neighbouring state, where Giri delivered a university-wide lecture in Urdu – a language he hadn't spoken for years. He started a bit tentatively but was so successful in the end that he was mobbed by students for autographs. 'Knowing Persian helps,' he quipped modestly afterwards. On returning to Hyderabad, there was more academic hustle and bustle of a similar sort. In the middle of it all, suddenly, one morning, Giri was taken ill. He could not pass urine and was in great pain. I knew one of the leading urologists in Hyderabad and telephoned him immediately. He advised me to get Giri admitted to the Hyderabad Nursing Home where he was a consultant.

In those days, before the rise of medical tourism, Indian hospitals were not quite what they are today. The room Giri had was modest, with a grey–black slate floor and unpretentious furniture. It was not even air-conditioned. I could see from Giri's expression that he was not quite sure that this was the right place for him to be treated. But he did not say a word. As the treatment progressed, however, he became more and more satisfied, not only with the calibre of the medical attention he received, but also with the politeness and consideration of the staff, not to speak of the cleanliness of the premises. He told me later, 'The quality of medical treatment was actually very good. My room was swept and swabbed every day. This country has a great future. Most of all, the people are much more caring and considerate.' Giri recovered quickly. I had the unique opportunity of being of some assistance to him.

Before he returned to the United States, Giri had dinner one evening with Sarina, my wife, and me at our flat in Mehdipatnam, Hyderabad. After we had finished, he told me a story: 'Once, a holy man had fallen sick in the house of one of his disciples. The whole family nursed him with patience and devotion. They never complained or even regarded this duty as a burden. In due course, the holy man recovered and left his disciple's home. In a few months, the disciple's income doubled.' He then looked at me and smiled. I said, 'So should I expect a similar turn of fortune?' He laughed, 'Don't be too sure of that, but it is puzzling, isn't it, that I had to fall ill at your doorstep?'

While I had a permanent position at the University of Hyderabad, Sarina, at that time, was professionally rather unhappy. Despite two post-graduate degrees from the US, she moved from project to project, getting neither enough money nor due credit for her hard work, let alone a permanent position. She had begun to apply outside Hyderabad to get a job commensurate with her qualifications. Soon after Giri left, she appeared for an interview for a very good opening with a bi-national organization in New Delhi. Before the results were announced, I had a dream in which the director of the organization, whom I did not meet till much later, told me that she had selected Sarina. I woke up with a sense of great hope and happiness. The dream turned out to be true. Not only was Sarina's salary more than doubled, but she was professionally secured for life.

These and many other incidents flashed through my mind when I saw that photograph. I remembered that it was taken in the year 1993 – the last time I visited Giri. He and his lovely wife Rima had driven up to the nearest airport, Springfield, Illinois, to receive me. As we motored back through the flat prairies of Illinois, I felt flooded with exhilaration and peace. It was a beautiful, sunny summer day. Cruising down the smooth freeway induced a sense of freedom and expansion of being. Life seemed to be so good, so full of possibilities.

Giri and Rima were happy too, but seemed rather alone. Their children were away at graduate school, one finishing his PhD in engineering and the other pursuing graduate studies in California. Rima had put on weight and looked jolly. Giri was still reading new books, thinking new ideas, but publishing almost nothing. About 'professional' academics, he had a simple formulation, '*Yeh sab bakwaas hain* (All of it is nonsense).' But he really believed in and lived the life of the mind. Already a full professor for nearly three decades, mere careerism never held any attraction for him.

During that visit, perhaps the most precious experience was our early morning meditation in his prayer room. It was not really a room but a large walk-in closet in his bedroom, full of pictures of various Gods and Goddesses. Dimly lit but beautifully decorated, it had such wonderful atmosphere. The faint smell of incense always lingered there. I felt that worship, which is the soul's contact with the divine, is an intensely private, deeply personal activity. Of course, millions can also pray together, but that is not the same as a secluded, almost intimate contact with God. This was clear as we sat together to worship that day.

It was Giri who had first taught me how to meditate some years earlier. His formula was simple: tell all your senses that you're about to conduct some serious business; tell them that you will not be attending to them for a while, and that they should not try to draw you outward with their perceptions or sensations. After that, you turn inward, closing the doors and windows of the mind to the outside world. Once you are reasonably comfortable in a particular place, cleanse your inner being of negativity. Cleanse the space around you, starting with the room you are in. Then send out positive thoughts in all directions – may all beings be happy; may they all be free from afflictions; may their hearts be purified. Consciously transmitting your positive vibrations everywhere. Your meditation may now commence.

I remembered his instructions as we prayed together that morning.

Prologue

All the pictures of the Gods and Goddesses seemed to glow when we offered them flowers from Giri's home garden. He made me read the Lalitasahasraman, a sacred Hindu text containing a thousand names of the Divine Mother Goddess – the supreme power who directs and controls our lives. This was the great tantric text he had asked me to peruse when I had turned to him for spiritual advice in 1981. He said, 'Study this; it's sufficient. It has everything you need.' Since then, I have been reading the text with almost unbroken regularity, little realizing what it was actually doing for me. That morning, as I read, he anticipated the next name. It felt like such a significant act, as if our combined energies were going out to heal and hold the world. The whole room, and everything beyond it, reverberated with a powerful, affirmative pulsation. He had introduced me to the text and now, making me read it and repeat the names after him, he seemed to be reinforcing the initiation.

Yet Giri never acted as if he was my guru; he not even admitted to playing that role. What bound us was a tie of reciprocal affection. But this did not mitigate his directness, even hurtful candour. Once, for instance, he suddenly said, 'You won't make it; you are too earnest, too literal. Loosen up a bit. All of life is a game. Play it to enjoy it, without taking it too seriously.' He demonstrated this by always kidding. Once, for instance, when he was approached by an Egyptian foreign student to sign a political petition, he joked, 'Yes, if you give me two dollars!' The student was too shocked to respond and retreated after staring at him open-mouthed. I asked, 'Why *two* bucks?' He replied, 'One for you and one for me.' After all, he implied, he couldn't simply ignore me, now that I was actually with him.

Thus, he took an interest in me and became deeply involved in my life. I, in turn, was devoted to him, considering him my teacher both academically and spiritually. When I look back on the role Giri played in my life, I am certain that it was more than that of a friend, philosopher and guide. He was all those but much more. He supervised my PhD dissertation on 'Mysticism in Indian English Poetry', though he was neither my official supervisor, nor dissertation director. He served as a member of my doctoral committee and even defended me during the viva when another member commented sarcastically that some sentences in my dissertation sounded rather bombastic, if not pompous. Giri said, 'Makarand should be excused for getting a bit carried away now and then; after all, he was dealing with highly inspired mystics.' Everyone laughed. The crisis was averted. I scored a 'distinction', the highest possible grade on the dissertation defence. I was so immature, but Giri overlooked my faults and kept encouraging my inner growth as a spiritual aspirant.

One day, I happened to see an old photo of his, framed in silver, and tucked away in a corner over the fireplace in his living room. The man in it looked totally different, with dark, thick, almost curly hair, a tweed suit and a cigarette in is hand, standing next to other well-dressed people. 'Who is this?' I asked. He pointed at himself silently. The picture was taken when he was an Indian Foreign Service diplomat posted in Tehran. 'But,' I cried, 'it does not look anything like you!' 'Yes, it does not. That is me, but in a different life.' I looked at him wondering, 'You mean, one can have several lives in this, *one* life?' He laughed and said, 'Just you wait and see.' Somehow, I didn't quite like the sound of that. I thought to myself not so much that I would never change, but that whatever changes took place, they would only occur in me, in this one life that I had. Of course, I was proven wrong, not once, but twice over.

In fact, it was he who had set me on my great adventure into the varieties of modern Indian mysticism. I say varieties advisedly, not only because it echoes the title of William James's famous book *The Varieties of Religious Experience*, but also because, if nothing else, that was the one thing I understood at the end of my PhD. Spiritual journeys were always diverse, if not divergent. There is neither origin nor closure in the realm of the spirit. Not just that, there is perfect freedom of approach and no laws or dogmas can circumscribe or curtail this freedom. God, being infinite, may be found in countless ways and places. Notions of right and wrong are man-made. There is no absolute rule or regulation; the 'republic of the spirit' is a democracy, not a dictatorship. In it, each of us has to chart his or her own independent and unique course. No one can dictate or prescribe it for us.

Similarly, even the discourse of spirituality is neither unitary nor oppressive. The limitless, even frightening freedom of its myriad manifestations and paths was one of the most valuable lessons that

Giri taught me: the pluralism of spiritual pursuits, the openness and wideness of methodology, the utter heterodoxy and excitement of its twists and turns. The multiplicity at the heart of mysticism could actually be threatening or terrifying to many. No wonder they slip into the dogmatism of conventional religion with its rigid hierarchies and cunning priests. Or worse, turn to bigots, fanatics or religious terrorists.

From our very first meeting in 1981 near the main card catalogue of the library, I knew there was something special in our relationship. He had greeted me as if I were an old friend. I had never met him before; I didn't know who he was, nor had I properly introduced myself. But we plunged right into what seemed to be an older conversation. Where and when had this conversation begun, and would it ever end, I did not know.

Though I responded positively, I was guarded. I wanted to know the coordinates. Who was he? What did he want from me? Was he just being friendly like many Americans are, without any real feeling? I wasn't even sure that he was an Indian; because he was fair and had light eyes, he could as easily have been Middle Eastern or Latino. As if reading my mind, he introduced himself, telling me his name, saying he was a Kashmiri Pandit, and designation, which was professor of comparative literature. Later, I found out that he taught Persian, having lived in Iran for several years before coming the US. From the library, instead of going our separate ways, we actually walked straight to his office in the Foreign Languages Building.

What Giri impressed upon me a few days after we had met was that academics would go on, since I had to study towards a degree, but what he was really interested in were 'other, more fundamental questions'. He did not, of course, spell out what these questions were. All he said was that we should be after the *asli cheez* (real thing). Perhaps, he was a bit insecure about calling this pursuit 'spirituality' or something else, thinking that it might turn me off, as it had so many others. But unlike most people who avoided this sort of inquiry, I readily fell for the bait.

I was, as Henry David Thoreau had put it, 'simmering, simmering, simmering' and it was Giri who brought me to a boil. 'What should I read?' I asked him, still smarting from a question which the famous Indian author Raja Rao had put me when he visited our campus, 'What

Prologue

do you really want?' I found that, just like Ramana Maharshi's question, 'Who am I?' Raja Rao's question too had no easy answer. When I said that I had come to pursue a PhD in English, he said, 'Of course, but what do you – all of us – *really* want?' I was stumped for an answer. Dimly, I recognized that he possibly meant something concerning the ultimate aim of human life. But I felt ill-equipped to take that on. I thought that if I could read or connect with something, I would know a little better. So I asked Giri. Unhesitatingly, he took a copy of *The Gospel of Sri Ramakrishna* from his bookshelf and gave it to me. Mahendranath Gupta's account of the life, times and experiences of Sri Ramakrishna seemed to offer answers to both of the vexing questions I had been harbouring secretly for years. Who was I? And also, if I was the ego, then how could I be free of myself? Sri Ramakrishna, with great love and authority, convinces us that nothing else is worth striving for in this world except God. You may call it by any name, realization, enlightenment, liberation, gnosis or emptiness. But it is for this that we are born – nothing else, no one else. Though I forget this from time to time, I always return to it because of the absolute clarity with which I first saw in those days.

When I wanted to return to India after my PhD, Giri was the only one who encouraged me. He himself had wanted to go back and once come very close to it, but had to stay in the United States for the sake of his family. So sure had he been of leaving that he donated all his books to the University of Illinois Library, including a signed copy of Jawaharlal Nehru's *Autobiography*. He was also on the verge of buying a house in Nizamuddin West, an up-market colony in New Delhi. So when I told him that I was keen on going back to 'serve India', as I thought, quite romantically, I might do, he actually said, 'Good. *Yahi karna chahiye* (That is what you ought to do).' While others thought I was being foolish if not impractical, Giri believed in both India and me.

Many years later, I met Giri's guru Swami Ramananda after I had returned and settled down in India. This had been my sincere wish for a long time: to meet the guru of my guru. So when Giri informed that Swamiji was passing through Delhi, I did not want to miss the chance to have his *darshan*. I visited him at the New Delhi Railway Station, of all places. He was on his way from Jammu to Mookambika, a famous shrine of the Mother Goddess in her mute (*mooka*) form near Mangalore in South India. I would have been honoured to invite him to my house, but he was surrounded by zealous devotees, who wanted him all to themselves. While in transit, he had chosen to camp at the railway station. This was the only window of opportunity to see him. So, on the busy platform of the railway station I sat awhile at his feet. People were dropping fruit, flowers and other offerings all over him in their eagerness to tender devotion. It would have irritated one to no end, but he bore it sportingly, without the least trace of discomfort or irritation.

I had the chance to eat a couple of grapes that had rolled off over his cropped, grey head and fallen into my hands as *prasad* or sanctified offering. Later, a little less beleaguered in the railway compartment, he turned to me and said rather enigmatically, 'He (meaning Giri) is a big *chor* (thief). *Bahut bada badmash hai* (He's a really big rascal).' I blinked uncomprehendingly.

Swamiji said, 'Suppose I have one rupee, how can I divide it between two?'

'Give each 50 paisa, Swamiji,' I said without thinking.

'Suppose it's a coin that cannot be changed?'

'Give it to the one who can use it for both,' I replied.

Swamiji gave me a toothless smile. The conversation ended.

I have often wondered about the significance of those words. Did Swamiji have 'passage fare' only for one person, that is Giri, and here I was being smuggled in, towards the fag end of his (Swamji's) life, two for the price of one? I don't know. On my part, I was perfectly content that the reserved berth went to Giri. His crossing was sure to benefit me too, however intangibly. Swamiji himself left his body soon afterwards. He was buried at the Sadhu Ghat in Haridwar, a special area by the banks of the sacred river Ganga reserved for renunciates and ascetics. In a profound sense, I am still not entirely sure who my own guru – the person who holds the key to my spiritual identity – is. I have encountered other godmen, great mahatmas and sadhus; many of them were so distant that I could hardly relate to them, while others were more intimate than my own relatives. One of these, Yogi Ramsuratkumar of Tiruvannamalai, was someone whom I felt very close to. Yet it was

Giri, to all appearances an 'ordinary' householder, who guided me in a language I could understand and pointed me towards the journey to the Ultimate, long earlier, when I was just starting out.

In a sense, I owe this book to him because he opened the door to the great mystery that lies at the heart of the universe. Who are we? Where have we come from? Where are we going? What is the purpose of life? Such questions are behind most human endeavours and our responses to them have shaped civilizations. Giri also led me to believe that these questions assumed a special urgency in India which, since its earliest recorded history, has come to be identified not with a particular religion or creed, but with the eternal quest of the human race. It is not that spiritual searching is absent in other parts of the world, or even that other human endeavours are devalued in India, but can anyone deny that a man's spiritual longing has found its most enduring, most varied, most inspiring expressions in India? That is why it is here that we find a superabundance of spiritual striving and finding.

It is this spirit of India that I have tried to capture in this book. The different chapters offer vignettes of contemporary India where the profane and the sacred intersect. The object of the book is to show how the terrain of the sacred in India is varied, but ever open. Usually, it is the modern, secular and non-sacred which is seen as the champion of liberal values in our society, thus setting up what I consider a false secular-sacred dichotomy. Unfortunately, what we have in India is a struggle between 'hard' secularists and religious zealots, while what we need is a 'soft' dialogue between the best of both. This would mean a combination of two pluralisms – religious and secular – in alliance against two intolerances. This book suggests such an alliance through a series of textured readings of texts and journeys to places of pilgrimage. My purpose is to reach, both through personal experience and research, that 'India of the spirit'.

Chapter 1

Na Hanyate

It is said that faith can move mountains. But when mountains do not move, it is we who must move towards them, as the famous saying attributed to Prophet Mohammad suggests. At the beginning of our journeys to sacred India, unless we are already blessed with a deep and abiding conviction, we too will have to traverse the jagged terrain of doubt and despondency towards the mountain of faith and the sea of hope. This chapter, then, is about faith or, more specifically, about its survival against all odds. That is why the well-known phrase from the Bhagavad Gita, *'na hanyate'* – it does not die, applies here.[2] The passage containing this phrase in the Gita is about what does not die even when the body is killed. Similarly, this chapter is about the fortitude of faith, about that which persists even after the apparent death of faith.

Any way you look at it, the crisis of faith has loomed large over the modern world. One way to confront it is by re-examining those famous rotting corpses in the spiritual backyards of our literary imagination. There is, for instance, the corpse of Father Zossima in *The Brothers Karamazov* by Fyodor Dostoyevsky.[3] A priest, a monk, a holy man of the highest rank and a well-loved elder of the church, whose own life has been exemplary, Zossima's body is expected to preserve long after his death. There may be no church promulgation to this effect, but that is the popular belief. By the afternoon of the next day, however, the odour of corruption is all too evident, slowly seeping out of the chamber of death like an incubus. Even the most faithful followers of the deceased holy man cannot deny it. Why is God testing their faith, they wonder. Soon, tongues begin to wag. There is a minor rebellion brewing in the monastery. Zossima's teachings must be false, some of the doubters aver. Young Aloysha – the guileless, faithful, devoted

Aloysha, who so doted on Zossima – is perplexed too. When Ratikin tauntingly asks him, 'But, surely, you're not so upset because your old man is stinking the place out? You didn't seriously believe that he'd start pulling miracles out of the air?' all poor Aloysha can do is to reply, 'I did believe, I do believe, I want to believe!' Ratikin mocks him further, 'So, you're angry with your God now, are you?' Aloysha says with a sudden, wry smile, 'I haven't taken up arms against God, I simply don't accept his world.'[4]

Was the putrefying corpse of Zossima really a sign from the heavens? Did it symbolize the end of an older order of faith and belief? Did Dostoyevsky presage a new era of atheism and anarchy, an age in which horrible crimes would be committed in the name of history, an epoch of torture chambers, concentration camps, and genocides? As he himself wrote in a letter to Katkov, the editor of *The Moscow Herald*, 'Our socialists . . . are conscious Jesuits and liars who do not admit that their ideal is the ideal of the coercion of the human conscience and the reduction of mankind to the level of cattle.'[5] Yet, in his time, few supposed that Dostoyevsky was warning his country against the danger of the new, anti-religious ideologies that were invading Russia from Europe; even fewer understood that he was advocating a return to the orthodox national church of Russia as the answer.

Years later, after the demise of the Soviet Union and the dismantling of the Berlin Wall, Dostoyevsky's political perspicacity seems utterly breathtaking. Like the restoration of the Cathedral of Dormition in the Kremlin, the cobbled fortress and seat of Russian might for over 500 years. When they captured power, the Bolsheviks closed all churches, including this 'mother church' of Russia. From 1547 to 1896 all the coronations of the Tsars had been held here. How many reverses had it suffered, being burned, looted and damaged so many times. During the French occupation of Moscow in 1812, it had even been turned into a stable. But in 1991, a little before the fall of the Soviet Union, it was restored to the Russian Orthodox Church. Today, it is once again Russia's national shrine.

Did Dostoyevsky 'predict' all this – the revolution, the imposition of atheism, then the restoration of the church? Probably not. Nor did the 'devilishness' of Stalin exactly resemble that of Stavrogin, the 'hero' of his novel *The Devils*. While Stavrogin's was an inner, moral corruption, Stalin created a system which could truly be considered diabolical. Indeed, it was on seeing the smooth, white, embalmed hands of Stalin as he lay in state in his coffin, that Gabriel Garcia Marquez was inspired to create his dead dictator in *The Autumn of the Patriarch*, the amalgam of all the despotic rulers of South America. In this novel on the unbearable solitude of power, Marquez's unnamed dictator of an unnamed Caribbean country is a fantastic creature – a compound monster who lives an impossibly long life, has the power of life and death over his people, and even sells the Caribbean Sea to his American 'gringo' patrons. This satire on power is not just funny, but grotesque and frightening.

That is why, some time or the other, most of us have cried out in the anguished and desperate tones of Goodman Brown, 'My Faith is gone.' In the story 'Young Goodman Brown' by Nathaniel Hawthorne,[6] Brown, against the admonitions and pleas of his newly wedded wife, also called Faith, has ventured into the forest on a secret and shameful errand. He has followed a familiar figure, perhaps the devil himself, who in fact, resembles his own father. On the way, he is astonished and frightened to see such personages as Goody Cloyse, who taught him his catechism, and Deacon Gookin, the very image of probity and piety, also hastening to the witches' sabbath. Not only are a great many of the good, decent and respectable folks of New England society there, but even someone who resembles the governor's wife. And yet, Brown believes that he can resist the Evil One: 'With heaven above and Faith below, I will yet stand firm against the devil.' But in the multitude of saints and sinners in the forest clearing, he thinks he hears the voice of his wife. 'Faith!' he shouts, in a voice of agony and desperation; and the echoes of the forest mocked him crying, 'Faith! Faith!' as if all bewildered wretches were seeking her in that wilderness. Just when Brown thinks he's imagined it all, down comes fluttering through the night a pink ribbon, such as Faith had worn that very evening. 'My Faith is gone!' Brown cries, 'There is no good on earth; and sin is but a name. Come, devil; for to thee is this world given.'

What happened to Brown in the forest? In his dark night of the soul, was the world revealed to him in its true, fallen state? Or did he simply have a bad dream, a nightmare in which he found evil lurking deep inside his own breast? Whatever it was, it changed him forever. When he returned to his village at the end of the story, he was no longer the carefree and naïve young yeoman who went into the forest on an unholy errand: 'A stern, a sad, a darkly meditative, a distrustful, if not a desperate man did he become from the night of that fearful dream.' Having seen evil within himself, he begins to see the whole world as fallen. He cannot let go of evil, but clings to it tenaciously, projecting it outwards upon everyone else. Regarding everything around him as fallen, corrupt and wicked, he dies a sad, lonely man whose 'dying hour was gloom'.

This powerful allegory by Hawthorne is, ultimately, about the 'discovery' of original sin. The Puritan mindset, obsessed by it, was unable to conquer or transcend its sense of doom and gloom. Even the message of Christ, promising redemption through love, could not overcome the profound Puritan awareness of the fallen state of all existence. Perhaps, these early American settlers were too literal and too reductive to allow the coexistence of contraries. Constructing their world in terms of binary oppositions: God/Satan, white/black, good/evil, virtue/sin, heaven/hell and so on, they denied the grey, the ambiguous and the doubtful. In their efforts to device a world of religious certitude, they simplified reality to a formula. Armed with such a ready reckoner, they assaulted life with enormous confidence and vigour. Their successes were great, so were their failures. But they lacked the negative capability to negotiate or hold contradictions. To them faith was a matter of obedience, of submission, of utter lack of choice. Just as there was no escape from original sin, grace too was irresistible – but only for the elect, the chosen. Faith was a deadly serious business, a matter not only of life and death, but of everlasting life and eternal damnation. No wonder that even today, the vast hordes of believers, the huge flocks of the faithful, so easily veer towards fanaticism and fundamentalism. The unattractive opposite of this faithfulness is the faithlessness, nihilism, extreme scepticism and alienation of the modern condition. Here, God is dead and man is condemned to be free. But there is little to comfort us in such faithlessness either. With its extreme scepticism and anomie, it leaves us gasping for some foothold, some solace in this world or the next.

Between these two extremes, is there a choice, a third way, a different path?

Away from Europe and America, in the remote Brahmin *agrahara* or village of Durvasapura in U. R. Anantha Murthy's *Samskara: A Rite for a Dead Man*,[7] there is another rotting corpse. The 'anti-Brahmin' Naranappa suddenly dies, leaving his Brahmin community in disarray. The latter did not know what to do with Naranappa when he was alive; in his death, he poses an even bigger challenge to the *agrahara*: 'Alive, Naranappa was an enemy; dead, a preventer of meals; as a corpse, a problem, a nuisance.'

Naranappa has broken every rule in the book. He has been a meat-eater, a wine-bibber, a fornicator; he has kept a prostitute in his house, fished from the sacred temple tank and has thrown the ancestral holy *saligrama* or sacred stone into the river. He has vowed to destroy Brahminism. Now, in his death, his threat seems to have come true. Even the learned and saintly Praneshacharya doesn't know what to do with the body. Naranappa's death rites have to be performed, but who will carry them out? Naranappa has no children and though he has renounced Brahminhood, Brahminhood hesitates to renounce him. Praneshacharya cannot find the answer to this dilemma in any of the ancient books. He fasts and prays before Maruti, the village deity, but to no avail.

Instead, on his way back to the village, he stumbles into Chandri, Naranappa's concubine. Before he realizes what is happening, they couple in the forest clearing. At midnight, the ascetic Praneshacharya wakes up: 'A night of undying stars, spread out like a peacock's tail . . . green grass smells, wet earth . . . and the smell of a woman's body-sweat. Darkness, sky, the tranquillity of standing trees.' The acharya, nearly forty, married out of choice to an invalid for almost 24 years, knows a woman for the first time in his life. Is it all a dream? The experience has been transformative, but when he wakes up the next morning, Praneshacharya feels like a man lost to himself: 'For the first time, a desolation, a feeling of being orphaned, entered his inmost sense.' Without knowing it, he has now become akin to Naranappa, his dead, demonic adversary. He remembers a Sanskrit chant, 'I am sin, my work is sin, my soul is sin, my birth is in sin.' What should he do? How should he face the Brahmins of the *agrahara* longing to hear his verdict?

The starving Brahmins, waiting for their leader, present a sorry spectacle. Vultures and crows, birds of ill omen, seem to have invaded their village. The poor villagers strike the gongs and blow their conches to ward off the scavenging birds. The din and clamour can be heard in the neighbouring villages who, ironically, think that the pious Brahmins of Durvasapura are at their daily worship and rituals again. But, unbeknownst to them, a terrible fate awaits the *agrahara*. Naranappa has brought the bubonic plague to their idyllic, little village. There are dead rats everywhere. And one reeking corpse, which they don't know what to do with.

Clearly, Naranappa's festering body is a symbol of the larger malaise that threatens to engulf the Brahmin village. It has brought the plague of faithlessness to this brotherhood of the chosen. Even their leader, the saintly Praneshacharya, is nonplussed. He doesn't know what to do. Worse, he finds refuge and solace, quite accidentally, in the arms of Naranappa's mistress. Neither Praneshacharya nor the other Brahmins of the village realize what has actually happened. The shadow of the Black Death has fallen upon them.

If anyone has her bearings, it is Chandri – the low-caste, 'fallen' woman who has been Naranappa's keep for ten years. While the Brahmins are fasting on account of the pollution caused by Naranappa's death, she walks to the plantain grove and feeds herself. She nurses and comforts the poor, starving and distraught Praneshacharya when Maruti gives him no answer. On her return to the village, she heads straight for Naranappa's house. Instantly, she realizes that what lies there, more than anything else, is a dead body that must be attended to: 'That was not her lover, Naranappa. It's neither a Brahmin nor Shudra. A carcass. A stinking, rotting carcass.' Acting swiftly, she enlists the help of a Muslim friend of Naranappa's. Together, they cremate the body, without the knowledge of the confused, suffering Brahmins.

I think we should follow Chandri's example. Good faith soon becomes bad faith. When that happens, it assails us like a decomposing corpse. We must then do what is demanded of us – cremate the corpse of the old, broken faith and dive into the vast ocean of truth. Simply speaking, there are no guarantees in this world: God may fail us, the guru may fail us, and we may fail ourselves. Our job is to confront and face the truth, the reality of our existence, and not to believe in half-truths and half-lies. Faith is not about dwelling in the Elysian Fields of comforting illusions, but about swimming in a whirlpool of discomforting truths. It involves an engagement with life, with people, with reality. There is no safe enclosure, insulated from the depredations of life. If we bind ourselves to doctrines or dogmas, we shall be forced like the Brahmins of Durvasapura, though the incursion of the death from the outside, to break out of our self-imposed confinement. Faith is about being free and fearless, not about trying to hide behind doctrines to escape from suffering.

To understand the mystery of faith, we have to learn a fundamental lesson. Faith *in* something – anything – is bound to be transient and limited. It is prone to error, and is susceptible to decay and death. The *objects* of faith, no matter how cleverly we define them, are always imperfect. An imperfect object cannot sustain a perfect faith. The deeper reason for this difficulty will be clearer when we shift our attention to the *subject* of faith. This subject, or the person who undergoes the crisis of faith, is itself unreliable, fickle, transitory, and ultimately, insubstantial. It seeks to perpetuate its regime of separateness by identifying with something that is more reliable and less transient than itself. But no matter what it invents, that invention will bear the taint of its inventor, and will have to share the latter's partiality and dissatisfaction. As embodied beings, how can we overcome this problem of inadequacy, of incompleteness?

It is only when faith is reposed not *in* something or the other, but begins to manifest itself *as* the very medium of our existence – the essence of our being – that it becomes meaningful. This is faith as a way of life, as the basis of living. This kind of faith is not necessarily unwavering or unreasoning. Nor is it blind or absolute. It is neither unquestioning belief, nor is it a system of beliefs or dogmas. It is closer to a confidence, a trust, a reliance, not *in* something, but *as* a sort of commitment to the truth, regardless of the circumstances or consequences. Truth, which is *what is*, which is not an idea or a thought, but the very essence of existence. True faith is nothing more or nothing less than cleaving to truth. It is sustained by awareness and openness to the ever-changing, ever-flowing river of life.

The Sanskrit word for faith, or something akin to it, is *shraddha*. The Bhagavad Gita has many passages extolling the virtues of *shraddha*. Without *shraddha*, Krishna says, true knowledge is not possible: '*Sraddhavam labhate jnanam tat-parah smayatendriyah/jnanam labdhva param santim acirenadhigacchati*' (4.39) or 'One who has deep faith gains divine knowledge, being full of zeal and devotion to it, and endowed with the mastery of the senses. Having attained that knowledge he is soon established in supreme peace.' Here faith is seen as the prerequisite for the knowledge which brings peace. Faith is therefore something that prompts right perception and action.

But it is in one of the creation stories of the early Vedic lore that we find a really fascinating account of *shraddha*. In this myth, Shraddha and Manu are the progenitors of humankind. Manu, or the one endowed with the mind, is the father, while Shraddha, or faith, the mother. Shraddha is the daughter of Kama or the life-principle. Kama is not just desire or expectation, but the creative force which seeks to express itself through life. It is that power, like the primal energy, which is responsible for all activities, all becomings. That is why, in Jaishankar Prasad's great epic *Kamayani*, Shraddha – the eponymous heroine of the tale – is named Kamayani, or the daughter of Kama. *Shraddha* or faith is thus the determination of the life force to manifest itself. That, combined with the conscious mind, makes up the human being.

This beautiful myth – making faith the daughter of desire – not only rehabilitates the latter but gives a new meaning to the former. The mind-endowed man (*manu*) is yoked to desire or will (*kama*); from their union is born trust (*shraddha*). Faith, born of intelligent desire, is necessary for life to prevail over death. It is nothing other than a profound trust in the ways of the universe. The myth contains a deep truth, which is that faith is natural to the human condition; we humans are creatures of faith. It is a part of the design of creation itself. There may be an individual defeat or death, but not a collective end to human aspirations. Nature, careless in her plenitude, allows all kinds of experiments, permutations and combinations. Through every possible setback or obstacle, she persists. Ever and anon; always. Such is her faith. We, born of her, must also keep our faith in the infinite possibilities of the universe.

Faith, then, is native to us. Life itself would perish without it. It informs every action of ours; it moves us in everything we do. It is faith that leavens our spirits to rise, to grow, to evolve. It is faith that motivates all our fumbling, groping and reaching out. Faith, like life, is indestructible. It is not found in something or someone – rather, it is the very essence of our being. We mustn't therefore worry about losing faith. It is anterior to any gain or loss; it is one with life. As long as life persists, so long will our faith last in one form or another. To have faith in the ways of the cosmos means to trust the force that has brought us into existence. It is, simply speaking, to go with the flow.

Yet, a part of me cannot avoid taking cognizance of the flip side of faith – extreme distress and suffering. 'Be a lamp unto yourself,' the Buddha told a grieving Ananda on the eve of his (the Buddha's) death – the *mahaparinirvana* or the great, final liberation. In anguish, Ananda had asked the Tathagata, 'Now what will become of us? Who will guide us and point the way to our liberation?' The Buddha consoled him thus, 'Be a lamp unto yourself – *atto deepo bhava*. Do not depend on others; do not rely on authority; examine for yourself what the right course is. Find the truth by your own inner light. Your liberation is in your own hands; take responsibility for yourself.'

This is one kind of message in spiritual life. The other kind seems to be the opposite: only true and perfect surrender makes you worthy of grace. Faith alone transforms us; without it, we are useless, like dried up twigs, fit only for burning. Both positions, on closer examination, do not appear to be all that far apart or opposed to one another. Both imply faith, but in the first case, the faith is in oneself – in one's own capacity as a moral agent. In the second instance, faith is reposed in someone else – superior, wiser and steady – who takes responsibility.

The spiritual life is no bed of roses; rather it is, to use another metaphor, like walking on the razor's edge. I respect those whose faith is strong, who trust in God, guru or some ideology, who, moreover, live according to their values and commitments. I also respect those who question certitude, who are doubters and sceptics, who seek only the truth, not any illusion that masquerades as truth, who take responsibility for their own lives to the best of their abilities. Faith which is never tested is no faith at all; faith for which one doesn't put one's life on the line is not worth holding on to; faith that comes too easily will not stand the stress of life. Only a faith based on recognition, understanding, clarity of mind and direct apprehension of reality will remain steadfast in adversity. Such a faith is fearless and free, not timorous and fettered.

Chapter 2

Sacred India

That is the eternal Asvattha tree whose roots are above and whose branches below. That is verily the pure, that is Brahman, and that is also called immortal. In that rest all the worlds; and none can transcend it. Verily this is that.

– Kathopanishad (6.1)

The Journey

Many years ago, I was in a train from Hyderabad to Delhi. After I had taken my seat in my air-conditioned compartment, I saw a sadhu enter. I wondered if he would sit next to me. Slightly nervous, I braced myself for that possibility. It was not that I had anything against holy men. Only that they were *different*. I wasn't sure how to conduct myself in front of them. My hunch was right; he came and sat in front of me. He was dressed in bright orange robes and had a companion to look after his needs. Gradually, the sadhu and I got to know each other.

As we spoke, the sadhu, for the most part, praised India and its 'glorious culture'. I found some of this eulogizing hard to swallow, considering the huge problems that we face, both as a nation and as individuals. In fact, in those days before the great economic boom and globalization, India's future didn't look very bright.

'Swamiji, what makes you think so highly of India when all this poverty, disease and underdevelopment stare us in the face?' I asked him.

He counter-questioned me, 'If that is the sole truth of India, then why is it that people from far-off "advanced" countries come here?'

'But, that's only a few,' I responded. 'The majority are quite happy where they are.'

'If you meet them, they say they want to find the meaning of their lives. If their system was perfect, why would even those *few* come here, again and again? Tell me, why this attraction? Could it be because this country offers something they don't have?' he asked.

'But, Swamiji,' I protested, 'so many Indians, in fact, some of our best, leave to go abroad each year. How do you explain *that*? Obviously, we don't have all the answers, do we?'

'That's easy to explain,' he shot back, 'but for that you need to know what happens before we're born.'

He paused dramatically. I waited, curious to hear what he would say next.

'You see, when we all go "upstairs", we realize how we have wasted our lives pursuing useless things. We are full of regrets for our sins of commission and omission. Then, in the world of the dead waiting to be reborn, we suddenly grasp what the real purpose of life is. So, when we get another chance we want to do it all differently.

'Over there, in the antechamber of the waiting room where our next birth is allotted, there is a great clamour for India. Why? Because we know that it will make our sadhana, our spiritual practice, easy. India is the land of dharma. Here, seeking God is a way of life. So it's easy to be spiritual here. Just living here is enough for you to make *some* progress. Elsewhere, there are far too many distractions...'

'Perhaps, Swamiji, that's why our population is increasing so much,' I said rather irreverently, 'after all, everyone wants to be born in India.'

He laughed easily. 'But, my dear man, the story doesn't end there. No sooner are we born than we forget all our intentions and resolutions. We get all caught up looking for money and the good life, and run off to the United States, England, Germany, the Middle East, Singapore, Australia or where have you.'

That night, lulled to sleep by the rhythm of the train, the sadhu and his companion on the other side, I reflected on the conversation. I suddenly realized that I did not know of anyone, not a single person, who had left India to pursue dharma or find some sort of spiritual truth. Everyone who went abroad did so only to improve his or her standard of living, to make money, or earn success or fame. The reasons for leaving India were largely material, not spiritual.

Consequently, I understood that for those who wished to explore spirituality above all things else, India might naturally be the best place on earth. Living in the sacred realm of India would be like living at the centre of the universe – that still, unmoving point from which everything is projected outwards in beguiling shapes and colours, making up our world of names and forms.

Choosing India

The most important insight I derived from my chance encounter with the sadhu was that it is not enough to be born in India. Though this in itself is a great spiritual blessing, it is not sufficient. You need to go beyond the fact of birth – you must *choose* India. But, to choose India, you have to first *know* India. Only a deep inquiry reveals that India is much more than a physical territory. It represents a worldview, a philosophy, a way of life.

What *is* it then that India represents? To appreciate this, let us go back to the Vedas, the oldest scriptures of India. Of course, there are a lot of people who don't know or care about the Vedas at all. This tradition of rejecting the Vedas is as old as the Vedas themselves. Such rejection of the Vedas need not, therefore, alarm us.

To me, the Vedas do serve the purpose of providing the basic orientation of our civilization. As Sri Aurobindo observes, 'If we would understand the essential spirit of Indian civilization, we must go back to its first formative period, the early epoch of the Veda and the Upanishads, its heroic creative seed-time.'[8]

The majority of Indians are not concerned with the antiquity of the four Vedas – Rig, Sama, Yajur and Atharva – even though some aver that they were compiled around 3000 BC, making them at least 5,000 years old. In fact, they are some of the oldest compositions known to humankind. It is believed they were not written by human beings but heard or apprehended by the refined and highly purified minds of our ancient rishis or sages. So the Vedas are both 'timeless' and *apaurushiya* or impersonal; what they contain does not depend on any individual or collective notion of authorship or authority.

Except for the Buddhists and the Jains, the Vedas are revered by all traditional schools of thought in India. Many modern Indians accept other sources of authority, such as the Guru Granth Sahib, or even capitalism or Marxism. But the Buddha, Mahavira, and later, Nanak, did not oppose the Vedas. What they condemned were harmful rituals, authority of the priests, and other corrupt practices such as animal sacrifices. As Swami Prabhavananda says, 'The teachings of the Buddha do not contradict the spirit of the Vedas but are in entire harmony with it; and the same is true of the teachings of Mahavira, founder of Jainism.'[9]

Perhaps this is a 'Vedantic' view, and some Buddhists and Jains will claim a total variance between their doctrines and ours. Indeed, some radical Sikhs have done the same in recent years, though I myself am convinced that the teachings of the Sikh gurus are not different from that of the several mystics, sages and saints of medieval India. Many of our modern spiritual masters like Sri Ramakrishna or Ramana Maharshi, of course, do not consider their message as contrary to the Vedas.

What, then, are these Vedas? They are a collection of highly complex and varied texts. They consist of four sections: the Samhitas, the Brahmanas, the Aranyakas and the Upanishads. The Samhitas are collections of mantras or hymns, addressed to specific deities such as Mitra, Varuna, Indra and Agni. The Brahmanas are concerned with more mundane activities such as sacrificial rites, duties and codes of conduct. The Aranyakas or forest books are also full of directions concerning rites, ceremonies and rituals. They supplement and correct the Brahmanas, going beyond them into the inner meanings of such observances. Finally, the Upanishads, which means 'sitting near', are about spiritual knowledge or the truth about the ultimate reality.

Though the Vedas, strictly speaking, are thus ancient anthologies, highly diverse and complex, the word Veda itself means knowledge or gnosis. As Swami Prabhavananda explains, 'The term Vedas, as used by the orthodox, not only names a large body of texts composed in times indefinitely remote, and handed down generation after generation to our own day, but in another sense stands for nothing less than divine truth itself, the inexpressible truth of which the Vedic texts are of necessity but a pale reflection. Regarded in this second aspect, the Vedas are infinite and eternal.[10] It is therefore obvious that the Vedas do not refer only to specific texts, but to the eternal knowledge itself. This knowledge is essentially knowledge of the 'self', of ourselves, and our world, which is also a part of ourselves. This knowledge is both old – very ancient – and very new – quite contemporary. It renews itself and needs to be refreshed generation after generation. It signifies not authority, but truth, the never ending human quest for it, and for higher and higher levels of its realization here on earth.

The Vedas are also knows as *shruti*, that which is heard or apprehended directly. This is another reason why the Vedas can by no means be restricted to the set of texts which they refer to. As Swami Prabhavananda says, 'A revealed truth is a direct experience, and as such it must be in the same category as the Vedas.'[11] The Vedas, therefore, resist any foreclosure of meaning. In fact, they are perhaps the only sacred texts in the world which assert time and again that Truth is greater than the Vedas themselves. As Swami Vivekananda says, 'It is the Vedas alone that declare that even the study of the Vedas is secondary. The real study is "that by which we realise the unchangeable".'[12] In other words, self-knowledge, creation or realization is even more important than revelation. It is not somebody else's knowledge or truth that will liberate us, but what we strive and secure for ourselves.

Given the system of traditional Indian epistemology, even vast bodies of knowledge can be encapsulated in pithy utterances or memorable phrases. Thus, the four *mahavakyas* or 'great sayings' exemplify the ultimate spiritual truth of the Vedas. These four statements are confirmed time and again by the entire subsequent history of our spiritual endeavours. They are: *Tat tvam asi* or That Thou Art (Chandogya, xi–xv); *Aham brahmasmi* or I am 'Brahman' (Brhadaranyaka, I.iv.10); *Prajnanam brahma* or Consciousness Is 'Brahman' (Aitareya, III.i.3); and *Ayam atma brahma* or This Self Is Divine (Brhadaranyaka, II.5). These great sentences assert the oneness of the Self and God, or of the *atman* and *Brahman*, or *jiva* and Shiva. That is to say that we are all divine, immortal and free, even when we are human, mortal and embodied. All these utterances assert that the ultimate truth is non-dual.

A lot of Indians, especially the Hindus, know this intellectually. These *mahavakyas* are actually telling us that we already are everything that we seek to become! We may worship as many Gods as we please, but we ourselves are divine. Other religions tell us that we have been made in the image or likeness of God or that we are His chosen people; the Hindu religion says that we are ourselves of the nature of *satchitananda*, or existence–consciousness–bliss.

It follows that the purpose of life is to attain this realization, not just mentally but as a fact of consciousness. It is India which proclaims this gospel through its numerous philosophies and traditions. It teaches us that all of us are one, regardless of our differences; it also enjoins upon us to achieve a harmonious co-existence with nature. Ultimately all are related and interconnected, and partake of the same ground of being. Choosing India, thus, does not mean that one must stay confined within its geo-political boundaries; it means to accept a particular worldview or way of life wherever we might be.

India's Quest

In *The Meaning of India*,[13] Raja Rao, the well-known novelist writes, 'India is not a country (*desa*); it is a perspective (*darsana*).' The word *darsana* is important because it is the Indian word for philosophy; it also means experience, vision, perspective, insight and outlook. And what *darsana* does India embody? 'Absolute, non-dual consciousness' according to Raja Rao. Even if there was no India in a physical, material sense, India as an idea would have always existed. As Raja Rao puts it, 'India has no enemies. She only has adversaries ... [and she] ... has to turn defeat into victory.'

If India's quest were to be summarized in one sentence, it would be for the Truth – for moksha, nirvana, mukti, ultimate reality, God, Shiva, *parabrahman*, *kaivalya*, Allah, Om, or its equivalent, depending on which tradition one follows. In the Adi Parva of the Mahabharata, when her husband Dushyanta refuses to accept her and her son, Shakuntala admonishes him for straying from truth: 'There is no virtue equal to Truth: there is nothing superior to Truth. O king, Truth is God himself; Truth is the highest vow.' A heavenly voice confirms the veracity of Shakuntala's words. Her son Bharata, the famous and just monarch who ruled for many decades, gives his name to India, which to this day is called Bharat. What Shakuntala said in this ancient text was echoed by one of India's greatest men, often called the Father of the Nation. Mahatma Gandhi also famously said, 'Truth is God.' No surprise, then, that the official motto of the Republic of India is the ancient Vedic declaration *satyameva jayate* – truth alone triumphs.

But, ultimately, not just India, but the entire universe, sentient and non-sentient, in its own infinitely rich and diverse ways, also seeks the Absolute. That, I think, is what the Buddha meant when he said that the whole universe is on fire. Again, to quote Raja Rao, 'There can be no world without duality, yet there can be no peace in duality.' Duality is primordial unhappiness (*dukkha*). Whatever exists experiences this *dukkha*, which is the very essence of duality. Duality or two-ness implies separation from the source. Everything that has individuality is therefore separated, ego-bound and *vibhakt* (divided), and seeks self-transcendence – in dissolution or union – as the means to regain its lost wholeness.

But if everyone and everything seeks the same 'thing' that India seeks, what makes her different?

The difference is that it is in India that this seeking has become self-conscious, reiterated generation after generation, over the centuries. Not just that, one might even say that India has not only sought, but *found* the Absolute. There is a prevalent Buddhist belief that if the world is to be saved from destruction, the inspiration for the radical transformation in consciousness must come from India. It was no accident, then, that the Dalai Lama sought refuge in India when the lamp of *dhamma* was in danger of being extinguished by the Chinese invasion. Indeed, several religions from alien shores have found here a most suitable and hospitable ground for their spiritual flowering. Mother Teresa's presence in India was the symbol of Christian charity and piety. Similarly, Jews and Parsis have sought and found a safe haven in India. More recently, the Bahais though persecuted in their ancestral land, Iran, have built their largest shrine, the world famous lotus temple, in New Delhi.

When Islamic rulers of various hues and nations invaded India from the twelfth century onwards, India responded by Indianizing Islam, giving a hospitable welcome to numerous Sufi lineages. Around the same time, the flavour of Hinduism itself changed; one great *bhakta*, or God-mad saint, after another walked the length and breadth of the land –Allama Prabhu, Akka Mahadevi, Lal Ded, Jnaneshwar, Narsi Mehta, Nanak, Namdev, Tukaram, Tulsi, Kabir, Mira, Dadu, Raidas, Shankaradev and so on. The southern traditions of devotion, springing from the lives and works of saint-poets of Tamil Nadu, the *alvars* and the *nanayanars*, are, of course, even older. But, from the twelfth and thirteenth century onwards, tide after tide of *bhakti*, or fervent love of God, swept the land right up to modern times, to Sri Ramakrishna himself. Finally, where Islam was most oppressive and intolerant, India produced a new, eventually militant religion, Sikhism.

When Western modernity challenged India, it once again responded by asserting the primacy of dharma. A galaxy of heroes, sages, saints and savants have walked the pages of Indian history over the last 150 years: Rammohan Roy, Shri Swaminarayan, Sri Ramakrishna, Swami Vivekananda, Sai Baba of Shirdi, Dayananda Saraswati, Rabindranath Tagore, Mahatma Gandhi, Ramana Maharshi, Sri Aurobindo, Swami Ramdas, Atmananda Guru, J. Krishnamurti, Anandamayi Ma, and contemporarily, Satya Sai Baba, Pandurang Shastri Athavale, Yogi Ramsuratkumar, Mata Amritananada Mayi, Sri Sri Ravi Shankar and so on – to name only a few of them.

Is India really as I have represented it to be? Is it really a sacred place or is this a poetic idealization, an escape from the material realities? When I make such claims for India, some of my friends complain that I am depoliticizing the inequalities, whitewashing the injustice, and running away from the intolerable suffering of the masses. One way to refute this is by clarifying that the notion of a sacred India does not deny the everyday reality of our grim struggle to survive as a modern nation state. It would, in my opinion, be a grave error to see India in an either/or manner – either as entirely sacred or as entirely secular. The sacred and the secular are not polar opposites, but flow into each other in a manner which makes them inseparable. Therefore, to believe in the sacredness of India is not to close one's eyes to its oppressing material realities. Every major saint also struggled to change society, Gandhi being a good example in recent times.

The tension between 'the idea of India' and 'the reality of India' is inherent in the very title of this chapter. When we say 'Sacred India', what exactly are we referring to? Are we saying that a part or a portion of India is sacred or is the whole of India sacred? I think if we understand the sacred part first, we can see what else remains.

What part of India, then, is sacred? And why is it so? If we look at the meaning of the word 'sacred', we will find that it goes back to the Latin word *sacer*, which means holy. The same root gives us words like 'consecrate', 'saint', 'sanctuary', 'sacrament' and so on. An important related word is 'sacrifice', a compound word which means 'make holy'. The etymological meaning of sacred thus clarifies that things become holy or sacred because we *consecrate* them. We endow them with a sense of the sacred. It is not because something is inherently holy that we consider it so, rather whatever we deem to be sacred, whatever we consecrate, becomes holy to us.

This is how we have evolved an elaborate sacred geography for this land. Everything about India is sacred – its rivers, mountains and numerous sites of pilgrimage. The whole subcontinent is studded with these centres of divinity. Such consecration has been repeated, augmented and enhanced generation after generation. Ultimately, the sacredness of India is not a matter of reason alone, but of faith and experience. India, then, is sacred to the extent that we *make* it so, to the extent that we uphold its sanctity.

Vande Mataram

'The mother is divine; the father is divine; the teacher is divine; the guest is divine,' says the Upanishad (Taittiriya, 1.11).[14] Note that in the order in which they appear in the injunction, the mother precedes the father. Earlier in the same Upanishad (1.3), the priority of the mother over the father is clearly established: 'Mother is the prior form, father is the posterior form, progeny is the junction, and procreation the means of joining.' Thousands of years later, we still tend to revere the mother, not just our own mother, but 'mother earth' and 'mother India'. Hence, *Vande Mataram*.

On a hot day of the Bengali calendar year 1176 (corresponding to AD 1772), Mohendra Singha and his wife Kalyani are leaving their ancestral homestead to tread the broad road to Calcutta. Though Mohendra Singha is a rich landlord, he and his family are starving. A famine rages in Bengal. Everywhere, men, women, children and cattle are dying of hunger. Famished and angry, the impoverished villagers have taken to dacoity. Yet, the tax collectors of the government are unrelenting. Clearly, the British rule, in its very first years, has reduced India to famine, beggary and robbery.

It is at this apocalyptic moment that Bankim Chandra Chatterjee's famous novel *Anandmath*[15] begins. Mohendra, searching for food, is separated from his wife. Both are eventually rescued by a group of sannyasi or monks called the 'Children'. When Mohendra is being taken to their hideout in the deep forests, Bhavananda, his escort, bursts into a song:

Mother, I bow to thee!
Rich with thy hurrying streams,
Bright with thy orchard gleams,
Cool with thy winds of delight,
Dark fields waving, Mother of might,
Mother free!

Astonished, Mohendra wishes to know who this mother is. Bhavananda replies by singing another verse:

Glory of moonlight dreams
Over thy branches and lordly streams;
Clad in thy blossoming trees,
Mother, giver of ease,
Laughing low and sweet!
Mother, I kiss thy feet.
Speaker sweet and low!
Mother, to thee I bow.

(tr. Sri Aurobindo)

Mohendra responds that what has been described is no mother, but the country itself. Bhavananda replies, 'We recognise not another

Mother.' Quoting the Ramayana, he adds, 'Mother and Motherland is dearer than heaven itself.' Mohendra asks to hear the whole song.

Later, the master of *Anandmath*, the abbey of bliss, Satyananda, takes Mohendra to a lofty hall. He is shown an image of Jagaddhatri, the Protectress of the world, 'wonderful, perfect, rich with every ornament'. This is the Goddess who sits on Vishnu's lap, 'lovelier than Lakshmi and Saraswati, more splendid with opulence and lordship'. This is the image of the Mother as she was. In contrast, Satyananda shows Mohendra another image, 'enveloped in darkness, full of blackness and gloom'. It is an image of Kali, 'stripped of all, therefore naked'. Satyananda explains, 'Today the whole country is a burial ground, therefore is the Mother garlanded with skulls. Her own Lord she tramples under her feet. Alas, my Mother!' Finally, Satyananda shows Mohendra 'a beautifully fashioned image of the Ten-Armed Goddess made in gold, laughing and radiant in the light of the early sun'. Satyananda explains that 'this is the Mother as she shall be . . . on her right, Lakshmi as "prosperity", on her left "speech", giver of learning and science, Kartikeya with her as her "strength", Ganesh as "success".'

What Bankim does here is identify Mother India as Durga or Narayani herself – supreme Mother Goddess, the sustainer of the world. Such a deification of the country, as we know, was to inspire millions of Indians throughout our freedom struggle. *Vande Mataram*, the anthem, was banned, as was *Anandmath*, the novel in which it had appeared. Yet, the worship of Mother India or Bharat Mata, once instituted, was here to stay. Across the Hindu political spectrum, regardless of ideological differences, the idea of the sacredness of the Motherland was widely acknowledged. Yet the inscription of the country as a Goddess, though credited to the extraordinary genius of Bankim, is actually based on much older myths and legends.

Even if non-Hindus do not participate fully in the seeming idolatry in the imagery, I am sure they share in the feeling of awe and reverence towards India as Mother. After all, a mother loves all her children, whether Hindu, Muslim, Christian or atheist. Tagore, who later criticized the excesses of such deification in *Ghare Baire* (1916), himself created an all-embracing 'Mother India' figure, Anandamayi, in *Gora* (1907–1909).[16] Anandamayi loves all her children, regardless of religion, caste or gender, though she is no one's biological mother. Tagore was obviously creating a symbol for India, in the tradition of Bankim, even if his emphasis and ideology were different.

Consider now the story not of a mother, but a wife and a daughter, Sati, in another Hindu myth. To know why she sacrificed herself, her father Daksha's yajna or sacrificial rite needs to be understood, however cursorily. Daksha's yajna was to gain mastery over all the three worlds and to make himself the overlord of Gods and men. This elevation of the ego to Godhead has always attracted retribution in Indian mythology. The stories of Hiranyakashyapu or Ravana bear eloquent testimony to this rule. The urge to dominate and enforce one's power over others is considered *asuric* or demonic. Similarly, to believe that the body is the Self and to live only for the enjoyment of the senses is also not well-regarded.

Daksha wished to elevate himself above others through his grand yajna. He had invited all the other Gods and Deities but deliberately slighted Shiva. In a sense, the yajna was designed to ruin Shiva, to defeat him once and for all, to marginalize everything he stood for. Shiva represents the supremacy of pure consciousness over matter. It would be ironic to regard his very presence as auspicious, considering how hideous and frightening he looks. But Shiva is auspicious because he denotes a supreme detachment and indifference to this world. Roaming about in skin and bark, body smeared with ash, unkempt and untidy, with poisonous serpents around his neck, Shiva is the very antithesis of the bourgeois gentleman that Daksha considered himself to be.

Daksha and Shiva thus represent two opposite principles – sense pleasure versus sense control, consumerism versus subsistence, indulgence versus restraint, matter versus spirit, enjoyment versus detachment, power versus truth, ego versus self. The success of Daksha's yajna would have meant the triumph of darkness over light, of untruth over truth. Not just to safeguard the honour of her husband, but to save truth, to save renunciation, to save all that was auspicious, Sati, which means the one who is true, jumped into the fire and thereby brought her father's diabolical plans to an end. Shiva, infuriated by the gruesome death of his beloved wife, unloosed a monster, Veerabhadra, who along with his *ganas* (attendants), devastated both Daksha and his world.

But the sacrifice of Sati and the discomfiture of Daksha is only the first part of the story. Now, disconsolate over his wife's death, Shiva began to roam the world with her dead body on his back. The Gods were alarmed. They sent Vishnu to stop this macabre grieving which was plunging the whole of creation into gloom and darkness. Vishnu, following Shiva from behind, began to dismember Sati's corpse. Wherever a part fell became a sacred shrine, a *shaktipeetham*. There are 51 such *peethams*, spread all over the subcontinent. These shrines can be found in such far-flung places as Ladakh (Sriparvat dedicated to Sri Sundari), Kashmir (Amarnath dedicated to Mahamaya), Nepal (Uchhait dedicated to Uma), Punjab (Jalandhar dedicated to Tripuramalani) , Gujarat (Prabhas dedicated to Chandrabhaga), Tamil Nadu (Kanyakumari dedicated to Sharvani), Assam (Kamakhya dedicated to Kamakhya), Shillong (Jayantia dedicated to Jayanti), Tibet (Manasa dedicated to Dakshayani), Pakistan (Hingula dedicated to Bhairavi), Bangladesh (Sugandha dedicated to Sunanda) and so on. The vengeful daughter and devoted wife, thus, became the universal Mother.

When the devotee, either physically or mentally, visits all or even some of these shrines, he is *re-membering* the Goddess, literally joining her different detached body parts into one unified whole. He is reconstructing the Goddess in his own mind and consciousness. But in doing so, what is also constituted is the image of a country, a territory, Mother India, the Goddess herself, whom Bankim consecrated. Our myths and beliefs thus help to form this sacred geography of our country. The political dominions of India may or may not fit this sacred geography perfectly, but they invoke it willy-nilly. The sacred and the secular are thus mapped onto each other.

Pauranic or legendary India is full of such pan-Indian groupings of sacred places. The four sacred abodes of Vishnu or the *char dhams* are thus located in the north (Badrinath), east (Puri), south (Rameshwaram) and west (Dwarka). Similarly, the five Kashis are distributed over the north and the south; the seven sacred cities or *puris*, which bestow salvation, are scattered across Uttar Pradesh, Tamil Nadu, Gujarat and Madhya Pradesh; the 12 *jyotir lingas* or fire shrines of Shiva are located in Uttar Pradesh, Bihar, Madhya Pradesh, Gujarat,

Maharashtra, Andhra Pradesh and Tamil Nadu. Likewise, Buddhist, Jain, Muslim and Christian holy places are also found all over the country. The Chistiya Sufi circuit, for instance, would take one from Ajmer, to West Punjab (Pakistan), to Delhi, Nagore, Hyderabad and Gulbarga in the Deccan, and through Bihar to Eastern borders of India. Another Sufi circuit would take one from west to east, from Pakistan to Bangladesh, via the great plains of north and central India – even perhaps beyond, to Malaysia and Indonesia. A Sikh pilgrimage would not only include shrines in East and West Punjab, but also those in Uttarakhand, Delhi, Patna and Nanded. The thousands of temples, mosques, gurdwaras, churches, dargahs and shrines spread across the length and breadth of India help fabricate its spiritual body, giving the sacredness of India a texture, a pattern, coherence and a unity.

Divine Polysemy

Many years ago, when I was completing my Doctoral dissertation on 'Mysticism in Indian English Poetry', my teacher Giri had already taught me an important lesson. I had finished writing all my chapters; only the conclusion remained. 'Is there something that needs to be emphasized in the conclusion?' I asked him. He had, of course, looked at my writing closely, but he paused before replying, 'You should emphasize the multiplicity, the plurality of the mystical experience. No one can put a closure upon it or assert that only one way is the right way.'

Following Giri's advice, this is what I wrote:

> ... no limitation may be placed on the mystic's expression. Herein is echoed the diversity of life itself. Mysticism, unlike theology, is democratic, lending itself to various approaches and ways of expression. No single interpretation may be imposed upon it. Mysticism is not logo-centric; it is not rigid or monolithic. In it no single authority tyrannises. The mystic tells us time and again to experience Reality for ourselves because Truth cannot be received second-hand, but must be realised directly by each person for himself or herself.[17]

I had not understood then just how important plurality and non-exclusion were in any democratic polity, let alone the domain of spirituality.

Later, when I wrote *Decolonization and Development: Hind Svaraj Revisioned*, I tried to apply this to the 'truth' of India: 'For me, India offers a culture of plural possibilities, but also a culture with certain emphases'; thus, 'there is no one truth about India. There are several contending truths.'[18] Yet, as I have tried to argue, these truths do have a general orientation, a direction to which they point, and this is spiritual.

The idea of the plurality of truth is as old as the Vedas. For instance, 'They call it Indra, Mitra, Varuna, Agni, and it is the heavenly bird that flies. The wise speak of what is One in many ways; they call it Agni, Yama, Matarisvan.' (Rig Veda, 1.164.46) This plurality, this openness, this freedom from fear characterizes the whole history of Indian thought. The famous Creation Hymn, the *Nasadiya*, from the Rig Veda illustrates this beautifully: 'Whence this creation has arisen – perhaps it formed itself, or perhaps it did not – the one who looks down on it, in the highest heaven, only he knows or perhaps he does not know.' (Rig Veda, 10.121)

This hymn, which has perplexed and tantalized us for thousands of years, is according to Wendy Doninger O'Flaherty 'meant to puzzle and challenge, to raise unanswerable questions, to pile up paradoxes'.[19] But surely, raising unanswerable questions has a deeper, more meaningful purpose. They imply that until our understanding is perfected, we must continue to inquire, to search and to venture, never to block or shut inquiry or questioning.

It seems to me that it is India which has solved the 'one-many' problem more creatively and successfully than any other civilization. Elsewhere, a monotheistic God displaced the pagan plurality, but when God shuts out gods, then other intercessors such as angels or saints come crowding in, from the backdoor, as it were. There was a sadder fate, however, for the primitive Goddesses who were driven out of the Kaaba. When the holy stone was cleansed of polytheistic matriarchal traces, though something was gained by way of clarity and purity, surely a lot was also lost.

In India, though the Goddesses were incorporated into the patriarchal pantheon as spouses of the Gods, they did not lose their independence totally. In popular iconography, the most well-known Goddesses – Lakshmi, Saraswati and Durga – are depicted without their spouses. Moreover, the Shaktas (practitioners of Shaktism) still accord primacy to the Eternal Feminine as the creatrix, sustainer, and destroyer of the universe. Every woman, consequently, is regarded as an embodiment of that primordial energy. To us, in India, the Motherhood of God is as acceptable as the Fatherhood of God.

One–many, self–God, male–female: all these, ultimately, are versions of the same problem. This is the problem of duality and non-duality. In India we have no difficulty in understanding that Truth has many levels; what is true at one level may not be so at another. The ultimate reality may be non-dual, but it is perceived as dual. It is, therefore, both non-dual and dual at the same time; from another perspective, it is neither dual nor non-dual. The first approach leads to the idea of *purnata* or fullness in Vedanta, the second to *sunyata* or emptiness in Buddhism. The very word, non-dual, indicates that this notion of reality is not monistic or singular, but the negation of duality.

A. L. Basham in *The Wonder That Was India* calls this 'a double standard of truth': 'Shankara's Brahman was not really different from the "void" or *nirvana* of Mahayana Buddhism, a fact well recognised by Shankara's opponents, who called him a crypto-Buddhist.'[20] While appreciating Basham's insights, I would still object to his use of the phrase 'double standard', which has negative connotations. Indians do not have *double* standards for Truth, but *multiple* standards. These multiple standards produce a rich and varied spiritual landscape, with many paths and options.

Without plurality, the spiritual quest becomes narrow, dogmatic, sectarian, and ultimately, self-defeating. The fossilizing, hypostasizing and ossifying of truth lead to untold violence and bigotry. It is in the nature of organized religions and churches to shut out free thinking and exploration for fear of loss of control over their flock. That is why, before modern scientific inquiry could to be established, the hegemony of the Church had to be broken. It is a great historical tragedy that spirituality in the Judeo-Christian tradition has so often had to bow down to dogma.

The Enlightenment liberated Europe from the stranglehold of superstition and dogmatism, but imposed instead the tyranny of secular reason. In destroying the dominance of religion, the salience of the sacred was also lost. The resultant world was spiritually bleaker. From this impoverishment, the West is still struggling to find a way out. No wonder that a terrible fear of the sacred persists in the collective mind of modernity. The sacred is immediately seen as irrational, sucking us into a vortex of atavistic and frightful chaos. Or it is dogmatic, intolerant, rigid and oppressive, linked to violence and terrorism. The modern mind, therefore, shrinks from the sacred, almost congenitally incapable of appreciating its beauty, grace and variety. Yet, only a genuinely religious mind can offer a holistic response to the hatred and fear which religious intolerance breeds.

Ironically, modern secularism is often itself as intolerant as religious fundamentalism – its 'other'. It therefore seems incapable of addressing, let alone solving, the problems of our times. Imposing an unchallenged hegemony of the 'irreligious' state is as dangerous as the hegemony of priests and mullahs. Both secular and religious fundamentalisms mirror each other. Both tend to be fascistic and totalitarian. Contrarily, genuine liberalism or humanism extends into both domains, secular and sacred, denying a dichotomy between them.

Sacred India, thus, is a wide-open territory, with plenty of space for the secular, even for the non-religious. It is a plural space, full of possibilities and potentialities. Out of such a space have emerged newer and newer notions of the spiritual. An important case in point is that of J. Krishnamurti. Denying the need of gurus or spiritual authority, denying the primacy of traditions, asserting instead the immediacy of awareness, Krishnamurti tried to give a new meaning to the sense of the religious. All you have to do is to look, he was wont to say. And in order to look you do not need any intermediary. You have to do it yourself:

> One has to negate the Gita, the Bible, the guru, the whole thing. One has to negate totally all the constructions that thought has put together, to wipe away and say, 'I do not know, I do not know a thing.' One has to say, 'I will not say a thing, I do not know. I will not repeat a thing which somebody else has said.' Then you begin.[21]

To rephrase this position, only *sruti* or direct revelation is important; *smriti* or authority is an obstacle. But I believe that what is required is not a rejection of *smriti* so much as its continual renewal and realignment. Since *smriti* is man-made, it can sometimes be renewed not only by affirmation, but also by deconstruction. To that end, all modernists and iconoclasts, including Krishnamurti, have an important role to play. But in the process, they offer yet another version of *smriti*, an anti-authoritarian authority, if you will. The perennial stream of tradition is thus renewed by those who affirm it, as also by those who deny it.

The Simplicity of Grace

Only 16, he was a restless, discontented student, travelling alone in Tamil Nadu. He had been to Vellore and Gingee, and somehow, he now found himself in Tiruvannamalai. He had read about a famous temple there, which he now wanted to see. His mind was sharp and bare like an unsheathed knife; he had no belief system to support him, only a wound in his heart and a hunger to understand life.

The courtyard of the temple was lined with sadhus, holy men, mendicants, beggars, all sorts of strange-looking people. Some had long beards and matted locks reaching down to their knees. They sat silently, neither extending their arms nor asking for alms. His head was swimming; he felt scared. Was he hallucinating? Was he being punished for his bad karma? Somebody whispered in his ears, 'Go to Ramanasramam.' The tone was insistent. He thought to himself, 'What the hell, why not?' It was evening. On entering the ashram, he found himself looking straight at a hill – very brown, not too high, and with gently sloping sides.

Suddenly, a man held him by the sleeve, 'Look!'

Baffled, he asked, 'Where?'

'At that!' the man replied, pointing to the mountain.

'But why?'

'Don't you know? It's holy. Don't argue, just look. Look!' the man insisted.

'But . . . I don't believe in these things . . . I don't even believe in God,' he blurted out.

The man turned pale and got angry, 'Then why do you come here? To mock us?'

'Please...' he pleaded, 'it's just that I neither believe nor disbelieve. I just don't know!'

The commotion attracted a kind-looking man in a white dhoti. 'He's just a boy,' the older gentleman said soothingly.

In the meanwhile, something extraordinary was happening. The boy, who had all this while been looking at the hill in the dimming light, found the voices around him fade away. He felt wide awake; he could see the hill and nothing else. Looming large ahead of him, almost advancing towards him, it had totally arrested his attention. His mind was captivated. The wild, whirling thoughts in his head subsided. He felt alert, quiet, still.

Later, the boy was told to go to the meditation room. He went less reluctantly. There, a huge portrait of the Maharshi looked down on him as he sat on the cool, tiled floor. The Maharshi was reclining on a couch covered with tiger-skin. The portrait now rested on the same sofa on which the sage used to sit. The eyes of the master looked at him with utmost compassion mingled, almost, with a faint amusement. The room was utterly silent. The boy felt rested; his feverish adolescent brain had never before experienced a calm like this.

Adjacent, in a large hall, was the sage's samadhi where his mortal remains lay buried 20 feet under the ground with a flower-bedecked linga on top. The boy stood hesitantly, not knowing what to do. Just then, someone said, 'Hey there, go in and eat. It's supper-time.' He was ushered into the dining room. Sitting on the floor, he ate the steaming rice and vegetable stew with great relish straight off the leaf-plate. There were several Westerners in the room. He watched them fumbling with their fingers, barely managing to eat their semi-solid meal. He particularly noticed a beautiful American woman with an intensely abstracted look. Was she in some sort of a trance? He wanted to talk to her, to ask her, 'Have you found it? Have you got what you came looking for from the other side of the earth?' Her absorption seemed too forbidding though. When he looked more closely, he found that she had great difficulty eating with her fingers. He asked, 'Why don't you ask for a spoon?' She frowned, as if he had disturbed her, shaking her head to indicate she was managing fine.

While putting on his shoes, he got his chance to ask about her. He asked the kind man in the dhoti, 'Sir, do you think that lady there has found enlightenment?' Surprised, the gentleman turned to look at him. Then he laughed, 'Bosh! Do you think it is so simple, young man!' With a faraway look in his eyes, he said, 'It's a very, very difficult journey. The ego must be shed completely. It's not just having a nice experience now and then...'

The guru draws you to him, holds you by the hand, takes you to the Ultimate Reality, shows you the Truth – right there in front of you, squat and solid, like a nice, rounded hill – and says, 'There! Seek no further. Rest here, free of all cares.' Then, after slaking your parched mind of its millennial thirst, he leads you to the dining hall, and says, 'Sit here and eat to your heart's content – the rice and dal of eternity.' You laugh, really relaxing for the first time in many lives. It's so simple and so funny, this divine play. Now you belong to Him for life. No donation you give can offset your debt. The debt to the guru can only be repaid by setting someone else free. Somewhere, your guru awaits you; you think that you're looking for him, but actually he has been watching over you, pursuing you from life to life.

The Sacred and the Secular

The idea that Indian civilization is primarily spiritual has been repeated so often and by so many eminent authorities that it has become a worn out cliché. An important proponent of such an idea was Sri Aurobindo himself. In *The Foundations of Indian Culture* nearly every chapter and section stresses on the spiritual nature of the Indian temperament:

> India's central conception is that of the Eternal, the Spirit here encased in matter, involved and immanent in it and evolving on the material plane by rebirth of the individual up the scale of being till in mental man it enters the world of ideas and the realm of conscious morality, dharma.

And:

> It is the formula of a spiritualised civilisation striving through the perfection but also through the exceeding of mind, life and body towards a high soul-culture.

In contrast, modern European civilization 'has become material, predatory, aggressive . . . Material comfort, material progress, material efficiency have become the Gods of her worship.' Both Europe and India have, of course, been changing and evolving over centuries, but 'still the differentiation of cultural temperament has on the whole been constant'. He calls it 'a cultural quarrel complicated with a political question.' What will be the result of this quarrel? In Sri Aurobindo's words, 'Either India will be rationalised and industrialised out of all recognition . . . or else she will be the leader in a new world-phase . . . and spiritualise the human race.'

New possibilities are open and visible when we look at the world today. A part of us is indeed dying; yet, we also see not just the persistence and reassertion of Indian spirituality, but also its spread all over the world, particularly in the West. An excellent example of this is the globalization of Mahayana Buddhism, owing chiefly to the charismatic and compassionate personality of the Dalai Lama. Similarly, ever since Swami Vivekananda went to America and England over a hundred years ago, there has been a steady and growing demand for Indian thought in the West. You could say that Swamiji globalized Vedanta. He also influenced Sri Aurobindo who said that humanity is indeed moving towards a 'unified world-culture', but this cannot be the kind of culture that dominates the world at present. 'The purely intellectual or heavily material culture of the kind that Europe now favours bears in its heart the seed of death; for the living aim of culture is the realisation on earth of the kingdom of heaven.'[22]

Most 'modern' Indians are, however, extremely uncomfortable with the idea that we are indeed spiritual. In a recent book on Indian philosophy, Professor Daya Krishna invites us to re-examine some popular myths about India, chief among which is the commonplace notion that Indian philosophy is spiritual. Indeed, Daya Krishna calls it one of 'the universally accepted ideas' which are 'treated as indubitable facts' but are actually 'myths'.[23] But, on closer examination, what Krishna proves is not that Indian philosophy is not spiritual, but that it is not *only* spiritual. Now who would want to quarrel with this? No philosophy or worldview can afford to be *only* spiritual. So the real question is about the relationship between the two. Daya Krishna contends that, ontologically, Indian philosophy recognizes the reality of both spirit and matter.

From the discussion of the *mahavakyas* it is clear how both spirit and matter are one and the same. The moot point, then, is what is accorded primacy. Again, Daya Krishna concedes, 'It is certainly true that Indian thought has held spiritual salvation to be the highest goal of individual effort.'[24] And, as Sri Aurobindo had stated much earlier, 'The tendency of the normal western mind is to live from below upward and from out inward... India's constant aim has been, on the contrary, to find a basis of living in the higher spiritual truth and to live from the inner spirit outwards, to exceed the present way of mind, life and body...'[25]

To be spiritual, then, is not to deny the body or the mind, but to assert, nay *experience* a higher reality that transcends these. Sri Aurobindo explains this very well:

> Matter, mind, life, reason, form are only powers of the spirit and valuable not for their own sake, but because of the Spirit within them – *atmartham*; they exist for the sake of the Self, says the Upanishad, and this is certainly the Indian attitude to these things.[26]

Changing India

I am happy to be an Indian, to live in this hallowed land, to breathe its air, to drink its waters, and enjoy the fruits of its soil. I am grateful for experiencing a sense of plenty in my day-to-day life – for having more than enough to eat, for having a nice house and decent clothes, for being able to travel, buy books, own a car, have domestic help, for having a reasonable degree of control over my time, for having a job that I like, for not having to work so hard for a living that I cannot think of anything but my survival from day to day, for having the wherewithal to look after my family, for being able to provide my children with whatever is necessary for their growth and well-being – in short, for having those things which are considered necessary for a meaningful life.

Even so, I am acutely aware of those 300 odd millions who are not just worse off than me, but who are so badly off that they not only lack most of the things which I take for granted including adequate food, clothing and shelter, but who are among the poorest of the earth's poor. Am I happy because I am well off? By this yardstick, most of our poor countrymen and women ought to be miserable.

Yet, when I look at them, I find that despite the most adverse life conditions, they manage to live reasonably positive, even joyous lives. They have a strength that most of us lack. They have fortitude, resilience, trust in life, wonderful determination, enduring courage and tremendous dignity. They are working people, toiling hard from dawn to dusk for their living, but still they are not broken or defeated. They not only survive on very little, but manage to give back to the society – to us, the better off – much more than what we give them. These common people have built this civilization. They are its backbone, its key agents. Their songs have contributed to the music of this country; their values have shaped our culture.

In contrast, the richest amongst us are not necessarily the happiest. They have their own share of problems and tensions, mostly prompted by the desire to own and consume more and more. They do not radiate peace or contentment. Rather, they come across as dissatisfied, aggressive, self-centred and violent. In other words, the lesson that India teaches us is that there is no automatic correlation between our material status and our inner well-being.

But this does not mean that all is right with our country. A civilization which is spiritual cannot afford to ignore the material realities that stare it in the face. A spiritual country cannot allow over a third of its people to live below the poverty line; it is duty-bound to pull them up, to share its wealth with them. The kind of spirituality that I have been talking about has an inbuilt, definite kind of politics. Sacred India is not callous and indifferent to the sufferings of its children.

Spirituality is not a retreat from the world. The ashram or hermitage has a dialectical relationship with the real world. It is like a nursery from whence the seeds of a new world can be broadcast far and wide. India, as I have been suggesting, is the world's spiritual nursery. But if it is to fulfil its role, it must put its own house in order. I believe that there is a tremendous energy lying untapped in our people. Our material difficulties can be solved by harnessing our *atma bala* or soul-force. This has been proven again and again in our history. We need good governance, greater equality, and social justice for the deprived millions.

Svaraj

More than 60 years after India's independence, we are enjoined, once again, to undertake some serious introspection. Is there anything special in the fact that we've completed six decades as a modern nation? Is the balance sheet of our successes and failures the best indicator of us as a people?

No doubt, also, that the state and its complimentary structures of civil society constitute the ground on which much of the material reality of our lives is constructed, both as individuals and as communities. Yet, being an Indian involves much more than merely being a citizen of this young nation, which is also an ancient civilization. The meaning and significance of India far exceeds its 64 year-old history and its various narratives. Thus, paradoxically, to commemorate these years is at once to exceed and transcend them – not be fixated upon them in a narrow literalistic manner.

This is perhaps an appropriate moment to re-embark upon our own discovery of India.[27] This invocation of the title of Jawaharlal Nehru's book is no accident. Written less than two years before India's independence, his book is both a personal testament and a record of a whole peoples' quest for selfhood and nationhood. Nehru's book is therefore one of the important acts of national self-constitution. At the least, it articulates the author's relationship to the society and civilization of his country – both how he was shaped by it and how he wished to shape it himself. Like Nehru, we shall have to undertake our own individual voyages of discovering what this country stands for.

But perhaps we also need to turn from the non-committal liberalism of Nehru to the compassion of Gandhi's vision of India. To Gandhi, independence would have no meaning if it only meant a transfer of power from the British to the Indians. Writing in as early as 1909, Gandhi clearly states that he does not want 'English rule without the Englishman'.[28] What he wants, instead, is true svaraj, which is 'when we learn to rule ourselves'. Elsewhere, he explained what he meant by svaraj: 'I submit that Swaraj is an all-satisfying goal for all time . . . It is infinitely greater than and includes independence.'[29] Such a society would consist of self-regulating individuals relating to each other in a cooperative and non-coercive manner. It would be a society based on truth and non-violence, where each person is free to practise his or her own religion. It would be a society without glaring inequalities or crushing exploitation, without class and caste distinctions or differences between the ruled and the rulers. It would be a society where the individual was not constantly at war with society, where freedom and responsibility were not always in conflict with each other. In short, *svarajya*, as conceived as a record of a whole peoples' quest for selfhood by Gandhi was nothing less than *Ramrajya* or the kingdom of God.

Though the term in its modern parlance has political overtones, the idea of svarajya is as old as the Upanishads. In the Taittiriyopanishad, svarajya is defined as the complete sovereignty and uncontrolled dominion that is obtained upon attaining oneness with the Ultimate Reality (Taittiriyopanishad, I.6.2). In striving for one's individual svarajya, one is therefore striving for svarajya of all. As Gandhi said, 'Swaraj of a people means the sum total of the Swaraj of individuals.'[30] Yet, looking at ourselves, we realize that we are far from attaining *svarajya* either individually or collectively. Therefore, 64 years of independence mean little to us. We must continue to strive for the *svarajya* that Gandhi spoke about, for without it our country would no longer be sacred. That is why Gandhi gave us the following talisman:

> I will give you a talisman. Whenever you are in doubt, or when the self becomes too much with you, apply the following test. Recall the face of the poorest and the weakest man whom you may have seen and ask yourself if the step you contemplate is going to be of any use to him. Will he gain anything by it? Will it restore him to a control over his own life and destiny? In other words, will it lead to Swaraj for the hungry and spiritually starving millions? You will find your doubts melting away.[31]

Gandhi wrote this to an unknown correspondent in August 1947 when India won its independence. Sixty years later, can we afford to ignore or turn our backs to Swaraj?

Chapter 3

India's 'Truths'

In the previous chapter we have seen how striking, if uncanny, the persistence of sacred India is. This is not the stereotypical 'timeless' or 'eternal' India which is easy enough to encounter in certain circles. It is not merely the Orientalist construction of India as merely spiritual. Though it is useful to invoke the resonance of Sanatan Dharma,[32] or the perennial path, when coming to terms with this India, it is also specifically locatable in time; it responds to explicit demands of history.

We have already seen that there are many truths about India as there are many paths to these truths. Compared to other countries which are largely mono-ethnic, mono-racial or mono-lingual, or even highly centralized, India is certainly a geopolitical space that is characterized by a culture of plural possibilities. But does it mean that it has no distinctive features or qualities? Perhaps, even if India does not have one single identity or essence, it has a certain set of emphases. A way to express this combination of plurality and singularity is the ancient Vedic dictum, '*Satyam eka, vipram bahuda vadanti*': truth is one; the wise call it by many names.

In India, where modernity is still not fully established, truth is seen as a unity, but not as unitary. Truth is entirely, endlessly plural, but not indeterminate or infinitely postponed like some post-modernists would argue. Nor is it one single truth that everyone must follow as the only way, whether from a religious or a scientifically imposed monism. Instead, we accept the unity of truth, but this unity is itself constituted as a field of difference, of plurality, diversity and endless possibilities.

In this context, it would be useful to touch on how the foundational ideas of nations and civilizations are established. Such entities have essentially two kinds of founders – conquistadors and sages. Most nations are founded on conquest – the so-called distinction between settler colonies (such as the United States, Brazil and Australia) and invader colonies (such as India, Malaysia and the Philippines) is only technical when it comes to this fundamental fact. The seizing of lands, the subjugation or elimination of local populations, the establishment of puppet regimes or client states, slavery or indenture, racism, expropriation – these are standard features of the colonial system. The conquest paradigm is thus the most common in history. Tribal, indigenous societies, of course, are not products of conquest. They trace their ancestry to mythical animals, birds and natural causes. But for most modern nations, conquest is the common factor. The United States, for instance, was founded upon the conquest and genocide of indigenous people even though its constitutional ideas came from the European Enlightenment. Most Islamic nations are also based on conquest and conversion.

In India, however, we believe that our society is based on the precepts of rishis or the ancient seers. Each clan and caste, to this day, traces its descent to some rishi or sage or at least to some mythical hero or heroine. From this method of tracing descent, it is evident that sages were considered as significant as kings. Even kings like Rama and Krishna are revered for their divine more than kingly qualities. The kings, whether elected or preferred by birth, were merely considered administrators, the keepers and protectors of dharma. The real founders of the society were the sages – those enlightened beings, who were also our ancient legislators.

Likewise, we might argue that modern India is formed by rishis such as Gandhi and Aurobindo, not by presidents and prime ministers. To thus mix the mythical and the historical is one way to maintain the notion of rishi *parampara* or wisdom tradition in our times. Like the indigenous people's respect of their ancestors, we too need to remember our spiritual forbears in contemporary times. If India is not a gladiatorial culture like the Romans were or the modern West is, we must acknowledge the debt we owe to our modern yogis and rishis. That is, my India is the India of Gandhi, Aurobindo, and Raja Rao, not just of Salman Rushdie, Arundhati Roy, or Aravind Adiga.

It was Sri Aurobindo who provided a different basis for Indian nationalism than the civic nationalism of France or the romantic nationalism of Germany. Unlike European nations, India did not have the common glue of one language, religion or ethnicity. Even Brazil, which is very diverse ethnically, has one dominant language to bind it. In contrast, Aurobindo proposed a 'Dharmic nationalism' for India. He said that each nation has a soul or spirit which it was uniquely blessed with and especially qualified to express. According to him, India's unique mission was to embody and articulate Sanatan Dharma. Not to be mistakenly identified with modern Hinduism, Sanatan Dharma for Aurobindo was the universal religion of humankind. Without Dharma, India is nothing; as Aurobindo put it, 'She does not rise as other countries do, for self, or when she is strong, to trample the weak. She is rising to shed the eternal light, entrusted to her over the world. India has always existed for humanity and not for herself, and it is for humanity and not for herself that she must be great.'

Most modern people, in contrast, are entirely secular in their orientation. But, as we know only too well, we may banish the religious, but it returns to haunt us, sometimes as our worst nightmare. That is why Jacques Derrida in his last writings called for a return of the sacred. Hence, post-secular thinkers and intellectuals need to engage with the sacred, not only in its pathological form, which is fanatical and violent, but in its benign and inspiring form, which is spiritual and nourishing.

Shakuntala or the Romance of India

One of the best ways to try to explain what India stands for is to tell one of its birth stories. Such a story sometimes tells us more about a nation than hundreds of volumes of history. The story of Shakuntala, as I mentioned earlier, occurs in the Mahabharata, but was later immortalized by India's most famous classical poet and playwright Kalidasa. Stories in India are always retold, which makes no one version of them authoritative. This story, too, has also been retold many times – there are even studies about the implications of these retellings. But this version may be seen not just as an Indian romance, but the romance of India, of the birth of a nation. And the first thing that strikes us about it is that it is, above all, a love story, which anticipates by over a thousand years the Bollywood romance.

But why is this the story of India? The conventional answer is that from the union of Dushyanta and Shakuntala is born the child, the boy Bharata, after whom India gets its pre-British, pre-Islamic name, Bharatavarsha. Even today, India is known in our constitution as 'Bharat Ganarajya'. But there is a deeper answer to which I shall come later.

We may call this the story of found, lost and found love.

The story of Dushyanta (the king) and Shakuntala (the forest nymph) starts, in Kalidasa, with the king going on a hunting expedition. Chasing his quarry, he approaches the ashram (hermitage) of Rishi Kanva. The king's horses are inflamed by the closeness to the game. The hunt is on, the king's sinews are taut, and he is about to shoot the deer that he is chasing. Just then a young renunciate from the ashram stands in the way: 'O King, stop! Desist from hunting this doe, for it is a protected animal. Don't you know she belongs to the hermitage of Rishi Kanva?'

The king immediately reins in the galloping horses, which of course, is a metaphor for the superior man's control of his own senses and passions. The king shows his mettle through his capacity for restraint. And yet, the hunt for the deer prefigures the king's pursuit of Shakuntala herself. Though the ashram doe escapes, Shakuntala does not. The young hermit, pleased with the King's self-control, says, 'Well done. You have acted as befits the house of Puru; you are supposed to be the protector of the weak, and this defenseless deer, which is running for its life, shouldn't be killed for sport. In any case, it is not a wild animal, but belongs to the hermitage.' The king is taught *rajdharma*, the duty of kings, by the forest-dwelling hermit.

Now fast-forwarding a little, the king gets down, goes to the ashram where he meets the enchanting and utterly virginal Shakuntala, whom he falls in love with. The king proposes to her, but because her guardian, the Rishi Kanva, is away, they contract a secret *Gandharva Vivaha*, a kind of love marriage, consummating it in the lap of untainted nature. Interestingly, more than 80 per cent of the marriages in India are still arranged, but in that ancient story, the progenitors of the nation go through a simple, covert marriage by a simple exchange of garlands, with no human witnesses.

Dushyanta goes away, promising to send for his wife later. Shakuntala is listless, thinking of her beloved husband when the short-tempered rishi Durvasa comes to the hermitage. So immersed is Shakuntala in anguished love that she neglects her duties to the distinguished guest, who promptly curses her, 'He whom you are thinking of now will forget you, as you have forgotten your obligations to your guests.'

What a crisis! When her companions hear of it, they rush to the aid of Shakuntala, pleading with the sage to revoke the curse. But that is impossible; once released, the words cannot be taken back and must come true. Mollified, perhaps by a good meal and the warmth of hospitality, the sage offers to mitigate the effects of the curse. He said, 'If you show him something that he has given you, he will remember you again.'

As the story proceeds, we find that Dushyanta does not send for his wife, and poor Shakuntala, in the meanwhile, finds out that she is pregnant. So she decides to go to the court of the king to present herself to him.

On the way to the palace, while bathing in the river, she loses the ring that the king had given her. Perhaps, she has become thin and careworn from anxiety. In any case, she feels so out of place; the city, with its opulent mansions and overflowing bazaars, is a different world from the sylvan hermitage where nature is itself as yet unfallen. In contrast, here, money and power rule human relations.

With great trepidation, Shakuntala announces herself to the King. Unable to recognize her, he says, 'Woman, I don't know you.' In the skeleton story in the Mahabharata, Shakuntala's response is rather forceful and spirited. She upbraids the king in front of all his courtiers for being a liar and base man. She enjoins upon him to respect her as his wife and also to accept his son. But in Kalidasa's tale, she is much more delicate, thus a figure of pity. Her escorts from the ashram also leave, saying that the matter is now between king and consort, husband and wife. The king, owing to Durvasa's curse, has forgotten who Shakuntala is. Alone and abandoned, she goes away, pregnant with the king's child.

After her departure, Dushyanta is extremely sad. Try as he might, he cannot understand why. I think this is one of the tragedies of the human condition that somewhere in our hearts is a yearning, a quest, for something much deeper than our mundane, material reality, yet we don't know what it is that our heart really craves for. Dushyanta too cannot find any solace in the pleasures of his palace. Several days pass, but he is unable to fathom the mystery of his melancholy.

Then, (un)luckily for him, the ring is restored. A fish in the river had swallowed it; a fisherman found it after cutting open the fish. The king's guards arrested the fisherman who was trying to sell the royal signet. So the ring is the mnemonic device which reminds Dushyanta of his lost beloved. Now his mourning has a cause and thus cuts deeper than the earlier sense of unknown loss. Along with the deep bite of the fang of sorrow, his heart also smarts from the shallower barbs of guilt.

Some years pass. The king is requisitioned to fight for Indra, the king of the Gods, because there's a war going on between the Gods and the demons. The Gods win with the help of humans. This, I consider, an interesting aside; the Gods need us, just as we need them. Both must fight the forces of evil together.

Victorious, Dushyanta is sent back from heaven to earth in a golden chariot, flying first class, as it were. On his way back to his kingdom, he has a stopover at another hermitage, that of Maricha Rishi. There he sees a fearless lad playing with lion cubs. Struck by the sight, he asks, 'Whose son are you, brave lad?' The child resists and says, 'Don't touch me; my father is the king and no one else can pick me up.' But the king, with a spontaneous rush of affection, does precisely that, much to the consternation of the onlookers.

Once again, unwittingly, the boy's words come true as the inmates of the ashram rush out to find Shakuntala's long-separated husband and the king of the realm, holding his own son in his arms. That boy is Bharata.

As we have seen, there are two journeys to two hermitages. The first is to the hermitage of Rishi Kanva and takes Dushyanta to Shakuntala. The second, to that of Maricha Rishi, unites Dushyanta with his long-lost wife, and restores his son, whom he has never even seen, to him. One journey brings the king to his wife, the other to his wife and son.

The two journeys are symbolic, as also the two chariots in which they occur. The first chariot is earth-bound; in it the king almost kills an innocent deer for his pleasure and later finds, marries and abandons his love, Shakuntala. This journey results in brief happiness but long desolation. The second chariot is actually a heavenly vehicle, the flying chariot of the Gods in which Dushyanta comes back to earth from the sky realm. It is this chariot that restores his wife and child back to him, giving him true and stable happiness, not to speak of the continuation of his line.

This story has been so ably retold in a modern version called *Shakuntala, or the Ring of Remembrance*,[33] a small, delightful book, just a hundred pages long, that is actually an English translation of a contemporary French rendering of Kalidasa:

> Love born in the paradise of childhood and innocence is regained, transmuted, and magnificently widened in another paradise that one could call divine. As there are two chariots, a terrestrial and a heavenly one, so there are two journeys, one, through the forest that leads the king to a world of marvelous purity, and the other through the regions of the sky, that brings him to a universe of light. From the union of the two is born Bharat, the support of the world.

Coming to the meanings of the word 'Bharat' itself, one is possibly to support, or uphold. That is how in several modern Indian languages, *bhar* means weight, that which is borne. This meaning brings us to India's responsibility.

As Gandhi said in a speech to Indian Christians in 1925, two decades before independence:

> I call myself a nationalist and I pride myself in it. My nationalism is as broad as the universe. It includes in its sweep even the lower animals. It includes in its sweep all the nations of the earth, and if I possibly could convince the whole of India of the truth of this message, then, India would be something to the whole world for which the world is longing. My nationalism includes the well-being of the whole world. I do not want my India to rise on the ashes of other nations. I do not want India to exploit a single human

being. I want India to become strong in order that she can infect the other nations also with her strength.³⁴

Or, as Aurobindo put it more succinctly in his famous Uttarpara speech in 1909, 'It is for the Dharma and by the Dharma that India exists.'³⁵

From Shakuntala to Aurobindo is a long leap. Yet, an underlying and continuous sense of India's special burden or responsibility is evident throughout history, right up to the newly-created Indian nation. The latter, which came out of a long and arduous struggle against the most powerful empire in history, was imbued with a sense of its special mission and destiny.

To reiterate some morals form the story, India is born out of love, not out of conquest or hate or war or opposition to anyone or anything, even the British. Moreover, it is born out of the union of the earthly and the divine. Shakuntala herself, the mother of Bharat, is the daughter of an earthly sage Visvamitra – a warrior who then becomes a man of religious power – and the celestial beauty Menaka. Hence two journeys, two chariots, two aspirations and two forces come together to produce the child Bharat. This combination of material and spiritual forces is evident in the statements of Gandhi and Aurobindo too.

For the more esoteric meaning of Bharat, we must go to the other root of the word: *bh* means to shine, radiate or light up. Thus you get *bhaskara*, one of the words for the sun – he who creates light. And a word like *prabhat*, which means dawn. Thus, the esoteric meaning of India is as a light-giver, the one who illumines. When we ask what the responsibility of India is, what is its *svadharma*, then we might venture to suggest that it in fact to illumine, to give light. But what kind of light should India give?

To answer this question, we might look at the material conditions of India right now. The growing population, the rapid pace of change, the economic expansion and the technological advances – India is actually living out what Alvin Toffler called *Future Shock*. Coping with the pace of change has now become so difficult that it is a psychological or cognitive challenge to most Indians. Sometimes we understand what is happening around us and sometimes we don't. For instance, my mother who has lived in Bangalore (now Bengaluru) for the last 43 years says, 'I'm so bewildered by the city. I can't recognize this road or that. There was no flyover here; I used to turn left here but now it's become a no-entry road. None of these buildings were here. This street looked totally different.' To me this symptomatizes a deeper sense of disorientation, or dislocation, that we experience in India. We are at home, but we are not at home any more, because home has changed so much.

Given these challenges, what is it that India stands for? Raja Rao, who died in 2006 at the age of 98, the author of pioneering and far-reaching novels such as *Kanthapura* and *The Serpent and the Rope*, offers an answer. In *The Meaning of India*[36] he says that India is not a *desa*, it is a *darsana*. *Desa* means country or nation, while *darsana* means a way of seeing, a vision, a perspective or a philosophy. According to Raja Rao, India is not a country, but a vision, a way of seeing reality. With due respect, I would modify that statement to say that India is both a *desa* and a *darsana*, both a country and a point of view – because a *darsana* cannot exist without a *desa*; even a revelation needs a form, local habitation and a name. Just as our consciousness is embodied, every perspective too is housed, grounded or located. This locus is a part of our reality. So, just as it would be an error to say that we are nothing but our bodies, to say that we are not our bodies at all would also be a mistake. India too, though it cannot be confined to its geographical location, cannot be totally removed from that location either.

Similarly, the vision that India offers, though not exclusive to India, is specially located here. Though few people have interpreted it in this manner, E. M. Forster's *A Passage to India* also makes a similar point.[37] The architecture of the book suggests affirmation, negation and transcendence, corresponding to the three sections: Mosque, Caves and Temple. Whatever else it may be, and it is a lot else including a social and a political book, *A Passage to India* is also a deeply spiritual book. In the last section, Godbole shows Fielding how in the celebration of Janmashtami, the birth of the mythical child-God Krishna, everything mingles in an embrace which is both cleansing and elevating. Duality, separation, evil and sorrow are all banished.

The other great Anglo-India classic, Rudyard Kipling's *Kim*, which comes before Forster's, is also read as a quintessential imperial text.[38] But it too, as it happens, is a spiritual book. Parallel to the great game, which is a metaphor for empire, is the wheel of law, the greater game of karma and reincarnation from which both the Lama, Kim's surrogate father and Kim, seek release. *Kim* ends not on the grand trunk road where the game of empire is played, but far away and high above the bustle of power and pelf, in the Himalayas, where the Lama at last finds his sacred river and where Kim too, through his selfless service, finds his redemption. While the two games are indeed related, even intertwined, Kipling seems to suggest that the real game is spiritual, not political. It is here that a marriage of east and west is also enacted by the author whose most quoted statement is 'never the twain shall meet'. In an audacious metamorphosis, the subplot flips over the main plot, while the imperial capers with which the novel began are rendered secondary. Whatever else it may be, Kipling reminds us that India remains deeply spiritual.

I would agree that Indian exceptionalism may be dangerous. This has been the tendency of some proponents of Hindutva, or right-wing Hindu nationalism. Similarly, there are those who hold that India is the greatest country with the greatest culture and the Vedas, the sacred books of the Hindus, hold all the wisdom in the world, and all that is glorious, great and wonderful has already been spoken of or written in our tradition. These are ridiculous claims; hardly anyone takes them seriously. But because there are these dangers and drawbacks, we cannot altogether turn our backs to what India has to offer. We cannot deny the 'truths' that India stands for just because some people neither understand them nor believe in them or because others wish to misuse or distort them.

Three Levels, Three Truths

In this last section, I want to actually name some of these 'truths' of India. They are abstractions or idealization drawn form both historical and mythical realities. These truths may be arranged in three levels, the metaphysical, the political and the cultural. This may be regarded not as a closed but expanding set. Indeed these 'truths' of India can be traced and deployed in many other domains. For instance, how do they apply to the realm of an alter-globalization and a new world order?

In the domain of metaphysics, India's truth, as Raja Rao reminds us, is non-dualism. In another remarkable book, *I am Thou*,[39] the philosopher Ramachandra Gandhi also makes the same claim. Non-dualism is different from monism – as it is from dualism. It is not the opposite of dualism or that which denies difference. The word is a negative, like decolonization, implying non-something. That something, in this case 'dualism', exists within it. Duality, the separation between you and me or subject and object, is the basis of our daily lives and ordinary consciousness. To deny it would be simple-minded and futile.

Is dualism, however, true ultimately? If it were, then our history of wrong-doing would be justified because we are doing these things to others, free from the consequences ourselves. But that is impossible. It is like destroying the earth believing that it will not affect us. Dualism allows us to treat others instrumentally, thus going against both the golden rule and Immanuel Kant's categorical imperative. If we are to treat others as we would like them to treat us or as ends in themselves, not as means to an end, then our ontological foundations have to be non-dualistic. Dualism, ultimately, is violent because it separates and divides. Non-dualism, on the other hand, is holistic and integrates. It enjoins upon us to treat others responsibly because there are no others; everyone is a different version of our self. Non-dualism recognizes two or three or more entities, but denies them sovereign individuality or unconnected separability. Non-dualism, as a compound, recognizes but refuses to accord ultimate legitimacy to duality.

After metaphysical non-dualism, let us come to its political equivalent. We could call it svaraj, after Gandhi. What is svaraj? It is a very old word, but comes into the vocabulary of modern India in the nineteenth century. When the struggle for freedom started acquiring a certain momentum, people like Dadabhai Naoroji, Lokmanya Tilak, Sri Aurobindo, and of course, Mahatma Gandhi used the word svaraj. The latter wrote a whole book on it, *Hind Swaraj or Indian Home Rule*.[40] To all of them, svaraj meant political independence, in varying degrees, but it also meant much more.

Svaraj is a variation or shortening of the Sanskrit word *sva-rajya*, which is an abstract noun. When applied to a single individual, the appropriate word is *svarat*, an adjective. It is a word that occurs many times in the Upanishads such as the Chandogya, the Taitteriya and the Maitri. But what is this *svarajya* and who is *svarat*? The base word is a compound, *sva* + *raj*; *sva* means self and *raj* means to shine. Hence the word means both the shining of the self and the self that shines.

The political meaning is secondary and derived from the capacity of power to shine or radiate. The root *raj* gives us many words associated with power including Raja, Rex and Regina. *Raj* means to shine ₣ '*raj deepnoti*'; that is why the word for silver is *rajat*, because it shines. The light metaphor is very important in the Vedas because it suggests the sun of higher consciousness – *Tat savitur verenyam* in the Gayatri Mantra, chanted by millions as the royal road to self-realization and immortality. It is a metaphor used in Islamic traditions as in Rumi, and in Christian traditions as in Dante. It is to that sun of spiritual radiance, *savitur*, that Sri Aurobindo refers to in his great poem 'Savitri'. So *svarat* is a self-luminous person, and *svarajya* is a state of being *svarat* or enlightened. You might actually say that svaraj is another word for enlightenment just as Bharat, the ancient name for India is.

It is in India that political independence is expressed in terms of enlightenment. Political independence, then, is a version of self-illumination, not necessarily the defeat of others, even if to obtain it, we must struggle against the colonizers or imperialists. Svarajya, then, is the principle of perfection, of perfect self-governmentality, because illumination comes from internal order, not from oppression. Originally, svarajya actually referred to the internal government of a person, the control and power over the limbs, the senses, the organs and of all the different constituents of the individual. When all these are well-governed, a person can rule himself or herself; he or she is in full possession of the power to function. Such a person is *svarat*. Thus svarajya is self-rule or self-governance or power over oneself.

But what is the *sva*, akin to the Latin *sui*? Self-rule means the rule of the self – but which self? The id, the ego or the superego, to use the Freudian set? In traditional Indian psychology, unlike in Freud, there was not only the unconscious self, but also the super-conscious. In each of us resides the higher self, the divine self. So svaraj would mean the rule of that self within us. Svarajya is the state of self-mastery; the master of senses is svarat. It is the yogi perfectly poised in himself or herself that is svarat. What is the opposite of svarat? It is *anyarat* – *anya* means other so *anyarat* means ruled by others. These others could be the British or the Americans, our own internal demons, or our unregulated sense organs. The Upanishad clearly says that those who are *anyarat* perish; they go to the worlds of dead. This is the smoky path of the night that leads to repeated births and endless suffering, while svarajya is that luminous path to the state from where there is no return.

Synonymous with liberty, freedom and independence, svaraj also suggests a host of possibilities for inner illumination and self-realization. Hence, svaraj is preferable to decolonization. It has greater resonance and complexity. It is also not directed against anyone else. One's own svaraj can only help others and contribute to the svaraj of others. In svaraj the personal and the political merge, one leading to the other, the other leading back to the one. We cannot be free unless all others are free too; they cannot be free unless we are free. Svaraj allows us to resist oppression without hatred or violence. Gandhi developed the praxis of *satyagraha,* the insistence on truth or truth-force, to fight for the rights of the disarmed and impoverished people of India.

The svarat person is one who has good self-governance. Gandhi and the others extended and applied this notion to the body politic. We do not want to be ruled by others, but this also means we should not try to rule over others. Svaraj also means self-restraint, self-regulation. If we are all self-governing, the state as we know it will wither away. For Gandhi, an ideal society consisted of highly evolved, self-regulating individuals who respected themselves and the others. Such a society did not need policemen or law enforcers because each citizen was looking out for the welfare of others.

Politically what India stands for is svaraj, even when we cannot practise it or are far away from it. But there is a deep and abiding quest in the Indian political psyche for autonomy. We do not want to be part of an American, European or a Chinese narrative. We respect their narratives; they are free to pursue their own narratives, but we want to be left free to work out ours. Whatever our civilizational narrative is, we want the autonomy and the freedom to develop it. If we become powerful we would not want to oppress others and force them to join our narrative. That is svaraj.

One of the clichés about India is that no matter how powerful the country was it did not send expeditions of conquerors to countries outside this peninsula or huge armies here and there to conquer and colonize, or to bring the loot back from these expeditions. This is how the Arabs, Turks, Persians, Afghans, Portuguese, Spanish, British, Dutch, French, Germans, and the others behaved. They went to other lands to conquer, plunder, exploit, appropriate and so on, but there is no record of Indian armies doing the same. Yes, there were expeditions overseas, especially to South East Asia. But here new, Hindu kingdoms were formed, which later as easily became Buddhist, and Muslim. It was a form of acculturation and adaptation, not of conquest and imperial domination from an Indian centre to a foreign colony.

There are no narratives of Indians bringing back loot from China, Egypt, Tibet, Indonesia Malaysia, or even Sri Lanka, sending huge ships to bring back the spoils of conquest, or land expeditions, returning with camels laden with gold – no, there are no such stories or records. It is not as if Indian kingdoms were weak or powerless. Though there was a large sphere of Indian influence, most of it was not through armed conquest but cultural osmosis and exchange. Thus the historical record of India does not show a desire to go and rule other people, to enforce its will on others, to trample upon them or exploit them economically, to destroy their temples and objects of reverence – that was not the Indian way.

But, by the same token, to be ruled by others is also unacceptable to us, and we will struggle against it. Throughout Indian history, the struggle for svaraj has gone on. We have records of villagers protesting against emperors, blocking roads, refusing to pay taxes, fasting, hugging trees, and so on. In the 150 years of British rule, there was a revolt practically every single year in India. Some part or the other of India was always up in arms against the British rule. So Pax Brittanica was a great illusion. There was no peace but only continuous war; an imperialistic power can only survive by the force of arms. For peace you need svaraj.

Svaraj is a political ideal, which comes from a deep spiritual ideal, resurrected during India's freedom struggle, defined and re-deployed by great Indian thinkers like Aurobindo and Gandhi. Writing in the *Harijan* in 1946, a year before independence, Gandhi outlined his vision of a good society or what svaraj will look like:

> In this structure composed of innumerable villages, there will be ever-widening, never-ascending circles. Life will not be a pyramid with the apex sustained by the bottom. But it will be an oceanic circle whose centre will be the individual always ready to perish for the village, the latter ready to perish for the circle of villages, till at last the whole becomes one life composed of individuals, never aggressive in their arrogance but ever humble, sharing the majesty of the oceanic circle of which they are integral units. Therefore the outermost circumference will not wield power to crush the inner circle but will give strength to all within and derive its own strength from it.[41]

In Gandhi's model of oceanic circles, we have a way of relating to one another which is very different from the pyramidal or hierarchical order of most societies. In the latter, you have a few people on top ruling the rest. As you go higher, the number gets smaller, until at the very top you have only one person. In Gandhi's model, the individual is the centre of the oceanic circle, continually expanding his self to include his family, his neighbourhood, his village, his state, his country and so on. What is wonderful is that Gandhi allows each person to be the centre of his or her cosmos, but does not limit any one to the confines of himself or herself. Each self has the capacity to expand outward, to reach out to others, to sacrifice himself or herself for their welfare. So the self in svaraj is not a limited but an expanding one – a potentially unlimited self which can stretch to embrace the whole cosmos. Ultimately, the self alone exists; there is no other. The Gandhian model is not one of conflict, but of cooperation. Progress does not necessarily come through clashes of opposites as in Hegelian and Marxian praxis.

Finally, in the cultural realm, the counterpart of metaphysical non-dualism and political svaraj is non-exclusion. Again, non-exclusion is different from inclusion. Inclusion is bound to be unfair because we cannot include everybody. Inclusion is often a myth, like tokenism, to keep most people out on the pretext of taking a few in. Usually, the status quo, with the dominant groups controlling the system, is retained with the justification that because no system can be perfectly inclusive, some people will always be excluded. The rich and the powerful rule in the name of being inclusive. When the marginalized protest, some scraps of privilege are thrown their way to quieten them.

Non-exclusionism is neither the opposite of exclusion nor the same as inclusion. It tries to create a just social order by refusing to accord exclusive entitlements to power or prestige to any group. Theoretically, no one will be excluded, though practically, some may still be left out. But if that happens, the system must constantly refine itself or make special attempts to include them. Non-exclusion implies the humility to know that we are not perfectly just, but that we would try to be so. It also saves us from the trap of political correctness.

While non-exclusion is humble, inclusion is arrogant. Claiming to be inclusive may camouflage a more flagrant kind of inequality, as in many so-called advanced countries. As immigrants or outsiders, even if we have jobs, homes, and contribute to society, we feel shut out socially, marginalized politically and alienated culturally. If we complain, we are told, 'Show us where a law is being violated,' to which we might wish to reply, 'It's not a matter of law, it's how you have designed your societies.' They are exclusive from start to finish; but because you have realized how unfair that is, you now try to include some of the others. The principle of exclusion has not ended, but is sought to be mitigated by tokenism. Once the quota is filled, the society remains as exclusive, racist or oligarchic as ever.

Perhaps, it is more important not to have closure than to try to include every single number in a system. Reality cannot be exhausted numerically. In India, there is no alpha point or omega point, no point of origin or conclusion. No single book, God or prophet, no one dogma or church, no one belief system or dictator. It is an open system, bounded by certain precepts, like a mandala. If you say that everything started with the big bang, an Indians would ask, what happened before the Big Bang? One of the creation hymns of the Rig Veda asks precisely such a question. Its answer is that the creator of the system knows or perhaps even he doesn't know.

Conclusion

India's 'truths', similarly, are not exclusive to India; rather they constitute a beautiful part of the heritage of humankind. It is for this reason that they should not be lost. The third way that India shows, which is to be neither the oppressor nor the oppressed, is not necessarily like Homi Bhabha's third space between nations. The third way of India is an alternative way of living and being, not always tied to power and its opposite, which is powerlessness. When we look at the world today, we see two clearly identifiable forces, at least in the political arena. There is US-led Western imperialism and in opposition to it is jihadism. One is systemic, the other counter-systemic. Similarly, there is the force of globalization and capitalism and then there are the anti-globalizers and the indignants. But the third way would be something different, not locked into the dominant either as an ally or as an adversary.

The dominant forms of post-colonialism, which are located in the West, do not offer this space. They are a part of the Western narrative, howsoever critically from the inside. Perhaps, countries like Brazil, Russia, India, China, and South Africa, the so-called BRICS, could show a differing path by realizing the third way. Our challenge is to produce viable social and intellectual systems which neither reproduce the contradictions of the dominant nor are at war with it. Our countries and societies are large and vibrant. The non-Western world is actually the majority. But much of this world consists of failed states and unviable systems. They cannot provide the alternative. That is why it may be left to some of us to do so. Shall we rise to the occasion?

Chapter 4

Pilgrims and Spiritual Travellers

Travel Writing and Empire

Travel writing, even when it concerns sacred India, is deeply involved in the broader historical, cultural, economic and political conditions of its times. Given that travel itself is often a disguised mode of exercising power, the politics of travel writing cannot be ignored when the travelling takes place across cultures. Furthermore, given that travel both as a means of recreation and as a mode of self-expression is available almost exclusively to the former colonizers, travel writing as a discourse is complicit in the larger project of post-, or rather, neo-colonialism. But are all travellers the same? Is there a special category of travel, and hence of travel writing, which defies this politics?

The moot question is whether pilgrimage as a mode of travel belongs to a distinctly different paradigm than the other modes of travel we know of. If so, are narratives by Westerners who come to India as pilgrims different from those written by conquerors or traders? Does the very idea of pilgrimage reverse the usual relationship between the traveller and the travelled?

I plan to explore such questions by looking at two texts, Paul Brunton's *A Search in Secret India*[42] and Roger Housden's *Travels through Sacred India*.[43] Both texts are written by Englishmen who were serious pilgrims, travelling to India in search of wonder. By historicizing these texts, I wish to discover their relationship with their times. Do they both project an identical, inalterable 'spiritual India' or do they instead reveal a changing and evolving cultural territory in which the sacred and the secular interact in an ever-changing dynamics? How would one account for the change in Western attitudes even to sacred India, which is supposedly timeless? By raising such questions, we might arrive at a better understanding of the relationship between prayer and power or between politics and spirituality.

But what of the increasing numbers of third world travellers? True, one sees more and more brown skin on international flights, but most of it belongs not to tourists or travellers of the Western kind. It is the skin of exiles, expatriates, people of the diaspora – living or going abroad in search of work – or, more recently, of business travellers – trying to make money in a global market. There are also new kinds of travellers, usually going for group holidays, herded together on cheap airlines or tour buses, dressed in Indian clothes and sporting inexpensive digital cameras. They travel with their own cooks and guides. Very few of these can be considered serious travellers. Certainly, almost none will write the kind of books about the West that Westerns have written about India for the last 500 years or more. As Salman Rushdie puts it, 'Adventuring is . . . by and large a movement that originates in the rich parts of the planet and heads for the poor.'[44] The Third World traveller, then, feels like an outcast outside the walls of the great city, aching for its bright lights, sounds and sensations, but unable to afford them. The experience of the metropolis inevitably becomes a painful and humiliating one.

A Map of Travel Writing

The major modes of travel writing may be categorized in terms of the relationship of the traveller with the land travelled to. In undertaking this exercise, the issue that interests me most, ultimately, is piety; even so, the question of power, which indeed is the fulcrum of any post-colonial analysis of travel narratives, cannot be wished away. Earlier attempts to map travel writing, however, have not met with spectacular success. In his overview of travel literature in *Encyclopedia of Postcolonial Literatures*, Patrick Holland calls it 'a huge field, without inventory, history, or theory . . .' He then goes on to outline four kinds of travel writing: 'imperial travel', 'inter-commonwealth travel', 'return travel' and, finally, 'within-the-country travel'.[45]

These categories may be useful even for within-the-country travel, such is recounted in this book. Yet, my own visits to sacred sites in India have not been uninfluenced by the accounts of Westerners. Holland's types, though useful, are not compete or even adequate. This is because they are based on a traveller's origin or affiliation, and therefore confusing and overlapping. For instance, imperial travel can also be inter-commonwealth or return travel. In special cases it can even be within-the-country travel, as when an Englishman goes to Scotland or Northern Ireland, feeling like an outsider. Other schemes try to offer graded, historical phases of Western travel overseas and to derive from them certain corresponding narrative types. Or they attempt to classify travel narratives in terms of their content or genre (see, for instance, Adams, Greenblatt, Pratt and Spur).[46]

What I propose is a somewhat different way of classifying travel. Off-hand, we can think of several recurring kinds of travellers that we encounter throughout history. Some of these are: conquerors, prospectors, explorers, traders, scholars, tourists, missionaries, job-seekers, exiles, immigrants, refugees, pilgrims, students and slaves. The real question is whether on the basis of these recurring types, we could construct a map of travel writing.

If we look at the list once again, we see a subtle order or gradient of changing attitudes from the conqueror to the slave. There is an incremental shift in the power relations between the traveller to the land travelled to. It is on the basis of these relations, then, that we can reduce these varieties of travel into three simpler types: domination, equality, and subservience. There are travellers who seek to dominate, there are those who seek parity or equality, and finally those who are subordinate or inferior to the place visited.

Applying this framework to our earlier list, we see that conquerors regard the places or people they visit as inferior to themselves. Spanish conquistadors, for instance, read out a speech called The Requerimiento to conquered people, enjoining upon them to submit to the authority of the Spanish crown and to accept Christianity. Those who didn't were often summarily executed, even if they didn't understand what was demanded of them. Later imperialisms may not have been as openly brutal or oppressive, but they too institutionalized the inequality between the rulers and the ruled in such a manner that this imbalance in power was reproduced across the board in all walks of life. Thus, even the explorers, scholars and tourists who followed in the wake of the conquest of a territory shared in the spoils of victory and took on the attitude of conquerors themselves. Conquest, thus, is as much an ideology as a physical fact and, furthermore, as an ideology, conquest can penetrate and percolate through the outermost layers of culture from its base in political and economic dominance.

If travel writing under such conditions of inequality is to escape from the ideology of conquest, the travellers or writers concerned need to find ways of actively deflecting, neutralizing or even abnegating their own economic, political and, hence, cultural superiority. Such a levelling is hard to accomplish in the first and second categories of travel which I have outlined above. For instance, it would go against a conqueror's very project to renounce the advantage of superior force that he enjoys over the conquered. Under all circumstances, if he is to maintain his power, this superiority has to be displayed and demonstrated. This may be done by a variety of methods such as disarming and disbanding the conquered people, relocating them, extracting from them signs and tokens of loyalty and submission and, finally, marking off the conqueror from the conquered, again by a variety of methods including dress, customs, places of residence, rank and status, and so on. So, for a conqueror to renounce his attitude of conquest would be a contradiction in terms.

Thus, even the genuine exceptions to this, those from the race or nationality of the conquerors, who seek parity and equity with the conquered, find it hard to do so. Such as these who seek genuine friendship and understanding, find their task fraught with difficulties. The pitch, so to speak, has already been queered for them. The best among these travellers may genuinely strip themselves off their privileges, even crossing over to the camp of the conquered, but the risks attendant on such defections are very high. To illustrate we only need to look at the vast body of Anglo-Indian literature which shows the dangers of the English mixing too freely with the natives. Any number of books suggest that no good comes of such promiscuity; it is best if each keeps his (or, especially, her) place. There is an invisible, but very definite line dividing the rulers from the ruled. This line can only be crossed at the character's own peril. There is always an innocent, well-meaning English man or woman who goes through the educative process of discovering the truth of this unwritten law, often by paying the price for having violated it.

But is there any possibility of a genuine forswearing of power in the third group of travellers – those who consider themselves inferior or subordinate to the land they travel to? I shall look at this group of travellers in the next section.

Pilgrims and Other Humble Travellers

There are at least eight groups of travellers who would have a deference and even a sense of inferiority vis-à-vis the lands they travel to: exiles, immigrants, refugees, slaves, students, job-seekers, missionaries and pilgrims. Of these, all but the last two – missionaries and pilgrims – are not travellers in the proper sense of the word. Many have actually been forced by circumstances to relocate from their homelands. Most of these involuntary travellers have not produced what is called travel literature.

It is not that they have been devoid of any literary aspirations or achievements. Usually, however, such literature as they produce is about their lost or, by now, imaginary homelands, rather than about the lands they have travelled to.[47] When the groups of such travellers are sufficiently large, they form a diaspora, complete with its own subculture and remembered heritage. But even with these groups, writing is one way in which they overcome their sense of voicelessness and powerlessness. They protest their erasure from history by speaking out.

Before coming to the category which most interests me, that of pilgrims, a word about missionaries. Even though they profess to be humble, carrying the word of God to the heathens and the benighted, missionaries or men of God cannot fully lose their imperial origins or moorings. The two, secular power and missionary activity, often go hand in hand, supporting one another. The modern missionary movement is linked to the overseas expansion of the West, and must therefore be considered as allied to conquest.

But what of older religious teachers and savants who travelled to distant places without the proppings of empire? Perhaps, the best examples of such travel are seen in the history of the spread of Buddhism all over Asia. The Dharma spread far and wide because its teachers travelled to distant places, inspired by the teaching. Their movement was thus, by and large, peaceful, though every now and then the conversion of the ruling monarch did help. A similar, though not identical, case may be found in the spread of Vaishnavism and, to an extent, of Sufism in the Indian subcontinent. In the case of the latter, there was some sort of state support or protection; sometimes, the missions were directly sponsored and were expected to report back valuable information about the local people and state, which was used during the subsequent conquest. Yet, there were many peaceful and non-imperial spiritual activists in pre-colonial times.

In all these cases of devotional travel, the traveller has an attitude of deference to the land or people travelled to. True, there is a difference if the traveller is a guru or a disciple. The gurus go to teach, while the disciples go to learn. So there is a great difference in the power relations between the gurus who are spiritual travellers and the followers. In fact, the tripartite framework proposed earlier of having superiority, parity or inferiority vis-à-vis the land or place travelled to can be applied to sacred travel in general too.

Thus, we might contend that there are three kinds of travellers: those who go to conquer, those who go to share and those who go to serve. The first wish to demonstrate their superior knowledge, the second aim at a relationship of parity or equity, while the third go to learn and assimilate.

I would now like to concentrate on the special kind of travel that a pilgrimage is. Here, axes of classification and difference can be traditional versus modern, colonized versus colonizer, east versus west, and sacred versus secular. These categories overlap and intersect in complex ways. Further, in each of these sets, the three different attitudes – dominance, parity and subservience – to the land travelled to are also evident.

Though it would appear that we have too many varieties here, most pilgrims display a reverence for the holy lands they travel to. This is because the very idea of a pilgrimage reverses the normal order of values expected of normal travellers. To embark on a pilgrimage implies that one wants to pay homage to a sacred site. The travel, too, is of a special sort. It is often accompanied by vows and abstentions, by ritual self-abasement or humility. Muslim pilgrims going on Haj, for example, observe great simplicity in dress and food. Those going for the annual pilgrimage to Sabarimalai, too, strictly regulate their diet, dress and lifestyles as a part of the pilgrimage. Similarly, Sri Lankan pilgrims in India will often turn vegetarian during their sojourn. Devotees at Tirupati often offer their hair to the deity. Several walk hundreds of kilometres, or climb tall mountains, or even cover vast distances with prostrations. There seems to be no limit to the pilgrims' self-abasement in their attempt to please their *ishta devata* or chosen deity. In all these instances, the pilgrimage becomes an event clearly demarcated from everyday life. Not only is it separated from the more mundane activities of the pilgrim's life, but it is characterized by a reversal of several of the values of daily life. Thus, there are traditions which encourage the voluntary practice of poverty, chastity, simplicity in food and dress, and several other such restrictions.

Cross-cultural pilgrimages, likewise, reveal some interesting reversals. The more powerful, affluent and materially advanced Westerners now occupy an even lower rank in the hierarchy of pilgrims than, perhaps, their middle-class Indian counterparts. Sometimes, these pilgrims also assume a poverty which is worse than their *desi* or native brethren. Thus, we have images of the down and out hippies wandering about India's sacred cities hardly better off than the local beggars. In the latter instance, their spiritual inferiority is reinforced by their material deprivations.

In addition, it would appear that such pilgrims, by the very nature of their enterprise, are traditionally less aggressive, less wasteful, less egocentric and less destructive than tourists. At least, this used to be the case traditionally before the days of luxury pilgrimages. In the olden days, very few of the pilgrims were really affluent, and those that were, were required to give away enormous amounts of money in charity. There is a memorable passage in the literature on Sri Ramakrishna when he forces his patron Mathur Babu to feed all the starving villagers he encounters during a pilgrimage to Banaras and also to give them enough money to apply hair oil. Even kings who would otherwise extract tribute or levy taxes on a territory invaded, when they visited the same territory as pilgrims, were supposed to perform lavish public acts of charity.

Does such a reversal of hierarchies exempt cross-cultural travellers from the kind of power affiliations outlined earlier? Is it possible for these travellers voluntarily to renounce their special privileges? Do pilgrims and seekers, then, escape from the normal attitudes of superiority which Western travellers bring to India? Does their reverence for India help them break free from the discourse of Orientalism? Or, contrarily, do they end up offering an obverse, but equally romanticized, representation of sacred India? Are these contrasting images merely symptomatic of the West's schizophrenic response to India or are they two diametrically opposite ways of understanding Indian realities? Can we conclude that these seekers and pilgrims are automatically better, more sensitive to India? Does a pilgrimage itself implies deference, respect for the land travelled to, and therefore cannot be oppressive in the same manner as secular travel is? Briefly, are pilgrims 'better' than conquerors? Or are both equally 'bad'?

In the next chapters, I examine the possibilities of genuine cross-cultural pilgrimage. As someone who shares certain assumptions with these travellers, I concede that there is a sacred India which attracts genuine seekers from all lands; furthermore that this India can be experienced, written about, and shared with others. Some Western travellers have done a commendable job of writing about it. Their narratives are not about dominance or parity, but about self-realization and transformation. Human beings from different and unequal positions can, it appears, dialogue with one another in a fruitful and productive manner. And yet, while being sensitive to the sacred and spiritual dimensions of these travel narratives, we cannot be blind or insensitive to their material and secular bases. It is only by being aware of both the sacred and the secular that we can arrive at a rich, complex and satisfying understanding of these journeys to sacred India.

Chapter 5
A Search in Secret India

*P*aul Brunton's book, *A Search in Secret India*, first published in 1934, has come to acquire the status of a classic. It is famous, not so much as a travel book, but as a guide to Indian spirituality. It has been considered compulsory reading for Westerners interested in the subject. Naturally, a certain class of Indians too has found the book useful. Its popularity in India is attested to by the number of Indian editions and reprints which the book has been through. Two years after its first publication, Brunton released *A Search in Secret Egypt*, following the same best-selling formula. But I don't believe this book did as well. Somehow, it was India, not Egypt, whose 'sacredness' was more readily accepted, at least symbolically, by the world. Soon, Brunton himself went on to become a guru. He wrote several other well-known books including *The Secret Path, A Message from Arunachala, Indian Philosophy and Modern Culture* and *The Spiritual Crisis of Man*. Yet, *A Search in Secret India* remains Brunton's best-known and most popular book.

Born in 1898 in England, Brunton's original name was Raphael Hurst. After serving in World War I, he began dabbling in spirituality and mysticism. He started, as many Westerners then did, as a theosophist. The whole premise of his journeys to India and the Orient was to find spiritually elevated beings or mahatmas, a belief that was most probably derived from theosophy. He found his first genuine calling as an interpreter of Eastern spirituality to Westerners. As a journalist and writer, he is credited with bringing the profound truths of the East to the West in simple and lucid prose. As a guru, however, Brunton took himself too seriously. By the time he died in 1981, he had more than 20,000 pages of philosophical and spiritual writings. Considering that his own master Ramana Maharshi taught through silence and hardly wrote anything, Brunton's output seems rather excessive.

Of all he wrote, his very first book, *A Search in Secret India*, remains his most readable and important book. This is partly because it is an absorbing account of spiritual India in addition to being a story of personal transformation. But its appeal also lies in that it reads like a great adventure book, full of unusual characters and incidents. It grabs the readers' attention and drives them from one wonderful event to another. The book's other claim to fame is that it contains the first Western account of Ramana Maharshi. It is not as if Brunton discovered Ramana, but he (Brunton) certainly brought the Sage of Arunachala international recognition. Brunton's book, in addition, has a formidable reputation in spiritual circles. It is believed that no sensitive or spiritually inclined reader is left untouched by its subtle influence. It is reputed to have brought many readers to the spiritual path, awakening their latent urge for the divine. It is after reading Brunton that countless other pilgrims from the West mustered courage to make that arduous trip to India.

The book, moreover, has considerable documentary value because it contains accounts of some well-known yogis, sadhus and holy men of India. Besides the detailed narrative on Ramana Maharshi, the other notable figures in the text include Meher Baba, Hazarat Babajan, Mahendranath Gupta (Master Mahashaya), the Shankaracharya of Kumbakonam [sic], Swami Vishudhananda of Banaras, Shahabji Maharaj of Dayal Bagh, and Yogi Ramiah of Tiruvannamalai. There are also encounters with several other faquirs, yogis, magicians, astrologers and miracle-mongers in the book.

Many of these accounts can only be described as thrilling, unexpected, strange and, sometimes, utterly incredible. Brunton, however, is as sceptical about what he reports as his readers might be; so he does not lose his credibility entirely. The book, replete with prophecies and predictions, ends with a reversal and a denouement; it thus has an effective plot and affords the satisfaction of a story well-crafted, controlled and concluded. In fact, it would not be inappropriate to mention that Brunton's book helped me in my own journey to sacred India.

Its year of publication, its authenticity, its documentary power and its appeal as a story, thus, make *A Search in Secret India* unique in the genre. The only book that I know of which has had a comparable impact is Paramahansa Yogananda's *Autobiography of a Yogi*.[48] Yogananda's book is an even richer and more fantastic than Brunton's; it is chock-full of miracles and paranormal occurrences. But it is also more detailed, with greater authenticating material such as names, address, dates, witnesses, written and oral testimonies, and so on. Having been written, moreover, by a practising yogi, it is perhaps more authentically located in an Indian spiritual tradition than Brunton's book which is by an outsider. Interestingly, Yogananda visits several of the persons named by Brunton and thus ends up corroborating and extending the latter's accounts. *Autobiography of a Yogi* serves as an interesting contrast to Western accounts of sacred India. It has also sold better and has brought more people, whether Western or Eastern, to spirituality. Yet, when it comes to Western accounts of India, Brunton's book remains a classic.

A Search in Secret India as Travel Literature

A convenient point of entry into Brunton's book occurs a little after the first half. Brunton has had one meeting with Ramana Maharshi, but then wanders on, not knowing exactly what he is looking for. His grand spiritual tour of India, so to speak, is still incomplete. Also, he has not yet had a proper opportunity to assimilate what he has seen and experienced. It is at this juncture that he encounters, in the dusty streets of Puri, a 'Literary Sadhu'. That, of course, is not his name, but is all that Brunton condescends to tell us about his interlocutor.

Lounging on the beach, Brunton is amusing himself with the 'rose-scented pages' of Omar Khayyam, when a holy man squats by his side and introduces himself in excellent English, 'Pardon me, sir . . . but I, too, am a student of your literature.' To prove his point, the sadhu unties the knot of his linen bundle to reveal, quite appropriately, if not the Minute, at least the *Essays* of Lord Macaulay! About the father of English education in India, the sadhu observes, 'A wonderful literary style, sir, a great intellect—but what a materialist!' The other book that the sadhu carries is *A Tale of Two Cities*, of which he says, 'What sentiment, what tear-bringing pathos, sir!'

But it is his third book which is most interesting – *Mammonism and Materialism: 'A Study of the West'* by a 'Hindu Critic'. Brunton says, 'It is written in a declamatory style by some Bengali babu and published in

Calcutta—probably at its author's expense.' Brunton does not think too highly of it, 'On the strength of the two degrees tacked on to the end of his name, but without any first-hand acquaintance with his subject, the writer luridly pictures Europe and America as a kind of new inferno, full of suffering and gloom, and peopled by tortured working-classes and sybaritic plutocrats engaged in debased pleasures.'

Brunton turns to the Literary sadhu and demands, 'Now tell me—do you agree with the writer of *Mammonism*?' The sadhu is not to be outdone so easily. He replies, 'Just a little, sir; just a little!' So far, the dialogue has proceeded along predictable, if entertaining lines. It is now that it takes an unexpected turn. The Literary sadhu adds, 'It is my ambition to travel to the West one day; then I shall see it for myself.' Brunton asks, 'And what will you do there?' The sadhu replies, 'I shall deliver lectures to transform the darkness of the peoples' minds into light. I would like to follow in the footsteps of our great Swami Vivekananda, who gave such captivating orations in the great cities of your lands. Alas, that he died so young! What a golden tongue died with him!' Brunton responds, 'Well, you are a strange kind of holy man.' The sadhu brings the encounter to a close by citing Shakespeare, 'The Supreme Playwright has set the stage. What are we but actors who make our entrances and exits, as your world-renowned Shakespeare says!'[49]

This intriguing passage can be read at several levels. It is as if in the deep of his Indian travels, Brunton has suddenly encountered his opposite number, someone who might have been Brunton himself and whom Brunton himself might have been, had circumstances been reversed. In this encounter we also see two different kinds of stereotypes and models of travel in evidence. Moreover, there is the inequality between the two which overrides all other impressions.

The Literary sadhu is very much a product of the colonial education system and yet, the dominant self is not a colonized, but a recovered self. Its model is, of course, Vivekananda, himself an English-educated positivist, transformed by Sri Ramakrishna. Vivekananda's triumphant travels in the West, which on closer examination are revealed to be not so triumphant after all, then, become the model for the east-to-west spiritual traveller.

The reason I foreground this relatively minor incident in the book is because it reveals the complex and paradoxical relationship of Brunton to India. As the representative of the ruling race, as an Englishman in India, as someone who has the money and the leisure both to examine and judge the various holy men he meets, he is at once superior to the land and its people. His privileges as a Western traveller are visible throughout – in the hotels in which he stays, in his mode of travel, in the baksheesh that he gives to faquirs who perform for him, in his access to the rich and powerful of the land, even to the extent of his receiving special treatment wherever he goes. For instance, he travels in a reserved compartment with Sahabji Maharaj, the head of the Radha-Saomis of Dayalbagh, part of the way, a privilege nobody else enjoys. At Banaras, when he visits Swami Visudhananda, he persuades Pandit Kaviraj, the principal of the Government Sanskrit College, to act as his interpreter. For all practical purposes, then, Brunton is the Sahib travelling amongst natives.

Nowhere is his sense of superiority to the natives more evident than at the beginning of his book, where he credits himself as a Westerner with higher powers of observation and logic. 'It is an unfortunate fact,' he observes, 'that the Hindus lack any critical approach to these matters and will mix hearsay with fact quite indiscriminately. Therefore such reports diminish greatly in truth as documentary records. When I saw the cataract of credulity which covers so many Eastern eyes, I thanked Heaven for such scientific training as the West has given me and for the common sense attitude which journalistic experience has instilled in me.'[50]

It is obvious that though Brunton's book is filled with the most incredible and 'unscientific' happenings – including telepathy, stopping one's breath, raising the dead (in this case, only a bird), tearing out an eyeball and restoring it, and so on – Brunton, because he is an Englishman, is, by his own assumption, above suspicion; his credibility is never called into question. At the same time, however, he can dismiss similar Indian accounts as unreliable fables. Critical thinking, scientific training and common sense are all conferred a priori upon himself (and the West) and denied to Indians. This makes Brunton's collusion with imperial cultural paradigms obvious.

Yet, as I argued earlier, the fact that Brunton is a pilgrim at once disassociates and distances him from the colonial functionaries in

India. He calls his book *A Search in Secret India* because he claims that the India he writes about is largely unknown to his compatriots who rule the country. He attributes this ignorance to 'the inevitable barrier imposed by this form of caste', – that is the caste divide between the rulers and the ruled, the whites and the browns, the colonizers and the colonized. 'Fewer still have taken the trouble to go out of their way to find the adepts in Yoga, while not one Englishman in a thousand is prepared to prostrate himself before a brown, half-naked figure in some lonely cave or in a disciple-filled room.' Evidently, Brunton is one such Englishman. In his figurative and literal prostrations before India's holy men, he is also prostrating before India and what it represents at its best.

Spiritual wealth, from this point of view, is more valuable than material wealth. Such a view is echoed by the leading Indian English novelist Raja Rao, who asserts that it was the search for the Holy Grail that led the English to India (*The Meaning of India*). When I mentioned this in a review, a friend accused Raja Rao (and me) of conveniently sidestepping the material realities of colonialism by recourse to this fanciful abstraction. A similar charge might be levelled against Brunton because he does not condemn, nor apologize for, the drain of India's wealth by the British. Yet, what is more important for this argument is that he does refer to a different kind of treasure which is not only intact, but which the British in their greed for material wealth, seem to have missed altogether. In this passage, the spiritual treasure is valorized over the material. Brunton's project, then, is mired in a complex politics of collusion and resistance. He respects India too much to trample on it; yet, by virtue of his racial, political, cultural and ideological affiliations, he cannot altogether escape from the colonizer's mentality and attitude to things Indian.

A Search in Secret India as a Spiritual Text

The source of the book's effectiveness as a spiritual text is the presence of several genuine spiritual gurus in it, but especially of Ramana Maharshi. There are two places in the text devoted to Brunton's encounters with the Maharshi, Chapter IX: 'The Hill of the Holy Beacon', and Chapters XVI and XVII, 'In a Jungle Hermitage' and 'Tablets of Forgotten Truth', respectively, which are the last two chapters of the book.

Both these encounters have been prepared for elaborately. The Shankaracharya of Kumbakonam has already predicted that the Maharshi is the person Brunton is seeking.[51] Even earlier, one of the Maharshi's devotees, Subramanya Aiyar, has asked Brunton to visit Tiruvannamalai, declaring that it is the Maharshi who is behind Brunton's trip to India, 'Because he [Ramana Maharshi] has led me to you! It is his power which has drawn you to India!'[52] In fact, the trail of premonitions and predictions goes back even further to Hazrat Babajan. Reputed to be 134 years old when Brunton sees her, she is the saint who had transformed Meher Baba with a kiss on his brow. Of Brunton she says, 'He has been called to India and soon he will understand.'[53] Indeed, both encounters with the Maharshi happen in spite of Brunton's great reluctance. On both occasion, his decision to go elsewhere is countermanded as if by a higher power, drawing him into the Maharshi's orbit.

During the very first darshan, Brunton has an important spiritual experience. The Maharshi says nothing, but his gaze is riveting, 'There is something in this man which holds my attention as steel filings are held by a magnet.'[54] The several thoughts, doubts and misgivings that arise in Brunton's mind gradually disappear, 'One by one, the questions which I have prepared in the train with such meticulous accuracy drop away....' What is happening is typical of the silent, but potent action of the greatest 'mind-slayer' of recent times. Of all miracles, the miracle of inner peace and equanimity is the hardest to attain; only a perfectly self-realized sage emanates it as his natural state.

This silent intercourse so overwhelms Brunton that he postpones his pressing queries for the meetings that follow. When he does get an opportunity, Brunton plies the Maharshi with questions, only to receive what appear to be a series of rebuffs, 'Why should you trouble yourself about the future?... Take care of the present; the future will then take care of itself.' Or, 'As you are, so is the world. Without understanding yourself, what is the use of trying to understand the world?'[55] The Maharshi seems to suggest that what Brunton has received is much greater and deeper than any question that he (Brunton) might raise.

Before he departs, Brunton has a major paranormal vision in the Maharshi's presence, which he calls 'a vivid dream'. He imagines that he is a boy of five, standing at the mountain path to Arunachala, holding the Maharshi's hand, who seems to be a towering figure, having grown to a giant's size. They ascend to the top of the hill, encountering several yogis and siddhas in subtle bodies on the way. On top of the hill, once again the Maharshi looks into Brunton's eyes:

> I become aware of a mysterious change taking place with great rapidity in my heart and mind. The old motives which have lured me on begin to desert me. . . . An untellable peace falls upon me and I know now that there is nothing further that I shall ask from life.[56]

In the days that follow, Brunton is unable to get any closer to the Maharshi, yet hears and participates in an important conversation. Its culmination is the Maharshi's explanation of the nature of the Self:

> The first and foremost of all thoughts, the primeval thought in the mind of every man, is the thought 'I.' It is only after the birth of this thought that any other thoughts can arise at all . . . you would discover that, just as it is the first thought to appear, so is it the last to disappear. [But the disappearance of the 'I'-thought does not lead a person to madness, unconsciousness or idiocy.] On the contrary, he will attain that consciousness which is immortal, and he will become truly wise, when he has awakened to his true self, which is the real nature of man.[57]

Brunton's doubts do not fade away, but he is aware of being in the presence of a very great truth.

Before Brunton departs, he is vouchsafed one more paranormal experience, once again coming to him via the Maharshi's gaze: 'His eyes shine with astonishing brilliance. Strange sensations begin to arise in me . . . His mysterious glance penetrates my thoughts, my emotions, and my desires . . .' Brunton is uneasy thus to lose control, but once again, begins to feel an 'extraordinary peace . . . a sense of exaltation and lightness. Time seems to stand still. My heart is released from its burden of care. Never again, I feel, shall the bitterness of anger and melancholy of unsatisfied desire afflict me . . . What is this man's gaze but a thaumaturgic wand...'[58] Gradually, the others leave the room: 'I am alone with the Maharishee! [sic] Never before has this happened. His eyes begin to change; they narrow down to pin-points... There comes a tremendous increase in the intense gleam which shines between the lids, now almost closed.' It is now that Brunton experiences nothing less than what the Buddhists call *bhanganyaya*, the deconstruction of the body itself: 'Suddenly, my body seems to disappear, and we are both out in space!'[59] After this, when Brunton finally leaves, his attitude is truly that of a pilgrim, who bows his head in farewell and attempts to mutter a few words of thanks as a poor recompense for a treasure so disproportionately immense.

After this memorable encounter, Brunton goes on in his wanderings all over India, still ostensibly searching for yogis, faquirs and miracle-workers. But there is a noticeable change in his attitude. Ironically, the very sense of wonder, innocence and novelty which has enabled him, without being judgmental, to encounter so many of these holy men of India, is now missing. Instead, a strange ennui gradually takes possession of him, until he finds himself tired and utterly exhausted, back in Bombay (now Mumbai). He has taken ill and is on the verge of a nervous breakdown. What Brunton is going through is, in the parlance of the mystics, the dark night of the soul, that vale of doubt and tribulation through which every earnest seeker must pass before arriving at the shoreless expanse of the final beatitude. A cry of anguish issues forth from Brunton's tortured mind: 'I realize unexpectedly that I have become a pilgrim without a God, a wanderer from city to city and from village to village seeking a place where the mind may find rest, but finding none.'[60] It is as if neither the secular nor the sacred can satisfy him.

As the defeated traveller, his purpose dissipated, prepares to turn his face towards home, he realizes how futile and limited his quest has been. Travel, at this point, takes on a totally different dimension, resembling the age-old metaphor of the round of lives that we go through, travelling from birth to death. This is no longer the travel of a European adventurer visiting distant shores in search of conquest or wonder, but the travel of a soul from life to life, in search for everlasting peace or freedom from process.

At the end of his spiritual tether, Brunton hears a voice which directs him to go back to Ramana Maharshi. While he is still in two minds, a letter arrives for him, quite unexpectedly, the next morning. It is from a prominent public figure, a member of the Madras Legislative Council and a devotee of the Maharshi. It bids him welcome to the hermitage of the sage once again, now that Brunton has had 'the good fortune to meet a real Master.'[61]

After altering his plans, he meets another Indian devotee, K. S. Venkatramani, the Indian-English author who had first introduced him to the Shankaracharya. Venkatramani is not surprised to learn that Brunton is on his way to the Maharshi; the Shankaracharya had already predicted it: 'Your friend will travel all round India. He will visit many Yogis and listen to many teachers. But, in the end, he will have to return to the Maharishee. For him, the Maharishee alone is the right master.'[62]

Yet, what happens in this second and concluding encounter in the book is somewhat different from what Brunton had expected. Brunton's conversion by now is complete: 'In my heart I know that I come as one seeking to take up the position of a disciple, and that there will be no rest for my mind until I hear the Maharishee's decision.'[63] The reversal of attitudes is amply evident here; the master, or at any rate, one who belongs to the master race, has now become a humble disciple. Sacred India, the land, has triumphed over the Western traveller.

As it happens, even the material advantages which Brunton came with are now withering away. He has news of some reversals from home; his own economic position is now rather precarious. Moreover, contrary to Brunton's expectation, the Maharshi does not accept Brunton as his disciple: 'What is all this talk of masters and disciples? All these differences exist only from the disciple's standpoint. To one who has realized the true self there is neither master nor disciple. Such a one regards all people with equal eye.'[64] A different kind of relationship develops between the Maharshi and Brunton. One old visitor, after travelling in India three times, even asks to be Brunton's disciple. It is Brunton's turn to play the guide: '"Your master is not far off," I told him and conducted him straight away to the Maharishee.' This, then, is the first of the thousands that Brunton is destined to lead to the Maharshi!

In the last pages of the book, the dialectical relationship between the sacred and the secular once again surfaces. When Brunton criticizes Indians for their 'neglect of material development', the Maharshi, unlike the author of *Mammonism and Materialism*, readily agrees with him: 'It is true. We are a backward race. But we are a people with few wants. Our society needs improving, but we are contented with fewer things than your people. So to be backward is not to mean that we are less happy.'[65] The whole focus of material development, according to this perspective, is only to fulfil our wants, not necessarily to multiply them. Development, then, cannot become an end in itself.

Brunton, however, can only understand this distinction in terms which he has invoked at the beginning of his book – spiritual treasure versus material treasure. The Maharshi to him is a 'child of a remote Past, when the discovery of a spiritual truth was reckoned of no less value than is the discovery of a gold mine to-day' and 'one of the last of India's spiritual supermen.'[66] Brunton's notion of spirituality, then, is backward looking. For him, it is a question of conservation and retrieval. That, indeed, has been the real thrust behind his travels – that there is something secret, hidden, inaccessible, which needs to be recovered, brought into the open, and made available to all. It is only in his later books he does talk about the future of humanity, of what is needed to save the race from self-destruction.

This process of going inwards reaches a quiet climax in the last pages of the novel. Here, Brunton tries to follow the Maharshi's advice to its logical conclusion, working upon himself in solitude, rather than looking for external props. He tries to trace thought to its source, to stand outside himself as it were. Given the way the book is constructed, this culmination of Brunton's search must happen; otherwise, the reader would feel cheated: 'Finally, it happens. Thought is extinguished like a snuffed candle. The intellect withdraws into its real ground, that is, consciousness working unhindered by thoughts. I perceive, what I have suspected for some time and what the Maharishee has confidently affirmed, that the mind takes its rise in a transcendental source.'[67]

Brunton is no longer a traveller; paradoxically, he is no longer even a pilgrim. From his heightened state of consciousness, Brunton seeks to bring back some 'memorials' of the 'starry truths' that he has gleaned, even though they must be 'translated into the language of the earth'.

These prophetic utterances are offered in italics, and are most certainly the 'Tablets of Forgotten Truth', which the chapter heading promises to reveal. After these profound interjections, Brunton describes one last meeting with the Maharshi in which they communicate perfectly in silence, 'In this profound silence our minds approach a beautiful harmony... my own inner life has begun to mingle with his.'[68]

Looking at Brunton's 'Tablets of Forgotten Truth', I cannot help but being struck by a curious paradox. At the very point that Brunton finishes his process, he ceases to be interesting. The 'Tablets' themselves, written in an archaic language, appear to be so many ineffectual clichés and truisms without the power to illumine or uplift. Brunton the traveller, even Brunton the pilgrim, has been a very interesting raconteur, a conscientious and engaging narrator. The moment he lays claim, however, indirectly, to sagehood, he becomes not just flat and boring, but somewhat incoherent and incomprehensible. His wisdom seems to express himself in vague assertions and generalizations. This difficulty persists in his later books as well. In this sense, the journey is far more interesting than the arrival.

Chapter 6

Travels through Sacred India

*R*oger Housden's *Travels through Sacred India* is an altogether different kind of text than Brunton's. Though it so obviously belongs to the same tradition, Housden's sacred India is not necessarily a secret one. There is no air of the mysterious and occult, no promise of the strange and the miraculous, and no suggestion of a carefully crafted plot in his narrative. The veil of romance that had shrouded the sacred in Brunton's book has been lifted.

There are no encounters here with acid-swallowing faquirs or miracle-mongering yogis. Housden's book, instead, is a travelogue through India's sacred geography. Its four parts take us through different aspects of the sacred in India – rivers, mountains, temples, texts, festivals, art, sadhus and ashrams, and finally, to other traditions like Sikhism, Jainism, Sufism, Buddhism and Christianity. So, the book is a kind of omnibus, offering an introduction to the notion of the sacred, and then following it up with detailed accounts and useful information. It is full of maps, charts, lists, addresses and explanations, thus, a combination of a handbook and travelogue on Indian spirituality.

Like Brunton, Housden is also an Englishman, born near Bath. According to his website, Housden, who now lives near San Francisco in the United States, believes us 'to be creatures with one foot in this world and one in another, less visible one'.[69] Through 'poetry, art and travel' he has found the appropriate language to experience this deeper reality. Now, like many New Age gurus, he leads others to it through his numerous books, readings and activities.

Travels through Sacred India, it would seem, was written when Housden was not yet a guru. Unlike Brunton, he begins not with the strangeness of India, not with its utter and unfathomable otherness, but with its disconcerting, even disappointing, familiarity. Contemporary India is very much a part of a global culture. This 'New India', which Housden talks of in the very first paragraph of the text, is the India of Pepsi and hamburgers, of Reebok and MBAs from America. Housden is forced to acknowledge this 'New India', with its much-touted middle-class, whose powers of consumption are supposedly fuelling the greed of transnational investors. The question, then, for Housden is what is the place of the 'Old India' – the sacred India – in this emergence of globalization and liberalization?

This exploration of what constitutes the sacred is carried out by a New Yorker who wishes to know 'what God means to the ordinary person'. He stops his car on the way down from Mount Abu and asks a farmer, 'Can you tell me what, for you, is the meaning of God?' The farmer offers a fitting riposte: 'Does he know what he is asking?' The American, with his cockiness, picks up a clod of earth and declares, 'This ... is dead matter ... If this is earth, what is spirit?' The farmer gets emotional: '"You call my Mother dead?" ... He kissed the earth, then knelt to return it to the ground.'[70] In contrast to the New India, this, for Housden, is the Old India.

But Housden clarifies that his book 'does not set out to paint some romantic picture,' rather 'it introduces the living dimensions of Sacred India.'[71] Thus at the very beginning of the book, Housden offers us a different way to understand India's idea of the sacred than does Brunton in *A Search in Secret India*. We may recall, that in his Foreword to the latter, Francis Younghusband had equated secret with sacred: '"Sacred India" would be as apt a title for this book. For it is a quest for that India which is only secret because it is so sacred. The holiest things in life are not bruited abroad in public ... The most sacred things a country keeps secret.'[72] While the *raison d'tre* of Brunton's book is to 'discover the secret' of India, Housden's approach is to regard the sacred as that which is not secret, but common, shared and practised. In contrast to Brunton's quest for the exotic, the mysterious and the romantic, Housden seeks that sacred India which is a part of everyday reality, living, evolving and changing. Like the clump of clay that the ordinary farmer declared was living.

In the chapter 'Sacred Land', Housden says, 'A sacred place is one that is graced with the presence of unconditioned being; where, through one agency or another, the unfettered energy and life of the domain of gods makes itself known in the finite world.'[73] But, one might argue, this can be any and every place because the 'unfettered energy' of spirit can push itself into our consciousness to make its presence felt, just as we too may respond to its presence whenever and wherever it wishes.

To meet the possibility of such an objection, Housden clarifies that though the sense of the sacred is actually everywhere, it is felt most palpably 'Wherever a saint is born, walks the earth, works miracles, and dies . . .'[74] The sacred, thus, is a bridge, a point of contact, a conduit between two dimensions of being: 'the infinite, the unconditioned, the unfettered' and 'the finite, the conditioned, the fettered'. Or else, a natural site that has displayed the sign of the supernatural is considered sacred. After describing several sacred sites crisscrossing the land, like arteries and veins or nerves in a body, Housden concludes, 'The pattern makes of the sub-continent a body-cosmos in which no local area is without its major and minor sources of sacred power. The entire country is a sacred land . . .'[75]

The Indian attitude to the sacred is not really confined to India, but extends to the whole cosmos because creation itself was an act of sacrifice in which Prajapati birthed the heavens and the earth out of himself: 'As the earth is a goddess, so the entire cosmos is a living organism.' There is a political dimension to all this, as Housden perceives only too well: 'The sacrality of the land of India, not any political vision, is what, still today, gives a sense of unity to this country of so many religions, cultures, races, and factions.' The modern cult of Bharat Mata or Mother India testifies to this: 'The nationalist movement of the 19th century capitalized on this sentiment by turning the land into a symbol of India as a national entity.[76]

Finally, the central paradox about the sacred: is it within or without? Housden realizes that without bringing in the inner dimension, no idea of the sacred can make any sense: 'The sacrality of the place is interior to the pilgrim, as well as being externally located in some physical place.'[77] After his wanderings all over India, Brunton is told by the Maharshi to look within, to inquire, 'Who am I?' Is that the final message of any pilgrimage? If so, why take the trouble of making the journey? 'Where is there to go, in truth, when everything is where you already are?' asks Housden. Then he replies to his own question: 'Yet you go anyway, because that is the nature of human existence. Round and round we go; what determines whether it is a sacred journey or not is the quality of our intention.'[78]

This subtle tension and opposition between the old and the new, the inner and the outer, the one and the many, and between pilgrimage and tourism is maintained throughout the book. Housden is aware, for instance, that without the right inner attitude, a pilgrim is only a tourist: 'Nothing more profound than tourism—seeing for seeing's sake—will take place unless the imagination of the pilgrim is sensitized to the deeper realities abiding there . . . Even so, among Hindus themselves, tourism is beginning to rival the traditional motive of gaining merit and blessings by embarking on pilgrimage.'[79] He emphasizes the difference between a traditional and a modern pilgrimage. A traditional pilgrimage used to be on foot, through dense jungle and vast tracts of land, across rivers and up mountains; often, those who set out would never come back. However, in the present times, Housden says, 'Pilgrimages are becoming a branch of the travel trade.'[80] The contemporaneity of Housden's text can be seen in this self-reflexivity which it often displays.

Another instance of this is provided at a rather unexpected juncture towards the end. Housden has covered the major texts, temples, rivers, mountains and cities of Hindu India. Now, he turns to the other traditions. After the Golden Temple of the Sikhs, he visits the Jain temples of Dilwara: 'From midday until evening the shoe-rack at the entrance to the Jain Dilwara temple on Mount Abu is stacked to overflowing with every conceivable kind of footwear.'[81] The shoes are out there not only because footwear isn't allowed inside most Indian shrines, but also because the Jains forbid any animal products inside the precincts of their temples.

The owners of the shoes, says Housden, have come from all parts of India and from abroad too, having read about the beautiful carvings of the Dilwara temples. Yet, those who are expecting to find a place of living worship, are bound to be disappointed because while tourists have the temple to themselves in the afternoon, the pilgrims, if they are Jains, can offer worship in the morning. The manager of the temple explains to Housden: 'What can we do? The government requires us to fulfil the needs of the tourists in the afternoons. It is understandable. Architecturally, this is a place of global significance. At least we have the morning to ourselves. Then only Jains are admitted. But come in the morning, as my guest. Then you will see a Jain temple instead of a tourist attraction.'[82]

Housden seizes upon this distinction between tourists and pilgrims: 'Sacred places all over the world are facing the same quandary. Tourism encourages a culture of observers, instamatic snappers, consumers of culture, sights, information, places of "interest".'[83] Obviously, there is something predatory about such visitors, even though Housden does not introduce issues of colonialism and cross-cultural travel in his analysis. With a remarkable admission of guilt, Housden includes himself in this category, even though his attitude throughout the book is demonstrably different: 'None of us, least of all me, an author of a book such as this, are untainted by it.'[84]

The very act of visiting such places even as a pilgrim, with the purpose of writing about them, Housden knows, makes him even more susceptible to the charge of desacralization. After all, any travel writer makes literary capital out of his journeys, thereby converting the places travelled to into products which can be marketed. '[O]ur motivation,' Housden continues, 'may well be that of a genuine pilgrim ... We may might even balk at being described as a tourist. Yet however we like to think of ourselves, we must know that our visit can only add to the pressures on the place and steer it that little bit further towards being a secular monument instead of a source of awe and veneration.'[85]

To this issue of tourist versus pilgrim, Housden adds that of a minority versus majority tradition. The dangers of predatory tourism, according to Housden, are less likely to threaten Hindu centres of pilgrimage because these are sustained by the living faith of about 800 million people and are, moreover, rooted in the local culture. But with a Jain shrine such as Dilwara, the additional dimension of a minority subculture of about 2 million staving off the pressures of an overwhelming majority is fore-grounded. The pluralism of Indian religious and spiritual traditions, which is so eloquently and extensively documented in this book, however does, to some extent, mitigate this pressure of tourism on a minority shrine. It is typical of this country that regardless of the denomination of the shrine, Hindu pilgrims frequent it no less than Jains. This is true not just of Sikh, Jain and Buddhist centres of pilgrimage, but also of Sufi and Christian ones. The Hindu is the quintessential indefatigable pilgrim.

Despite this overlap, Housden is clear about what separates a pilgrim from an ordinary traveller: 'What matters—what will set apart a pilgrim from the ordinary traveller—is whether you are willing to make the crossing, via the tirtha, from this world of mundane reality to one (the same one!) in which the journey, the goal, and the pilgrim himself, are all expressions of the One Divine Whole.' Once again, we notice how Housden makes distinctions only to blur them. The pilgrim, he says, is someone who makes the crossing from this world to another, but that different, sacred or divine world is also, paradoxically, the same as the mundane one. The dichotomies, the oppositions, then, are provisional and heuristic, not final or definitive.

In Housden's book, therefore, a more complex picture of sacred India begins to emerge. Not only is the relationship between the secular and sacred, between the New and the Old India, formulated in a more nuanced manner, but the definition of the sacred itself is less categorical. As Housden observes in the Introduction, 'Everything in the universe is related, and the divine, rather than being somewhere above and beyond life, is right here in the middle of it—even somehow in the squalor that seems to be its very antithesis.'[86] While Brunton emphasized the specialness or the sacred experience, Housden stresses its ordinariness.

Consequently, there is no dramatic or climactic encounter with the guru in Housden's book, no build-up towards some miraculous transformation, and no climax in a mystical or self-transcending experience. Instead, a quiet and easeful wisdom permeates the entire narrative. This ripeness is a quality which is distributed through the very texture of the book, circulating in each chapter. There is also no dark night of the soul as in Brunton, no plunge into depths of despair and despondency. Similarly, though the book does profile a host of well-known holy men including the Kanchi Shankaracharya, Sri Jayendra Swamigal, Nanagaru, Mata Amritanandamayi, Poonjaji, Satya Sai Baba and Chandra Swami (not the infamous one), the emphasis is really on scores of lesser-known sadhus and ordinary men and women whom we encounter in practically every other page of the book.

In addition, the author's acute awareness of the political dimensions of travel is evident in the deliberate lack of any obvious sense of superiority on his part. There is no evidence of his considering himself to be a part of the ruling race, no reference (nostalgic or otherwise) to the British empire, no attitude of condescension to Indians, no assertion of superior scientific training, no reference to the credulity and childishness of Indians, and no racial slurs or innuendoes. The book does, of course, make distinctions between Westerners and Indians, nowhere attempting to elide over the differences in outlook and mentality between the two, yet, even when disapproval is expressed, say about the growing consumerism of a certain section of Indians, it is done so very gently and cautiously.

Housden does not let anything detract from his primary purpose, which is to offer an account of spiritual India. So, even when scores of gurus, traditions and techniques are discussed and analyzed, the critique is always balanced and eminently sensible. Housden certainly seems to have understood Indian traditions better than many of us have understood either Western or Indian ones. All these qualities make this book one of the better books of its kind.

There have, no doubt, been scores of books on Indian spirituality by Western writers. The interest in sacred India has not waned in spite of the commonplace presence of Indian godmen and gurus in the West. Why? If we were to vocalize Roger Housden's implicit answer, then it will be that India, notwithstanding all its modernization, globalization and liberalization, remains perhaps the only place on earth where the pristine purity of the spiritual quest remains inviolate. What makes Housden's book special is the conviction and moderation with which he articulates this position. Housden is not merely a curious travel writer, secure in his modern scepticism, pursuing the exotic and arcane in inhospitable terrains. Neither is he a glorified tour guide, offering a brochure for prospective spiritual tourists. Housden is himself a serious practitioner, a *sadhak*, a seeker: his account of sacred India is born out of a loving and lengthy engagement with this quest.

What is more, Housden is one of the few to have written about the spiritual traditions other than Hinduism. His book has extremely insightful sections on Sikhs, Jains, Sufis, Buddhists and Christians. What Housden shows us is not only the primordial unity of the indigenous religions in spite of their significant differences, but the unique and transforming spiritualization which imported faiths have undergone in India. Perhaps, nowhere else in the Islamic world are Sufi traditions as widely prevalent and influential as in India. Similarly, Christian spirituality has found a hospitable home in India, a space from which Christianity itself may be rejuvenated into a non-sectarian, deeply spiritual faith based on love and sharing.

Housden's book not only gives us the sacred geography of India – mountains, rivers, ashrams, *dhams*, tirthas, *puris*, dargahs, temples, gurdwaras – but is also full of insights and comments on how this sacred India copes with modernity. In other words, the author's spirituality does not make him blind or uncritical to the pitfalls and contradictions of contemporary India. He is quick to notice the continuing poverty, inequality, dirt, disorganization and corruption which one encounters everywhere.

The other great strength of the book is its careful discriminations between various traditions and gurus. The book serves as a subtle commentary and critique on the various practices which he encounters. For instance, about Poonjaji of Lucknow, he says: 'The Lucknow mantra is "I had it, but I lost it." Some, it appears, have been driven to the edge of despair, even suicide, by the realization that what they thought was final enlightenment was another passing stage.' If pursuing the spiritual quest is like walking on a razor's edge, then Housden has succeeded in performing this arduous balancing.

Conclusion

The previous chapters have addressed the issue of pilgrimage as a distinctly different mode of travel than tourism. If so, are narratives by Westerners who come to India as pilgrims different from those written by conquerors or traders? Does the very idea of pilgrimage alter the usual relationship between the traveller and the travelled?

It ought to be clear that while the accounts of pilgrims are different from those of conquerors, there are also different kinds of pilgrims and pilgrimages. Pilgrims display greater sympathy to the land travelled to and to its people; their attitude is one of deference, even reverence, quite unlike the instrumental, predatory approach of conquerors, traders or even scholars associated with imperial expansionism. These pilgrims, moreover, seem to subscribe to a different set of values than secular travellers, who often treat tourist destinations as products and items of consumption. The attitude of pilgrims is different because their worldview often entails a reversal of the normal system of values in which the material always takes precedence over the spiritual. Because pilgrims have access to this altered ideology, they are better able to appreciate the spiritual treasures of a country like India, turning a blind or indulgent eye to its other real or imagined defects. The sort of recoil or revulsion to things Indian which is so common in Westerners' accounts of India is, therefore, missing in their writings. Their representations, too, are consequently less damaging to the wounded colonial or postcolonial psyche.

Yet, what emerges is that pilgrims are not entirely free from the prevailing attitudes and material circumstances of their times. Their narratives too are a part of wider historical, cultural, social and political narratives, conflicting and colluding with the latter as the case may be. For example, we have seen that Brunton shares many of the established attitudes of the ruling race, but his sincerity as a pilgrim helps him overcome most of them. We have also seen how Brunton constructs the sacred in rather exclusive terms as something secret, remote and totally removed from the ordinary world, while Housden does exactly the opposite, arguing that the sense of the sacred permeates throughout our quotidian existence. Brunton's mindset appears to share in certain colonial ideas and modes of thinking, while Housden's text is clearly postcolonial in the positive sense. Brunton approaches sacred from a modern, while Housden does so from a postmodern standpoint. Despite their different starting points, their paths merge in the sacred, the noumenal and the spiritual. Both, thus, display a certain adherence and fidelity to what might broadly be termed as a respect for the spiritual quest, which stresses the journey inwards.

It should be clear that the secular and the sacred are not two mutually exclusive or opposite domains, but that they are related, interconnected and overlapping. When we turn to the sacred, we do not necessarily turn away from the secular. The world follows us, so to speak, into the sacred space; we cannot escape it. However high we might fly in our spiritual aspirations, we remain, as the Rig Vedic hymn asserts, children of the earth. There is always a materiality to our pursuits. Also, our quests have a specific historical ground whose limitations we may not be able to overcome. Our ideas, thoughts, perceptions and self-images are all influenced by these material conditions in which we function.

Does this mean that the sacred, the transcendental and the noumenal can all be reduced to the secular, the material and the phenomenal? This, indeed, has been the practice in many contemporary strategies of reading texts, especially Marxist, New Historicist and postcolonial. I think not. These strategies fail because they cannot address the whole question of the spiritual. On the other hand, those who profess to the spiritual point of view tend to ignore or negate the very contingencies which frame their anti-materialistic turn.

My approach here has been somewhat different: while the sacred is to be understood by its secular articulations, it cannot be exclusively decoded by these. Ultimately, the sacred needs to be understood on its own terms, which defy precisely such binary oppositions as the secular versus the spiritual. After going beyond the binary opposition between the secular versus the spiritual, we need to articulate what is most important to us, but not to the exclusion of everything else. This way, the spiritual enriches our understanding of the secular and vice-versa.

Both these texts are valuable because they show how Westerners have tried to understand India in ways that defy conventional Orientalist notions. Indeed, both books offer valuable insights about sacred India that may not be found in Indian texts. Yet, each text is also a product of its time and speaks of concerns, values and ideas which were in circulation when it was written. Both these travellers are pilgrims, but this fact does not erase their national, cultural, racial or historical locations. Ultimately, however, it is their relationship with sacred India that endures.

Chapter 7

A Passage to Tiruvannamalai

Stalking the Self

Many years back, as an undergraduate in St. Stephen's College of the University of Delhi, I spent one winter vacation in the hostel instead of going back home. There were very few people about and it was quite cold. Both the season and the moment were conducive to an intensification of the quest eternal. It was almost as if I had been given that special interlude only for that purpose.

But very soon, I came up against a block. Was seeking the self also a kind of self-seeking? That is being selfish, doing things to enhance oneself? Thus was seeking the self actually another way not to liberate oneself but only to strengthen one's bondage? For an undergraduate student of 18, seeking liberation was perhaps special. But being aware of that only added to one's ego and came in the way of the professed objective of being free of the ego. I felt trapped. Everything that I did to get rid of the ego might actually end up inflating it.

Were there two selves? The ego self and the 'real' self? Was the goal of life to shift from being one to the other? I began reading J. Krishnamurti's *Commentries on Living* to find out.

The more I read, the more I seemed to be blocked. The person seeking the answers was himself the cause of the questions. The inquiry was only perpetuating that from which liberation was sought. What to do? Where to go? Everything I did, thought, or wanted was within the orbit of the very self which I wanted to transcend.

Frustrated, I wandered about the bookshops on Bungalow Road, near College. In the Motilal Banarsidass store, I suddenly picked up a slim booklet, *Who Am I?* 'Who am I?' What a stupid question, I thought. But it upset my mental poise immediately. I realized for a fact that I simply did not know the answer to an apparently simple question. I had no idea who I really was!

Of course I was so and so, son of so and so, studying such and such, of such height and weight, and so on, but is that what I *really* was? If that was all I was, then who was it that was aware that I had been unsettled by the question and this was an inadequate response? Was I the thoughts racing in my head? Or was I the awareness of these thoughts? If I was the former, then did I have a past and a future? Did two thoughts, or thoughts upon thoughts upon thoughts, add up to 'me'? If I was just a sequence of thoughts and memories, was I 'real'? If on the other hand, I was the awareness of the thoughts, then how could I have a past, present, future or be a separate person?

Krishnamurti had pointed out over and over again that thoughts were merely products of conditioning, created by the interaction between the world and the perceiving device. So was I merely my conditioning or was I something else? If I was my conditioning, then who was it that was aware of the conditioning? On the other hand, if I was awareness, then did awareness have individuality? Was awareness a person? If I was my thoughts, then I was 'unreal'; if I was awareness, I was not a person. In either case, 'I' seemed to be in trouble!

The simple question, 'Who am I' had unsettled me completely. Nothing I knew, nothing I had read or understood, nothing anybody told me had quite prepared me for what followed such an inquiry. 'Who am I? – *I* simply don't know – and the one who *knew* was not 'me.' My inquiry which had begun so bravely during a lonely Delhi winter ground to a halt rather unceremoniously. I was left humbled, even defeated.

Then I went to study at the University of Illinois. I have already narrated earlier how I came to work on mysticism for my PhD. I thought my life's quest and my professional interest could thus be coupled. My teacher, Giri, gave me *The Gospel of Sri Ramakrishna*. More self-seeking? Lifestyle changes, days and nights of stalking the self, studying, teaching, subject to a gruelling schedule in the coldest of mid-Western winters in the flat, snow-smothered plains of Illinois. So far from home, but the hill of fire shining within the heart-space, like a blazing flame!

Soon, I returned to the question that had confounded me and to its author, Ramana Maharshi. I found in his *Collected Works* the most direct path to the self. There it was again, the question which had bothered me, the question for which I had no answer: 'Who am I?'

One morning, a year or so after my quest resumed in earnest, after weeks of intensive meditation, something happened. It went like this: I was delighted with a new insight. But immediately, the counter-thought presented itself. My insight wasn't *true*. It was merely a personal opinion. For a moment, I felt trapped again. My realization could only be as true as myself – a partial and transient being. My insight, in other words, was only another thought in an endless chain.

At that instant, there was a breakthrough, like a shaft of lightening showing everything clearly in the darkest night. 'But there is no such entity,' came the spontaneous counter-response from within. Suddenly, it dawned on me that there was no such person as 'me'. Therefore, there could be no anxiety about the impermanence at all. Even feeling the pang of transience was only momentary. If there was no 'me', there was only insight, neither mine nor any body else's, somewhat like awareness as opposed to the series of thoughts. 'I' referred to a non-existent entity or at any rate was the name of something that had no real or ultimate existence, but was merely an ever-changing, never-permanent flow of thoughts and experiences.

Since there was no 'I', there was no one seeking freedom and no one bound either. Bondage was just a thought as was freedom. Thoughts and experiences would come and go, dancing like whirling sparks in the dark chamber of consciousness. Similarly, bodies would come and go. The flow of reality was continuous and uninterrupted, unaffected as the white screen is by whatever is projected on it. I was not thoughts, but awareness: thoughts could not exist without awareness, but awareness did not need thoughts to exist. Awareness was aware of itself and therefore needed no Other, not even thoughts.

I felt an immense sense of relief and joy. A great internal block had been removed. There was light everywhere. I had wanted the 'truth' very badly and now I had a definite glimpse of it. Rather, *It* had chosen to manifest itself.

Arunachala

Though the Maharshi had died in 1950, his ashram at Tiruvannamalai was a famous centre of spiritual endeavour, frequented by thirsting souls the world over. The ashram is located at the foot of Arunachala, which has been described as 'the Holy Hill which beckons those rich in *jnana-tapas*'.

What is so special about Tiruvannamalai? The name itself is a Tamil compound made up of *tiru* or *sri* (which means holy, auspicious or prosperous), *anna*, which usually means elder brother, but also means powerful or great, and *malai*, which means mountain; so *annamalai* means the great or all-powerful mountain. The hill is known as Arunachala in Sanskrit. *Arun* is the morning sun and *achala* means place (unmoving or situated). According to the Skanda Purana, 'It is the heart of the earth. It is Shiva Himself.' On the great night of Shivaratri, the God assumed the form of an infinite pillar of fire to show Brahma and Vishnu – the other deities of the Hindu pantheon – that He is really limitless. Because this fiery-linga in its original form would be unbearable to ordinary mortals, Shiva assumed a more benign form as the hill. 'Though in fact fiery, my lack-lustre appearance as a hill on this spot is an act of grace for the maintenance of the world.' (Skanda Purana)

Another text, the Arunachala Purana, makes Tiruvannamalai the culmination of Parvati's austerities to unite with Shiva. It is here on the day of Shivaratri that the Lord absorbed His Shakti or spouse into himself, She occupying the left half of the body. Hence, the *ardhanarishwara* or the 'half-woman God', which is the androgynous form of Shiva. 'Her going round the hill was like Parvati's earlier circumambulation of the sacred Agni on the day of her marriage! As she neared the east completing her *pradashina*, the Lord absorbed her as his left-half.' (Arunachala Purana)

There are many other legends and beliefs about Tiruvannamalai. The Maharshi recited a verse, '*Darshanad abhrashadashi, jananat Kamalalaye,/Kashyantu maranan, muktih smaranad Arunachalam*' or 'To see Chidambaram, to be born in Tiruvarur, to die in Benaras, or merely to think of Arunachala is to be assured of Liberation.' Just thinking of the sacred hill is enough; it slays one's ego as the tiger slays the deer.

Arunachala Ashtakam, attributed to Sri Shankaracharya, links Arunachala to the Sri Chakra – the geo-mandala of supreme knowledge and cosmic power. Indeed, it is believed that the hill is the *adi* or the primal linga; the path around it is thus the sacred yoni. Linga represents the male generative principle, somewhat like yang in Tao, while yoni is the female power, like yin in Tao. They are always a unity, like word and meaning, together constituting the sum and substance of the dance of creation. Hence, the *pradakshina* or circumambulation of the hill is at once the *pradakshina* of all lingas. *Pradakshina*, according to one interpretation, means *prada* or giver of boons, *kshi* or destroyer of karma and *na* or giver of *jnana* or supreme knowledge. Arunachala is the one *kshetra* or holy place where the hill, the deity in the temple, and the city, all possess the same name.

In the Skanda Purana, Shiva tells Nandi, 'I, the Lord, ordain that those who reside within a radius of three *yoganas* (about 45 kilometres) of this place (Arunachala) shall, even in the absence of initiation, etc., attain union [with God] which removes all bondage.' It was this verse which Ramana Maharshi quoted to a follower of the Shankaracharya who wanted him to be formally initiated into sannyas.

Each place of pilgrimage has its special features and characteristics. What makes Tiruvannamalai so unique is that the worship of a natural object, the hill, has been identified not only with Puranic temple-ritual, but now also with the force of modern Indian Advaita. In the cult of Arunachala are thus combined centuries of rich spiritual tradition, from very ancient nature-worship to very modern Vedantic metaphysics. Arunachala combines magic, myth and reason into a power vehicle for emancipation and knowledge. As the Skanda Purana declares: 'What cannot be acquired without great pains—the import of Vedanta—can be attained by anyone who looks at [this hill] from where it is visible or even mentally thinks of it from afar.'

The hill has attracted numerous great saints and sages in the past. Indeed, it is believed that at least three mahatmas or great souls reside here at any given time to guide those who seek the divine. The roster of great ones associated with the hill include Arunagirinatha, Esanya Desika, Guhanamashivaya, Virupakshadeva, Seshadri Swami, Ramana Maharshi and, more recently, Yogi Ramsuratkumar.

Ramana Maharshi came to Tiruvannamalai as a lad of 16, already fully self-realized. He had had a death experience in Madurai which convinced him that he was not the body. He spent several years on the hill, speaking little, living a life of exemplary austerity and boundless compassion. Then, his widowed mother joined him. After she attained *mahasamadhi* or the great merger, she was laid to rest at the foot of the hill. Because the Maharshi had given her liberation, a linga or emblem of Shiva was installed over her Samadhi or mortal remains. Aptly termed the Matrubhuteshwara, the Lord of the Mother-Element or God-in-the-form-of-Mother, a temple came up above it and an ashram grew around it.

The Maharshi taught mainly through silence which he considered the most potent medium of communication. He emphasized both the way of devotion and the way of knowledge. 'Either surrender or find out who you are' is the essence of his teachings. We are already the Self and therefore nothing new needs to be sought or discovered; all we need to do is to get rid of false-identification, to stop seeing ourselves as mortal, perishable, embodied creatures, but rather as the infinite, undying, omnipresent consciousness.

Getting There

Tiruvannamalai is a mid-sized town in what used to be the North Arcot district of Tamil Nadu until it became the headquarters of its own eponymous district in 1989. With a population of about 2,50,000, it is approximately 200 km by road from either Chennai or Bengaluru. Though there is a rail link, road travel is much more convenient.

There are the usual lodges, of course, and some new 'three-star' hotels, but the best place to stay is Sri Ramanashramam, at the foot of the holy hill. It has several spartan but adequate rooms and suites, which can be booked in advance by a written request to its president. Free accommodation inclusive of meals is provided for three days by the ashram to serious seekers, but donations are welcome. A special bonus is the food served at Sri Ramanashramam – healthy, simple, vegetarian fare, which nourishes both the body and the soul.

The Deccan plateau has scorching summers followed by a relatively early onset of the monsoons. The months to avoid are March through June; November to January is possibly the best time to visit. So rich in sacred relics and lore, Tiruvannamalai offers much to pilgrim and sceptic alike. The cynosure of the town is, of course, the sacred hill. Going around it in a clockwise direction is supposed to be extremely beneficial. Such a leisurely *pradakshina*, well-equipped with a picnic lunch and rest on the way, is quite enjoyable. Those who can't walk may go on a bicycle or even in a car. The whole loop is a little less than 14 km.

The more adventurous may actually climb up the hill. Even a short climb offers stunning views of the big temple and of the town. Not too high up the hill are the Virupaksha cave and Skandashramam, where Ramana Maharshi lived for several years. The hill is an enchanted place with several caves, rills and groves. It is good to go up with an experienced guide and a good stock of food and drink. A climb to the top is what the modern mind may consider the acme of the pilgrimage. But the Maharshi never recommended it. He preferred people to go around the hill. On top, where the *jyoti* or the flame is lit during the Kartikai Deepam festival, there is a permanent deposit of ghee and ash, considered very auspicious. The view from the top is magnificent.

Apart from the hill, the big temple of Lord Arunachaleshwara and his spouse Goddess Apeetakuchamba is a big draw. It is one of the larger temples of India, with massive walls, beautifully laid out and designed courtyards, sculpted gates, *gopurams* or vaulted towers, tanks and courtyards. The outer, walled circumference is about 4 km long. It is, really, a temple city in the best traditions of South Indian architecture, a monument which may be classed with the Madurai Meenakshi or the Thanjavur Brihadeshwara temples.

The traditional importance of this shrine derives from it being one of the *panchamahbhutasthalas*, that is the site where Shiva takes the form of one of the five elements. The linga here stands for fire. The town has several other temples. Of these the Ashtalingas or eight Shiva shrines dedicated to Agni, Yama, Niruti, Varuna, Vayu, Kubera,

Esanya and Indra – the eight deities – located around the hill on the circumambulation route are significant. Also worth seeing is the Adi Annamalai or the original temple, which has been renovated recently.

Devotees of Ramana Maharshi will be interested in visiting sites hallowed by him. Several of these are within the ashram premises or up on the hill, but rest include the temple tank, Ayyankulam, the 1,000-pillared hall, the Pathalalingam in the basement, the Subramanya shrine – all in the big temple – and the Illuppai tree, Gurumurtam, Pachaiamman Koil, around the hill.

Near Ramanashramam, the colony of devotees, Palakottu is notable. Other ashrams in Tiruvannamalai include the Seshadri Swami Ashram next to Ramanashramam, the Esanya Math, the Yogi Ramsuratkumar Ashram in the Agraharam Collai, and the Nithyananda Ashram near the hill.

Yogi Ramsuratkumar

From Chengam, a good half-hour away from my destination, the milestones begin to announce the town that bears the name of the hill of fire, Tiruvannamalai, the happy hunting-ground of the Self. From the world over seekers come, first as hunters, but then as the hunted.

I gaze out of the window as the road curves slightly, straining to discern the shape of the holy hill in the horizon. In my waking dreams and in the twilit consciousness of sleep, how often have I seen it – arising ever so gently from the ground, the seven-faced auspicious hill, sometimes bare and brown, at other times lightly tufted with downy grass, and after the rains, verdant all over. Composed of the oldest rock on earth – the hill that represents rock solid gnosis, truth that stills the chattering mind, granting nothing short of the knowledge of the self.

How often have I longed for its auspicious sight, not necessarily out there, lit up by the glory of the morning sun or crowned by fleecy white clouds, but in here, inside my mind and heart – a presence which reminds me of who I really am. And in moments of prayer and penitence, utterly defeated by my own stupidities and inadequacies, how often have I cried out, 'Arunachala, O Arunachala, You are my Father and Mother and Everything, O Arunachala! Take away my sense of doership.' Then, if grace follows, not an outcome of prayer but of the divine's own, sweet caprice, you coast along effortlessly, on the tides of time, joining and leaving this world and all its vagaries as a sport of the Gods.

Nowhere else in India is the principal deity the hill itself. Even the magnificent Arunachaleshwara temple, one of the biggest in India, houses Shiva in the form of Arunachala. When you go around the premises of the temple, by the northern wall, you see lingas or emblems commemorating the samadhis or graves of seven saints. In modern times, the town is famous all over the world on account of Ramana Maharshi. The Maharshi showed a new path to self-realization through the practice of the simple method of inquiry, 'Who am I?'

Today, another big ashram has come up in Tiruvannamalai, the Yogi Ramsuratkumar Ashram. The yogi, who got his divine madness from his guru, Swami Ramdas, wandered all over India before making Tiruvannamalai his home. He spent nearly 18 years living in the streets, sleeping in the verandas of shops or under trees, mingling with the mendicants in the temple, shunning all publicity or attention. But gradually, his greatness became irrepressible and irresistible. Even the late Paramacharya of Kanchi declared that the Yogi was a great soul, a veritable spiritual dynamo. Calling himself 'this dirty beggar', Yogi Ramsuratkumar had a simple one-line blessing for everyone who came to him: 'My Father blesses you.'

Until he shed his body in February 2001, Tiruvannamalai was blessed with his presence. Originally from Bihar, Yogi lived as a homeless wanderer before his devotees decided to make a grand ashram for him. His teaching is simple but powerful: 'My Father alone exists; no one else, nothing else.' He never gave talks or preached, but only blessed those who came to him. He spoke English, besides Tamil and Hindi. Several prominent men and women from Tamil Nadu, from other parts of India and from abroad were his devotees.

Yogi Ramsuratkumar used to say, 'This beggar has nothing to teach. Whatever was needed has already been taught by Ramana Maharshi, Sri Aurobindo, my master Papa Ramdas and others. This beggar has only his name to leave behind.' When we ponder on this statement, its many levels of meaning gradually unfold. First of all, Bhagawan does not prohibit anyone from reading other masters and learning from them. He actually recommends them to us, urging us to read, study and broaden our spiritual horizons. But he does insist that we repeat his name.

He used to say again and again, 'My father alone exists, no one else, nothing else.' The name 'Yogi Ramsuratkumar' immediately reminds us of this great saying, which is in itself an assertion of supreme non-duality. Father alone exits, not many but one – not you, me, he, she, and it, but only Father, Father everywhere. Behind all this apparent diversity, there is unity – this is what Yogi reminds us. True, it does appear as if we are many, but we have always to bear in mind that in actuality, we are all one – in fact, none of us really *is* outside Father. 'Father' refers to the supreme transcendental principle, Satchidananda Parabrahaman itself.

The glories of the name are endless as are its powers. The more you speak of them, the greater they grow. When we utter his name, the Lord himself answers. It is like a direct connection with 'Father'. When we chant the name 'Yogi Ramsuratkumar', he renews our charter to his pledge of love and protection. We remember his *leela* (sport) and our minds get purified. Yogi himself chanted his own name to show us that the name was greater than any individual or person.

'My Father Blesses You'

During one of my numerous trips to Tiruvannamalai a few years back, it was to Yogi Ramsuratkumar that I was heading. As the taxi neared the town and I set my eyes on the sacred hill, my spirits lifted up. I felt that there was some hope for me, after all; I must have done something to deserve such closeness to the hill of fire. Arunachala was so still and strong, solid and true – just there – reminding us of the sheer presence of Reality.

I remembered my early morning *pradakshina* around the hill in the company of a senior devotee and an attendant. We had started at 3:30 am, treading the mountain path in a clockwise direction. The person whom I was accompanying had been this way dozens of times. She had suffered untold hardships and traumas in her life – an alcoholic husband who committed suicide, leaving her almost penniless; a son who seemed to have inherited his father's fatal flaw; a daughter, trying to get out of an unhappy marriage; years of hardship and struggle to

A Passage to Tiruvannamalai

secure a roof over her head and a modicum of comfort for her children. Yet, today, this same lady looked utterly untouched by the sorrows of the world. At 65, she was youthful, stylish, radiant and full of fun and laughter. Though barefoot, she set the pace for our circumambulation. Later, when she told me that she also had asthma, I was even more astounded. We walked steadily for four hours, with little conversation. At the end, we entered the temple and returned to the Yogi Ramsuratkumar Ashram after paying our respects at the Seshadri Swami Ashram and at Ramanashramam. When I asked her how she managed the long trek barefoot, she said, 'Oh, I'm used to it now. But the first time was so difficult. The skin peeled off, but I bandaged my feet and walked right on.' In those days, the road around the hill wasn't smooth and tarred as it is today. This lady is just one of the hundreds of thousands of people whose lives have changed after visiting Tiruvannamalai.

The first time I was drawn to Tiruvannamalai was when I was a callow teenager, too young to understand the meaning of grace. It was sheer chance which brought me here. Someone told me about the grand temple of Arunachaleshwara and, on my way to Chennai from Bangalore, I decided to stop to take a look. It was only several years later that I realized how fortunate I had been. Somewhere, your guru awaits you, stalking you in the shadows like a tiger watching his prey. You think that you're looking for him, but actually he has been watching over you, pursuing you from life to life. As Ramana Maharshi had said, 'Arunachala! You root out the ego of those who meditate on you in the heart, O Arunachala!' The Maharshi himself had come to Tiruvannamalai, as a youth of 16, after his death-experience in Madurai.

Now more than 100 years after the advent of the Maharshi and 50 years after he left his body, I was once again in Tiruvannamalai, on a quest too ancient, too urgent, in fact, all too common to be spoken about. I had been here many times in between, once even being led to the summit of 2,668 ft hill. I had been to many ashrams and holy places, not just out of academic curiosity, but propelled by the same primeval thirst which sets the course of numberless adventurers of the spirit to lands of no return. On one of these trips, I was 'introduced' to Yogi Ramsuratkumar. If I keep going to him, I can only say that it is his wish, his doing. A far cry from the new breed of gurus, Yogi Ramsuratkumar was a rare saint who forced you to look into your innermost being.

Sighting a white Ambassador at Agraharam Collai in Tiruvannamalai, the line of pilgrims straightens out; folded palms and bowed heads. The chant starts: *'Yogi Ramsuratkumar, Yogi Ramsuratkumar, Jaya Guru Raya.'* The holy hill looks on serenely.

From within the car, a man in a green turban, white beard and piercing eyes looks upon the assembled devotees and raises his hand. 'My Father blesses you,' he seems to be saying. Who is Yogi Ramsuratkumar? If anyone were to ask this question in front of him, it might provoke a peal of infectious laughter. Those who have known him for years recall several such sessions of mirth during which the most depressing and obdurate problems dissolved into harmless fun.

Bhagawan himself says little: 'This beggar has nothing to say.' When prodded for a message, he declares: 'Only my father exists, nothing else, nobody else – past, present, future – here, there, everywhere!'

Paradoxically, this assertion of sheer non-dualism requires a rather dualistic, even mechanical, method of realization – *japa*, the continuous repetition of the Lord's name. Ramsuratkumar remembers his initiation under Papa Ramdas, a famous spiritual master in Kerala: 'At that moment, some force entered this beggar's body, mind, soul or whatever you may call it. It began to control all the movements. Then this beggar died. Now only this force directs everything.'

Papa Ramdas gave the mantra, *'Om Sri Ram Jaya Ram Jaya Jaya Ram'* to Ramsuratkumar. 'Recite it for 24 hours,' ordered his guru. Initially, Ramsuratkumar was unsuccessful. Then a sudden burst of energy brought about total transformation. The recitation became effortless. In Ramdas's works, Ramsuratkumar has been called the 'mad Bihari'. In those days, Ramsuratkumar would roll on the ground in uncontrollable ecstasy. He wanted to stay with his guru forever, but Ramdas sent him away in 1952.

'Where will you go?' asked Papa. 'Tiruvannamalai,' came the spontaneous answer. Ramsuratkumar arrived at the sacred precincts of Tiruvannamalai in 1959. He had wandered all over India for seven years. Arunachala was hallowed by the presence of an unbroken line of yogis, the latest being Ramana Maharshi who had himself blessed Yogi

A Passage to Tiruvannamalai

Ramsuratkumar as he had Papa Ramdas – Yogi Ramsuratkumar's guru.

For over three decades, Ramsuratkumar traversed the streets of Tiruvannamalai, and his spiritual greatness unfolded gradually. Then, in the mid-1970s, some devotees asked him to shift to a house on Sannidhi Street, near the big Arunachaleshwara temple. Later, in the early 1990s, he reluctantly consented to his devotees' request for an ashram. That dream is now a reality. The Yogi Ramsuratkumar Ashram is the latest attraction of this ancient pilgrim town. It houses a huge auditorium, which can accommodate over 15,000 people. There is a beautiful, circular meditation hall facing Arunachala. Ramsuratkumar predicted that, in the coming years, this ashram will be flooded with devotees, 'like the Vatican'. The ashram is well-administered by Justice T. S. Arunachalam, former acting chief justice of the Madras High Court. It holds a promise to serve *sadhakas* (seekers) for many years to come.

When he was alive, only a few lucky ones were called for a private audience with Ramsuratkumar, which was an exhilarating and memorable encounter.

It starts as an ordinary conversation but ends up taking you to an absolutely different level of consciousness. If you are meeting him for the first time, the Yogi usually asks general questions. And he ends the darshan with: 'My Father blesses you.' The person's name is clearly pronounced as if it is being entered in Father's secret register. Unlike many other spiritual guides or gurus, understanding Yogi is difficult. His actions are inscrutable. But in his presence you feel a subtle inner transformation. You actually have to experience this alchemy to believe it. It is a higher form of love in which the soul's detritus is washed away and the being is left cleansed.

In the presence of Yogi Ramsuratkumar I once again experienced the strange alchemy of subtle transformation. I did not stir outside the ashram, but looked at the hill – morning, noon and night – from where I was. The whole town of Tiruvannamalai was in my consciousness, though. The busy bazaars, the blaring songs, the gentle, dignified and cultured people in white dhotis, the strong, proud working women of Tamil Nadu, the clean houses with rangoli (coloured patterns) in the courtyard, the smell and sight of flowers in white, fragrant garlands for the deities in the temples or in the black tresses of the women, and mendicants wandering about the town, ash-smeared, with *rudraksha* beads and *kamandalus* (calabashes). And above all, the hill which brought you back to yourself, beyond sense or thought, to the timeless ground of being.

Once hooked to the sweetness of the Visri Swami, so named because of the *visri* (fan) he carries, you will long to visit the place again and again. As my taxi moved towards Bangalore, I kept looking back at Arunachala. Maybe it would keep calling me back until my dust mingled with its red soil. What could be better than being buried there, trodden over by numerous pilgrims on their path to the ultimate reality? The reality, which is our final resting ground.

Seri – It's Ok

One's first meeting with a spiritual master is always memorable. Mine took place quite unexpectedly one afternoon in November 1992. I was visiting the Aurobindo Ashram in Pondicherry[i] (now Puducherry) for the first time. Though I had booked a room at the International Guest House of the Ashram, there was some misunderstanding and I had to seek alternate accommodation. It was already 7:00 pm; all I could find was a dormitory called Samarpan. *Samarpan* means surrender. I thought it was a cue to me. I had to change my attitude from trying to control everything to simply yielding. 'Surrender, surrender,' I said to myself. I took my room and went to pay my respects at the samadhi.

I should have gone to the samadhi first. There was a note for me at the Ashram office with details of my reservation at the International Guest House. I found out all this only later, after I had already checked into Samarpan. The lesson I learned is report first to the sanctum sanctorum on arrival; worry about everything else later.

But it was at Samarpan that I met a man from Tiruvannamalai. His name was Pushkar. He was short, bearded and had long hair. His eyes were bloodshot. I was so struck by where he lived. 'I went there once, many years ago, when I was 16 . . . I wish I could go there again,' I said. 'But you can,' he shot back. He invited me to see him there. He added, 'I will take you to a great living master, Yogi Ramsuratkumar.'

So I took a bus via Villupuram to Tiruvannamalai the very next day.

A Passage to Tiruvannamalai

It was to be a one-day trip because I needed to get back to Pondicherry by the evening. My luggage was still there, shifted to the International Guest House that morning, when I moved into the room booked for me. I spent the afternoon at Sri Ramanashramam, and then went to Pushkar's house behind the post office around 4:30 pm as planned.

We took an auto to the Sannidhi Street, behind the magnificent Arunachaleshwara temple. There outside a small house was a large crowd, mostly of urchins. I thought the Yogi must be famous. He was; nevertheless, the onlookers had come to see one of the most iconic music composers of Tamil cinema, Illiyaraja, who was already inside the house.

I stood on the steps with the meagre offerings in my hands, an assortment of fruit bought in a hurry. In the meanwhile, the street urchins were making a nuisance of themselves. Some scrambled up to the windows like monkeys to get a glimpse of the Yogi with the musician. Others were screaming and shouting beneath, on the street. Twice somebody came out to shoo them away. I was afraid that I too would be asked to leave. I stood there, uncertain and somewhat afraid.

After a while, Illiyaraja stepped out. He was a short, dark, unimpressive man, in a white dhoti. But what a great musician he was. I had heard and loved his songs. As he walked down, I walked in. Very briefly, our eyes met, but my first impression, much to my later embarrassment, had been one of recoil. I should have wished him, told him how much I respected him and his music.[87] Before I could recover, the moment had passed. Illiyaraja was in his large cream-coloured car, tinted windows rolled up, and I was inside the dark, covered veranda of the Yogi's abode.

In the corner, I saw some ladies singing. One of them, I would later identify as Devaki Ma. There was another man seemingly in charge, like a major-domo, who asked me to take a seat. But wonder of wonders, the Yogi, whom I saw at last, with flowing locks and beard, was actually smoking! There were packets of Charminar cigarettes strewn in the room. There were also heaps of flowers and fruit.

I made my *pranaam* (salutation) and proffered the fruit offerings. Yogiji did not seem that much interested in me. He spoke to some of the other devotees in Tamil, frequently punctuating his remarks with '*seri*' (all right) which turned out to be his favourite word. He would often burst out laughing, with happy and childlike glee. His face would light up as his eyes shone with merriment.

One young man entered, bowed, left a large invitation card at his feet, and quickly made his exit. The devotee-in-charge, when motioned to do so, opened the card and began to read it aloud. It turned out to be an invitation to the young man's forthcoming wedding! The Yogi laughed, as did all of us. The groom, before he could be blessed properly for what, more than most occasions, required blessings, had vanished. Evidently, he had much else to do.

Yogiji now turned to me. His gestures were unhurried, measured, as if he had all the time in the world; in fact, as if time itself did his bidding.

'What is your name?' he asked, pronouncing each word slowly in clear English.

'Makarand Paranjape.'

'Makarand Paranjape, Makarand Paranjape. *Seri*,' repeated the Yogi.

'What is Makarand Paranjape doing?'

I didn't quite know what to say so exclaimed, 'I am working on a book on Sarojini Naidu.'

'Good, good. Sarojini Naidu. Great lady. Great national leader.'

Then he gave me an apple and said, 'Makarand Paranjape, my Father blesses you. You may go now.'

I prostrated before him. He thumped my back twice, laughing in happiness. That was all. My first encounter couldn't have been simpler.

But when I left, I felt a surge of power and lightness of being. I had observed the Yogi minutely. When he raised his hands to bless anyone, the whole air seemed charged with strange electricity, like a current of grace. I was also struck by the fact that though he smoked incessantly, there was no smell of cigarettes nor a trace of smoke in that stuffy room.

Outside, I thanked my friend Pushkar, who had brought me here. As we walked to the bus station, I slowly and very deliberately ate the consecrated apple, seeds and all.

Afterwards, I kept sending the Yogi copies of my books, a practice that I still continue. It was started with the ulterior motive of seeking his blessings for their success, but now I also do it as an offering, an act of surrender, even though Bhagawan is no more. Incidentally, the

Sarojini Naidu book was a great success, selling out two hardback and one paperback editions. Recently, it was reprinted with a revised and enlarged introduction.

Father's Will

Tiruvannamalai – the abode of Shiva and the Siddhas – the name is itself thrilling. I arrived at 4:00 am (when I mentioned this to Yogi later, he said, '*Seri*. Very good!'). I had taken an overnight bus from Kalasipalyam, near the City Market in Bangalore, going to the bus stand straight from the airport, having just flown in from Delhi. This seemed the best way to save time – I didn't want to wait another day! I didn't even go home to see my mother, but headed straight for Arunachala. The bus started at 11:30 pm instead of the scheduled departure time of 10:00 pm. I was so irritated – 'Let's go, let's go,' I wanted to scream time and again.

I could hardly sleep, not just because of the discomfort of the bumpy bus-ride, but because I wasn't sure when we were supposed to reach. I didn't want to miss my stop and go on towards Pondicherry. I thought we would take four hours to reach Tiruvannamalai. So I was up by 2:00 am, trying to look for signs which could tell me how far we were from Arunachala. But it was pitch dark outside; I couldn't make out a thing from the tinted windows. I stumbled to the conductor, dodging some sleeping bodies on the floor of the bus. He said we had another 50 km to cover. 'Go to sleep,' he said.

Finally, we reached. I was dropped off outside Ramanasramam. I felt a strong urge to go inside to pay my respects. The shrine of the great sage of modern India seemed to beckon me, but I decided not to deviate from my goal, which was Yogi Ramsuratkumar. So I headed straight to the Yogi Ramsuratkumar Ashram.

The watchman was sleepy and crabby. He muttered some incomprehensible protests as he very reluctantly let me in. Once inside, however, things seemed to work like magic. I located Sarvanan, one of the workers, got the keys to my cottage from him – it was the third cottage this time, very clean and comfortable. I felt wonderful. Drank some water, unpacked a bit (I'd forgotten to get a towel), then rested. It was good to stretch out.

I got up again at 6:00 am, had a bath, washing out the chill of Delhi in January from my bones. Then I went straight to the *darshan* (blessed sighting) line at the gate of the ashram. All of us stood silent and still, barefoot in the dawn, waiting for Yogi's car. I looked at the sacred hill in its majesty and prayed silently: 'Arunachala, O Arunachala, you are my father and mother and everything!' Just then, Bhagawan's car became visible as it turned to the road approaching the ashram.

Very slowly, quite majestically, the car entered. *Samajavargama.* We stood with breaths bated – who would be beckoned? Who would have the privilege of breakfast with Bhagawan? I was standing next to the gentle, blond American giant, Brett Carlson. Brett was busy building a small ashram for Mr Lee, an American guru, and his devotees. We both stood with folded hands. Justice Arunachalam was not with us, nor any other senior devotee.

The car passed. I was left standing in the line. Before any disappointment could register, the car stopped half way to the breakfast cottage. Ravi, Yogi's driver, got out. He beckoned to me. I waited for a microsecond to ensure that I wasn't making a mistake, stepping out of line before I was called. But it was I to whom he was pointing. I ran to the car, which had begun to move, following it as it halted in front of the cottage.

Bhagawan stepped out, wrapped in shawls, a bearded, turbaned figure, bundled up cosily, a garland of necklaces around his neck. His gait was slow, but steady. There was no hurry or anxiety in any of his gestures. We followed him in. He had his back turned to the door and he was facing Devaki Ma. I remained standing till he called out, 'Makarand, *vokara* (sit down)!'

'How did you come?'

'Bhagawan, I took a bus, going to the terminus straight from the airport – I didn't even go home to see my mother. I got the only available seat left, number 30!'

Devaki Ma repeated what I'd blurted out so rapidly. 'Such madness,' she said.

She should have known! Who could be as mad as she when it came to Yogi Ramsuratkumar? She had left a teaching position in a college, her home, and her whole world to become his 'slave'. Everyone had given her up as mad.

Bhagawan picked up a morsel of his 'special' food that Ma had brought. This food was without spices, sugar and fat.

We began to eat. The idlis were delicious, as usual, but though I enjoyed the food, I was too intensely alert to Bhagawan to bother about it.

Bhagawan said, 'Somebody told Ramana Maharshi that Sri Aurobindo had brought down the Supermind. Do you know what Ramana Maharshi said?' He peered at Devaki Ma and me. Neither of us spoke. 'Well, Ramana Maharshi said if it has come to Pondicherry, then it will also come to Tiruvannamalai.' Somehow, it seemed incredibly funny. We all laughed.

'Did you understand that, Devaki?' Ma didn't say anything, but nodded. Bhagawan said all this in a high-pitched voice. He did not seem to be very enthusiastic about divinizing the human body. 'We thought this body as mud, no Devaki?' Then he added, 'The Theosophists also keep talking about evolution. So, death itself is to be abolished, is it, in the future?' The way he said it, I thought he was a bit sceptical, as if there was no need for all that in order to achieve the aim of life.

We then sang some *bhajans* (devotional songs), did the *japa* (repetition), 'Arunachala Siva, Arunachala Siva, Arunachala Siva, Aruna Jata.' Finally, we all repeated the Kanchi Paramacharya's beautiful song, '*Maitrim bhajata,*' which M. S. Subbulakshmi had sung at the United Nations:

Maithreem bhajatha akhila hrith jeththreem
Atmavat eva paraan api pashyata
Yuddham tyajata, spardhaam tyajata, tyajata pareshwa akrama
  aakramanam
Jananee prthivee kaamadughaastey
Janakodeva: sakala dayaalu
Daamyata Datta Dayadhvam Janataa
Sreyo bhooyaath sakala janaanaam (thrice)

Cultivate friendship, which can conquer all hearts
Consider others even as your own self.
Renounce war, forswear competition, give up the use of force to
  get others' possessions.

Our mother earth has enough to fulfil all our needs
And the Lord, our Father, is supremely merciful.
(O people of this earth) show restraint, be generous, and practice compassion.
May all beings be prosperous (repeated thrice).

The song had a deeper significance for not only were there rifts and divisions all over the world, but right here within the ashram. Perhaps, that is why Yogi wanted us to repeat the words in Sanskrit, Tamil, and English.

After breakfast, I returned to my cottage and slept right through till the phone rang at 10:00 am to remind me of morning *darshan*. Again, we stood in line to do our *pranaams* to Bhagawan. As soon as everyone had done so, I was called to Bhagawan. He sat on the green cushioned chair. My white moulded plastic chair was placed at a little distance from him. I felt like moving it a bit closer, but wisely refrained. The Yogi disliked anyone tampering with his arrangements, let alone doing things out of turn or unasked. But, as if reading my mind, in a few minutes, he motioned me to move forward, leaning towards me, as if trying to catch what I was saying!

Yogi asked me to read Sri Aurobindo's *Savitri*. When I had met him on Christmas Eve, December 1998, he had said, 'This beggar has got a lot from Sri Aurobindo and his ashram. This beggar first read of Sri Aurobindo in a magazine published in Hindi by the Gita Press, Gorakhpur. The magazine was called *Kalyan*. Then he ordered a copy of the book *Lights on Yoga* by Sri Aurobindo from Calcutta.'

Now Bhagawan was asking me to read to him from the great epic *Savitri*. I read Canto 1 of Book 1, then the Epilogue, and then started Canto 2 of Book 1. I read continuously for almost all of the two hours that I was with him.

Though the task seemed simple, it was one of the most difficult readings I had ever done. I felt so drowsy and heavy, as if I would either fall off the chair or into a swoon. There was no reason to feel this way; it was as if every ounce of my energy was being demanded in that simple task. With all my power, I fought to keep awake, to continue reading steadily.

It was nearly noon. It was time for Bhagawan to go and my ordeal came to an end. What a relief! It was one thing to 'want' Bhagawan and another thing to be able to 'take' him. I helped Bhagawan to his car. He asked me to hand over the book *Savitri* that I had brought for him, and some incense sticks. He blessed me and gave me two bananas, then drove off.

I had lunch by myself. Brett came later, but we had time for a chat. He said, 'The work Yogi is doing on you is not simple. Later, you'll find that it will consume you entirely. You will have nothing of your own to live for!' I listened in silence to what seemed like a dire sentence though in fact presaging the end of the ego.

After lunch, in the afternoon, I dozed off again, till I was woken up at 3:30 pm for tea. I said I didn't want any, and drifted back into a slumber. At 3:50 pm sharp, the phone rang again. It was almost time for the afternoon *darshan*. I hurriedly washed my face and rushed to the line. After *pranaams*, I was called once again to sit with the Yogi!

This time I read and finished Book 11. While reading aloud, it occurred to me that though *Savitri* was a great epic with a magnificent sweep, there was so much repetition in it. The same things seemed to be said over and over again, but in different ways and at different places in the text.

In the middle of the reading, Bhagawan seemed to go into a trance. Devaki Ma came from inside and called him four or five times before he opened his eyes. Suddenly, he said, 'Is there something written in the pages that you've read? Mark it with a pen.' When I took out a pencil, it became clear that he was referring to some other book that Mataji had. The latter was trying to explain a complicated situation pertaining to some devotee. This man was receiving several threatening calls after he and his sister had decided to split the property on their father's death. Bhagawan said, 'We'll think of that later, Devaki. Let me talk to Makarand for some time.'

So the reading continued. He asked me if anyone had guided me in my study of Sri Aurobindo and the other mystics of India. I mentioned Professor Giri Tikku of the University of Illinois. Bhagawan asked me about my PhD, and then suddenly said, 'Illinois . . . can you tell me which states surrounded it?'

I was totally taken aback. I muttered, 'Indiana to the east, Kentucky to the south-east, Missouri to the south-west, and . . .' I had totally forgotten Iowa to the west. When I said that on the north, it was bounded by Lake Michigan, Bhagawan immediately said, 'Chicago!' The Yogi had a great penchant for geography. Whenever someone visited a foreign country or city, he would ask the name of the river or some other detail about it. Often the questioners did not know. I realized that this was one more lesson in mindfulness. We visited so many places but failed to register the most obvious details about them.

After that I watched Bhagawan deal with a devotee and his family. The man owned an offset printing press. He had two daughters and a son. He wanted his son to get a job. Bhagawan said, 'No need to look for a job so soon. Let him come with you to the press rather than remain idle at home.' But as an afterthought, he added, 'I will pray to Father that your son gets a job soon.' He then blessed the two girls. The parents were worried about the elder one's marriage. He then blessed the elder daughter again, 'With Father's grace your wedding will take place early.' I watched the visible relief spread across everyone's faces.

When the devotee's wife bowed down to Bhagawan, he was visibly moved. Not only his visage, but his whole being seemed to expand and become incandescent. He said, 'Do you know who this beggar is?' The lady rose up hastily and looked frightened. She started to stammer something, 'Yes, Master . . .!' Bhagawan said, 'No Master, only a dirty beggar. That's all!' The man left, placing some money at Bhagawan's feet.

After they left, I carried on reading at his command. He asked me to read my favourite lines. I turned to Book 11, the joust between Savitri and Yama. Death, throwing off his dark mask, is revealed to be Light itself.

Now and then, Bhagawan looked at me, his gaze full of power and authority. His look seemed to penetrate me. I felt shy, like a woman. Suddenly, he picked up the money at his feet and gave it to me, the first and last time he had ever done so. I felt overwhelmed, but tried not to show it. The reading continued. Then the book ended. In between, he would make some small talk. 'What are you doing in Bangalore? What is your conference about? Who are the participants?' I had, of course, told him nothing about my work in Bangalore, but then I suppose he knew it well, having arranged it all to give me this opportunity of being with him.

It was nearly 6:00 pm. He blessed me and gave me some bananas. He sent blessings for my mother, who was in Bangalore, and then said, 'You may leave.'

I said, 'Bhagawan, please call me again to your lotus feet.'

He replied, 'Father's will, Makarand. We must do Father's will.'

That was a great teaching, perhaps the greatest I've ever received: At all times and under all circumstances, 'We must do Father's will.'

Chapter 8

Lessons from Svadhyaya

Searching for Svaraj

*I*ndia may have made remarkable progress in the last 20 years, but there is something terribly amiss. Despite all the hype and 'feel good' self-image, we know that the stark reality of a dark and depressed India beyond the slogans of 'India Shining' or 'Incredible India' cannot be wished away.

The whole country is gradually but surely forgetting about that section of the population which is impoverished, undernourished and wretched. The poor have disappeared from our public discourse and from the television screens, even though we have more than 300 million people living on less than a dollar a day. It was on behalf of these that Mahatma Gandhi struggled for our independence, but these very people now seem to be disenfranchised in the brave new knowledge society that we are promoting. True, freedom was won, but the society which this freedom was meant to produce is yet to be achieved. In a word, we have failed to attain real svaraj or self-rule.

Perhaps, the first one to realize this failure of our dreams was the so-called father of the nation, Gandhi himself. On midnight, 15 August 1947, the very moment that India was keeping its tryst with destiny in a glittering ceremony at the Viceroy's Palace in New Delhi, Gandhi was keeping another tryst at Calcutta with the poor, lowly victims of the bloody Hindu-Muslim riots. While Jawaharlal Nehru and his Congress colleagues became the beneficiaries of the transfer of power, the lonely Mahatma was continuing the other struggle to bring about *purna svaraj* or full independence.

At the very inception of independence, we thus see two Indias: one centred in Delhi, representing the power and authority of the state – and the other in the little villages and localities of India, representing the unfinished agenda of independence.

This struggle of the other India is not merely a political or social struggle, but a moral and spiritual one. Every society finds ways and means of preserving itself. If the official and available channels of finding satisfaction – the state, the political system, the bureaucracy and so on – fail, then it will look elsewhere. It will find alternatives. It will raise new leaders who will intervene directly.

A perfect example of this new initiative is Svadhyaya, a mass movement inspired by the teachings of Pandurang Sastri Athavle, also known as Dada-ji. Svadhyaya tackles three of our most intractable social problems relating to caste, religion and gender, in addition to bettering the material life of its adherents. It does so through a spiritual approach to building human relationships. The empowerment that results from Svadhyaya is both real and radical, yet it is qualitatively different from what is expected or produced by modern methods.

The Challenge of Svadhyaya

I encountered Svadhyaya by travelling to some of the sites where their work has been notable. I belonged to a group of distinguished citizens who were invited to go on a *prayog darshan* or an experiential vision of Svadhyaya in August 1996. Our circuit was Ahmedabad–Veraval–Rajkot–Mumbai, with trips to Bhangi (janitor) and Vaghri (a backward community) settlements, two Amritalayam villages, a fisher folks' village, a Shri Darshanam, Nirmal Neer, Vruksh Mandir, Bhav Nirjhar, Tatvajanana Vidyapeeth, and finally to Dada-ji's *pravachan* or public address at Madhav Bagh, Khetwadi.

From the very first meeting that introduced our group to Svadhyaya, I felt attracted to it. I was no stranger to its principles, premises or objectives; I shared its cultural, civilizational, philosophical outlook. Not only was I in agreement with its aims and objectives, I was also attracted to its methods.

I quickly realized that one of the things that made Svadhyaya so unique and so effective was that it offered a way of translating theory into practise. *Kriti-bhakti*, by its very definition, implied a devotion which was expressed through action. Without such a translation, there could be no Svadhyaya Movement.

Svadhyaya uses India's native cultural resources to bring about social change. It is, thus, nothing but a process of self-acknowledgement. This approach is at great variance with that of the Westernized intellectual class, which looks upon all relationships in terms of power or self-interest. But the renewal of India needs all kinds of people – farmers, shopkeepers, carpenters, fisher-folk, sweepers, vegetable sellers, domestic servants, daily wage earners, blue-collar workers, and so on, not just the Westernized upper classes. What can bind all these by a common thread of self-renewal is a deeper sense of belonging to a common culture and civilizational ethos.

Svadhyaya is a unique way of bringing diverse people together in such a manner that they learn from each other and share each others' talents. They also relate to one another in an affectionate, familial manner, thereby giving them a sense of belonging, togetherness and community. Where political processes fail, while Svadhyaya succeeds is precisely in this: the former concentrate on external changes, while Svadhyaya brings about an inner transformation. What human beings need is dignity and recognition which can only come from genuine mutuality and caring, not just from some political programmes of social justice.

I first heard Dada-ji speak at a mammoth meeting in Kurukshetra – a city in Haryana, believed to have been the site of the ancient war of the Mahabharata. Never in my life had I seen such a large group of people assembled together for a socio-spiritual cause. From near the dais where we were seated, we could see an undivided and unhindered sea of humanity. What is more, they were totally disciplined. The total number of people must have been more than 1,00,000. All of them had come on their own, paying for their own tickets and food. On the way, I had seen families from distant places enjoying the outing. There was a carnivalesque atmosphere.

The sheer efficiency of Svadhyaya is stupendous. The people in charge are superb managers. Because the whole taskforce consists of volunteers, there is no motivation problem. The communication systems are incredibly efficient; the speed with which orders are conveyed and obeyed is amazing. Such efficiency, moreover, enhances pride and self-esteem, especially in an otherwise totally inefficient system like ours.

On the way back, in the bus, I suddenly understood how the great social movements in the past – that I had merely read about in books – must have been like. Today, with my very own eyes I had seen a large mass of people mobilized for a cause of self-realization coupled with social transformation. As Dada-ji said in his sermon, 'God has not turned his back on humanity. We can still save ourselves if we are self-reliant and help one another.' This must have been how Gandhi brought people together. And so many social, spiritual and political movements in India in the past must have worked along similar lines. All my life I had been seeking the flowing river of enlightenment, not just within myself, but outside too. I had thought that it could only be found within. But now I know that it could also run outwards, bringing people together, creating a new social order.

The *Prayog Darshan*

It was raining very heavily when we reached Ahmedabad – the main city of the state of Gujarat in western India. My co-passenger on the flight said that when he had called Ahmedabad from Delhi, they told him to postpone his arrival. The conditions were flood-like; there was practically no transport available. I thought we would be stranded. But the Svadhyayis were well prepared. A series of cars and jeeps had lined up to await us. We were shepherded through the dark and wet streets of Ahmedabad to a comfortable country club. I was impressed not just by the unfailing courtesy of the Svadhyayi volunteers, but by their unassuming friendliness. Later, we were taken to the house of one of our hosts for dinner. We ate there throughout our stay. What delicious food! The whole family looked after us, including the children. Nobody complained about the extra work involved in feeding guests. Every member of this blessed family worked so hard in extending their hospitality to us. Svadhyaya, it seemed, knits families together.

The next morning, we went to Ramdev Para, a *chawl* or lower-class tenement near Jawahar Chowk. This was where the Bhangis, traditionally the clearers of night soil and toilets, lived. Before the abolition of the caste system, they were the outcastes among the outcastes, the lowest of the low among the 'untouchables'. Gandhi wanted to dignify all the untouchables so he called them 'Harijans' – the children of God. In Svadhyayi parlance, this word is not used. Instead, Svadhyaya has coined another one, *bhavlakshis* – those who wish to be esteemed.

We sat together in the house of one of them, Ramesh-bhai. The house was clean, full of shining brass utensils. Ramesh-bhai's old father had tears in his eyes as Samdhong Rinpoche-ji, a senior Buddhist lama and head of the Tibetan Parliament in Exile, stepped into his home. Traditionally, the upper-castes would never visit the home of an 'untouchable' for fear of ritual pollution. Now most of us, who were upper-caste, not only crowded into that little house, but were also accepting victuals from them. It was the miracle of Svadhyaya that had brought all these distinguished people to this home.

We heard what was to become a familiar refrain. Before Svadhyaya, this used to be like most other 'untouchable' colonies – filthy, impoverished, neglected; the residents had low self-esteem; drinking, gambling, wife-beating were rampant; very few children went to school; and though the reservation policy had ensured jobs for some, there was terrible social discrimination against these people. After Svadhyaya, everything changed. The drinking and wife-beating stopped, as did the deadly quarrels between neighbours. Marriage customs were reformed; superstitions which had cost a lot of money were abandoned; children started going to school; the houses became clean and tidy; what is more, every child in the *basti* learned Sanskrit *shlokas*.

In the community centre, I found a very high degree of awareness. Ramesh-bhai said that after becoming Svadhyayis all of them had got a lot of respect. The *savarna* Svadhyayis had visited their homes, invited them to their own houses, fed them, and treated them properly. It is this attention, caring and respect that had reintegrated them into society. Earlier they were filled with hatred and anguish, now they were well-adjusted and happy. They even felt sorry for those who still treated them like untouchables, the *savarnas* who had not yet been touched by social reform. 'I know I am better off than such people,' Ramesh-bhai said simply. 'I can only feel pity for them.'

For the first time in my life I heard a man call himself a Bhangi with unselfconscious pride. 'I am a Bhangi, but I also do the work of a Brahmin. A Brahmin is one who spreads knowledge; so I too am a Brahmin. I go on *bhakti pheris* to spread the liberating message of Svadhyaya. So I am a Bhangi-Brahmin.'

This one statement contained the seeds of a social revolution in the Indian context. The lowest and the highest ends of the caste spectrum combined in this unprecedented self-description, Bhangi-Brahmin, defying all ideas of hierarchy and taboo.

Later, an 'untouchable' medical doctor told us how he had vowed to kill at least ten upper-caste Hindus. That, he thought, would be the only way to take revenge on those who had oppressed him and his people for so long. But now, after the enlightening touch of Svadhyaya, the same man said that he would not claim any reservation for his own son because he did not feel the need for any special privileges or protections. 'Dada-ji has taught us not to beg, not to accept anyone's leftovers, not to take what doesn't belong to us, or to claim what we haven't earned. I no longer need handouts.'

Svadhyayis feel that such a change should come voluntarily. They believe that reservations, though necessary, are not enough. What the Dalits need is social warmth, human sympathy, personal attention, love and respect – not just economic or political sops. It is only in Svadhyaya that I saw the solution to one of India's most intractable problems: the continued oppression of the Dalits and the counter-casteism unleashed in their name by the politicians. Both extremes mirror each other; both divide society and threaten to rend the national fabric. Only in Svadhyaya did I see a so-called 'Bhangi', without the least trace of an inferiority complex, calling himself as such. Only in Svadhyaya did I see a Dalit declare that he was a Brahmin. Only in Svadhyaya did I see a scheduled caste man foreswearing reservations. The cultural traditions of an 'untouchable' enrich our society as much as that of a Brahmin. Such, after all, was Gandhi-ji's idea of *varna*: diversity, occupational security, self-respect, without stratification or inequality. In Svadhyaya we see a combination of the Ambedkarite drive for self-respect combined with a Gandhian emphasis on self-transformation. The two standard ways of opposing caste discriminations are through counter-violence and hatred or through a politics of caste-based reservations and compensations. But the method of Svadhyaya, without succumbing to either, achieves greater results.

We found a similar experience in a Vaghri village on the outskirts of Ahmedabad. The Vaghris or Devi-Pujaks are another despised tribe of India. Though they are now vegetable-sellers by profession, many were originally considered thieves and scoundrels by society. Ranjit-bhai, of Jawahar Nagar, summed up the impact of Svadhyaya: 'Earlier we were like animals, living outside the village, drinking, fighting, cursing; but now we are flowing in the current of *prem bhav*, the flow of love. Today, far from being a nuisance to society, we have become its leaders and sustainers.'

Later, in Veraval, on the coast, we went to a community of fisherfolk, where again we witnessed a self-reliant, proud society being built up. The whole village got together to 'invest' in a communal fishing trawler, whose produce was used by the poorest. Every member of the community took turns to offer free services to this ship, running it, fishing on it, and repairing it. The community fishing boat, like the community vegetable cart, the community farm or the community dairy were some of Svadhyaya's experiments in abolishing poverty and knitting people together. Svadhyaya, by emphasizing the indwelling Divinity in every human being, gives a message of hope and strength to the most despised and abandoned sections of our society.

The empowerment that comes with Svadhyaya is not external; it is not brought about by economic handouts or social props. It is not based on doles and subsidies given by the government. Svadhyaya transforms a person's self-concept: from seeing himself as helpless and weak, a person begins to see himself as self-sufficient and strong. Communities which have been alienated from society are reintegrated. People who could not read or write today recite Vedic hymns. Their faces shine with pride as they intone these mantras; they wish to tell the world that they too are children of the rishis and the seers of Aryavrata.

In Kajli village, near Veraval, we saw how Svadhyaya had tackled another one of our almost insoluble problems: the communal canker. This village had 250 Harijan families, 100 Muslim families and 100 Karari Rajput families, all living together in harmony. The village was an Amritalayam, which means that more than 80% of its inhabitants were Svadhyayis. What was the secret of their communal harmony? It was, we discovered, not just *sarva dharma samabhav* – Vinoba's message for equal respect – but *sarva dharma sveekar* – the equal acceptance of all faiths.

When supporters of the Ramjanmabhoomi Movement who wanted to build a Ram temple on the ruins of a medieval mosque came to this village to collect money and volunteers, they were politely told that the villagers would build both a Ram temple and a mosque in the village itself. There was no need to get involved in a temple–mosque conflict far away. The coexistence of a temple and mosque in Kajli was the best defense against the communal violence unleashed in the wake of the destruction of the Babri Masjid.

Salim-bhai, the secretary of the Muslim *jamaat*, offered his views on how to ensure peace and amity between the two communities: 'No conversion; mutual respect, tolerance; and the Loknath Amritalayam, where people of all faiths can gather together.' Before Svadhyaya, the two communities were separate, neither eating nor drinking from each other's houses, but now they even worshipped together. We asked Salim-bhai if he, as a Muslim, objected to coming to the Amritalayam which had photographs of Hindu Gods and of Dada-ji. Was not idolatry prohibited in Islam? He did not wish to get involved in doctrinal controversies, but insisted instead that there should be mutual tolerance and that the core of both faiths was similar: both stressed a belief in God and the living of a virtuous life. In effect, the Muslims of Kajli had openly accepted that Hindus would, unlike them, continue to worship idols, but that did not mean that the latter were non-believers or *kafirs*. There need be no conflict between members of different communities; after all, the basis of Indian culture was pluralism.

Maulana Wahiduddin, one of India's most distinguished Muslim clerics and a member of our group, got up to speak. He said that Svadhyaya was the hope for the new India, an India whose foundations had been laid by the freedom struggle, but whose promise had been belied by the post-independence developments. He felt that he was a Svadhyayi himself. He worshipped in the mosque at Kajli, while many of us, heads covered, watched silently.

The more astounding event, however, occurred later. Maulanasaheb did his *namaz* in one of the Svadhyayi temples during our tour. True, he did not prostrate before the photographs of the Hindu Gods, but instead faced Mecca like a true Muslim; yet this was the first time I had ever seen a Muslim offer prayers in a Hindu house of worship. This was one of the miracles that I had seen during my trip. Now, whenever anyone told me that Muslims were fanatical and intolerant, I would point out how I had seen, with my own eyes, a learned and pious Muslim Maulana offering prayers in a Hindu temple. He told me as if in explanation that a Muslim could pray anywhere. There was no insistence on a particular sacred place or spot.

Not only has Svadhyaya succeeded in empowering Dalits and in tackling the so-called minority problem, wherever it has spread it has also raised the status of women. I felt this most keenly at Shanti Para, a village in Saurashtra. The whole village had gathered at the Amritalayam. There, in front of over 500 people, Rudi Ben – an illiterate, rustic housewife – stood up to demonstrate the extent of her self-confidence and emancipation. She spoke out clearly and fearlessly, explaining exactly how Svadhyaya had changed her life and reformed her family. Earlier, women from the village were more or less confined to the house. They were not educated. Their functions were restricted to domestic chores. After Svadhyaya, the village women have become community leaders, with an equal voice in determining how they want their lives to be run. As one rural woman summed it up, 'Svadhyaya *nahin, toh gaurav nahin*' – there is no respect without Svadhyaya.

True, Svadhyaya is not like Western feminism or its *desi* (indigenous) versions. It preaches neither the equality of woman, nor the upliftment of women per se. Rather, it emphasizes the value of cooperation in every family and in the whole community. It has special programmes for women which raise their consciousness without being problem or issue based. Because of Svadhyaya, the status of women has not only risen greatly within the family, but in the wider community because women also go out on *bhakti pheris*. They accompany their husbands in most of the important activities. They have learned not only to read and write, but also to teach, to spread the message of Svadhyaya. The evils of dowry have been eradicated in Svadhyayi families. Mothers-in-law and daughters-in-law, considered natural enemies traditionally, have learned not just to coexist, but to love and support each other. These changes have come about through innovative programmes such as *saas-bahu ka milan* or *sakhi milan*. All the conventional relationships are idealized; Svadhyaya builds up communities by revitalizing relationships.

Svadhyaya has not only succeeded in empowering Dalits, minorities and women, but it has helped rebuild entire communities. The best example of this was Shanti Para itself. It felt like a model community – a self-reliant, highly enlightened village, made up of upright, responsible and caring individuals. It was a village which used to be plagued with politics earlier; now, there was no need here even for elections. The leader was chosen by common consent. The man in question told us that it was with great reluctance that he had accepted the charge of sarpanch or head of the village. He knew it would be a thankless job, but he had agreed only out of a sense of serving the community. How did the change in him come about? He said that when Krishna was his *hriday samrat* (the emperor of his heart) he felt no need to seek power. After all, we seek external recognition only when we feel impoverished inside. Svadhyaya makes each person feel wealth within, thus reducing his or her craving for external rewards. In fact, the *trikal sandhya* (triurnal prayer) is based precisely on such a notion of self-renewal. One becomes great by renewing one's contact with the indwelling God.

There was no poverty in this village. The standard of health care was quite high. After the arrival of Svadhyaya, the village had been cleaned up, the open drains sealed. Malaria, which had earlier been a killer, had been nearly eradicated. The local doctor spoke of how impressed he was with the community spirit. In fact, he himself became a Svadhyayi after seeing how progressive these villagers were. Wells had been recharged, old water bodies repaired. Nearly every house had a soakpit and clean toilets. When a cyclone had devastated the power lines, the villagers put up the poles and wires themselves, merely requesting the electricity board to switch the current on.

This was the kind of village in which a farmer would have an MA in Philosophy. The villagers had planted over 16,000 trees – not just planted them, but nurtured them. The method was simple: each person adopted a certain number of trees and took full responsibility for raising them. Krishna broke the pots of butter and milk so that the produce of Gokul did not go to Mathura; the local youth could consume them and become strong. Similarly, Shanti Para had a *Gorus Kendra*, another brilliant idea of Dada-ji, whereby the farmer sold his milk to a cooperative in the village from which all the other villagers could get pure and unadulterated milk. This enhances the status of the cow, which was earlier thought of merely as a source of money and thus tortured to produce maximum milk. It also ensures that the profit from the centre was the *prasad* or offering of God.

Such a village, to my mind, was exactly what Gandhi-ji might have had in mind when he had spoken of *gram svaraj*:

> It will have cottages with sufficient light and ventilations, built of a material obtainable within a radius of five miles of it. The cottages will have courtyards enabling householders to plant vegetables for domestic use and to house their cattle. The village lanes and streets will be free of all avoidable dust. It will have wells according to its needs and accessible to all. It will have houses of worship for all, also a common meeting place, a village common for grazing its cattle, a co-operative dairy, primary and secondary schools in which industrial education will be the central fact, and it will have Panchayats for settling disputes. It will produce its own grains, vegetables and fruit, and its own Khadi. This is roughly my idea of a model village...[88]

Perhaps, Shanti Para is far more urban and modern than Gandhi-ji imagined an Indian village to be, but it has the kind of ideal community that he envisaged.

Notable Svadhyayi Experiments: Bhav Nirjhar

Located in a spacious campus on the outskirts of Ahmedabad, Bhav Nirjhar is an educational institution with a difference. Here boys from reasonably well-off rural families are trained to become farmer–philosophers. To enter, they must own or expect to inherit at least ten acres of land. They come here after schooling in similar Svadhyayi institutions, and must, following their 'graduation', return to their villages. No degrees are awarded. With one stroke, the whole lure of salaried jobs in the city is eliminated, as is the problem of the drain of human resources from our villages.

Dada-ji started these institutions so that a different kind of human being could be created, someone who is not a slave of degrees and diplomas or merely a recipient of a lop-sided and practically irrelevant education. What a radical break it is from the competitive, examination-oriented, colonial education system in which we are all trapped. All the ills of the present system – the false disciplinary hierarchies, the soul-denying, culturally alienating kind of knowledge, the obsession with marks and grades, cheating and copying, tutorial colleges, tuitions, and so on – have been eliminated in this alternative system.

Here students get a rounded, integrated, vocational education. Besides agricultural sciences and training in cottage industries, they also practise yoga and philosophy. The emphasis is on *samskar* – moral training – more than *shiksha* or education. Those who wish to study further can go to Tatvajnana Vidyapeeth in Thane, where Dada-ji himself supervises the teaching of comparative philosophy, Indian culture and civilization, and other such topics.

Yogeshwar Krishi, Shri Darshanam, Vruksh Mandir

All these are ways of creating *apaurushiya Lakshmi* or impersonal wealth. Cooperative farming in which volunteers from one or several villages participate, not as farmers, but as pujaris, or worshippers, helps create wealth which belongs to the entire community. This wealth is then used to help and support those who are most needy, yet it is not seen as charity or dole. It is the *prasad* of the worshipful work of the whole community and can therefore be given and accepted in a manner as impersonal as it was created. A Yogeshwar Krishi is confined to one village; a Shri Darshanam is the combined effort of 15–20 villages; and a Vruksh Mandir involves an even greater number of villages. The sizes of the communes vary, ranging from two or three acres in a Yogeshwar Krishi, to dozens of acres in Shri Darshanams and Vruksh Mandirs.

The idea behind these experiments is not just to produce wealth and profit; in fact, during our visit to the Vruksh Mandir near Rajkot, we were told that the costs almost equal the proceeds. The main purpose behind these schemes is to bring people together. Several families work on these farms turn by turn. They stay there for two or three nights, work together, study together, and listen to each other. People of different villages come closer together through such meetings. There are spin-offs like *Gaon Milans*, in which entire villages visit each other. The first village may go during Dussera, while the hosts may return the visit during Diwali. In this manner, all communities get to know each other.

Underlying Svadhyaya is the notion that all human beings are related by the indwelling God within each of us. There is a repeated experience and reinforcement of this deeply felt truth in these meetings. During our visit to the Dhora-ji Shri Darshanam, a lady told us how the whole Svadhyayi family, which meant not just the village, but Svadhyayis from outside, helped in solemnising and celebrating the marriage of her daughter. Her own financial resources were strained, but without asking for help even once, the whole village came to her rescue. Similarly, we had earlier been told how the highest Brahmins had helped in arranging for the weddings of their Bhavalakshi brethren. Svadhyaya makes unselfish love and giving both personally and socially rewarding.

The same idea of creating impersonal wealth and building communities informs projects like Matsya Gandha. Here, instead of community farming we have community fishing. Likewise, there are community vegetable carts where the same concept of cooperative volunteerism is employed.

Other experiments include recharging wells, building or rebuilding tanks and water bodies, organic farming, etc. All these are meant to redress the ecological damage caused by the over-exploitation of the earth. The image given to us as explanation was that we have drunk too much milk from mother-earth; now her breasts are withered and she has been reduced to a skeleton. We must replenish her and nourish her so as to save her life; otherwise, future generations will call us murderers and never forgive us. Indeed, water management is the key to sustainable agriculture and rural reconstruction. Dada-ji's emphasis on *rishi krishi* or divine farming reflects the urgency of eco-friendly means of self-sustainment.

Dada

The greatest soul-stirring moment during the Kurukshetra trip was Dada-ji's *pravachan*. He had just come out of a heart surgery; it had been touch-and-go for days. He was speaking against the advice of doctors. He said, 'How could I not come to meet you and talk to you after all the trouble you have taken to assemble here from distant parts of the country?' I remembered how the meeting itself had been in doubt because of the unseasonably heavy rains. Yet, now, listening to the great man, all the fatigue and hardships were forgotten.

What was the gist of Dada-ji's talk? It was very inspiring, no doubt, but what I remember most is Dada-ji's unique interpretation of the Bhagavad Gita or 'Song Celestial', one of the most sacred texts of the Hindus. I too had read the Gita, but I had never felt its inner truth in the manner in which Dada-ji had expounded it. He declared: 'In the Gita, the Lord has assured us that he is always with us *and* within us, to guide us, to help us live our lives. He will never let his *bhakta* (devotee) down. This is a promise. God always keeps his promises.'

Dada-ji's words had a strange power. They entered right into my soul, giving me a great sense of confidence and peace. Then Dada-ji added: 'What does the Gita say? It says, "Stand up. Don't give up. Don't despair. You are not alone. I am with you. Come on, face life."' Dada-ji taught me that the Gita is not just an abstruse or esoteric philosophical text, but an assurance of help and hope. It preaches a positive, affirmative attitude to life. It uplifts and encourages. That is how the Gita may be read.

Later, we met Dada-ji briefly. He greeted us as if he knew each of us individually. When someone said something to him, he listened with genuine interest and attention. I had seen that unhurried self-confidence before in other great souls, but not that sense of curiosity. He really was keen to know us, to find out who we were.

Most of us normally have absolutely no curiosity or interest in others. We tend to look upon them with indifference, if not suspicion or hostility. When we meet anyone, we are guarded and cautious. We even avoid people, not wanting to deal with their problems. We are simply not interested in their realities. In contrast, here was a man who actually saw divinity in all of us. It was not just a slogan that God resides within each of us. He actually saw people as embodiments of divinity. The simplicity and sureness of this attitude were totally disarming.

When we met him again in Bombay, my earlier impressions of him were confirmed. He was simple and totally unassuming. There was a straightforwardness and clarity in his vision. At the same time, he had a sharp grasp of human beings and the ability to avoid useless discussions. The man we saw before us, however, was certainly not at the peak of his powers. His movements were slow and speech slurred. He was also wont to forget names, even of his close associates. Yet, he was by no means a man who had given up. On the contrary, though his greatest achievements were behind him, he still had the ability to plan ahead, to dream.

When we gathered around him in a group, Dada-ji asked Maulana Wahiduddin only one question: 'Do we have your blessings?'

There was no attempt to engage in polite conversation; Dada-ji had got to the root of the matter. When the Maulana had given his assent, Dada-ji was very pleased. He said, 'It is my belief that the communal problem in India will be solved if we accept Jesus Christ and Paigambar Mohammad as avatars of God.' This was *sarva dharma sveekriti*, the acceptance of all faiths, taken to its limit. I wanted to ask Dada-ji if the Muslims and Christians would reciprocate.

As if guessing my thoughts he added, 'In the Gulf, Svadhyayis donate blood on the birthday of Prophet Mohammad. The laboratories are usually closed on this day, but the Sheikh specially had them opened to receive our blood. After all, that holy day has significance; we are not interested in donating blood on any other day. So, you see, if we try to go to others, to talk to them, most of the problems will be solved. Our sincerity will overcome all resistance.' That was the secret of Svadhyaya: to genuine love and devoted fellow-feeling we cannot but help responding.

Later, Rev. Samdhong Rinpoche, the then Prime Minister of the Tibetan Parliament in Exile, spoke. 'I cannot consider myself a Svadhyayi,' he said, 'though I am in full sympathy with its aims and objectives. This is because as a Buddhist I do not believe in God. Yet, I believe that this is the kind of movement that I had been looking for, for years. We believe that the world will only be saved if India, *Arya*

Bhoomi, provides a spiritual leadership to it in these troubled times. I had almost despaired of finding something like Svadhyaya which has the capacity to raise a new society on the basis of our ancient spiritual principles. Now that I have found it, I wish it every success.'

The next day, after his lecture, I asked Dada-ji to comment on what Rinpoche had said. We spoke of other ideological differences which tend to be incommensurable. Dada-ji smiled and told me, 'I have yet to come across an atheist.' The theism of Svadhyaya is, thus, not to be taken as a dogmatic creed. Dada-ji believes that only a creator could have created this universe, but those who don't believe in an *Ishwara* or God need not feel left out. Svadhyaya is for everyone who believes in human brotherhood and a higher cosmic law to which we all must submit. Yes, the spirit of Svadhyaya does militate against the modern notion of man as the supreme arbiter of his own destiny, as an autonomous being responsible only to himself for his choices.

In his lecture, Dada-ji had stressed *nisvarth prem* or selfless love. He had praised actions performed without an ulterior motive and with purity of heart. I asked him, 'What about the desire or wish to attain moksha? Isn't that also a desire? And the desire to help others? The desire not to have any desire? And so on?' He smiled and replied cryptically, 'But these don't harm you.' Once again, his ability to cut through theoretical quibbling to get to the heart of the matter was evident. Dada-ji's altruism was, ultimately, only a programme of self-realization and inner development.

Changing the topic, he told us how the district commissioner of Rajkot had once appealed to him to help make the district 100% literate. Dada-ji told him, 'This is your job; we have nothing to do with such missions. But, yes, now that you've asked me to help you, I will. Let's divide the district into two zones. You take one, we'll take the other. It's your responsibility to make everyone literate in your zone and it's ours in our zone. But note, we'll make them literate by teaching them mantras and shlokas; you do what you like.' The result was predictable: while the Svadhyayi zone become literate in six months, the government zone is yet to achieve its target. Dada-ji concluded, 'Voluntary work done in the spirit of worship is far more effective than all sorts of expensive government schemes. Material incentives do not encourage us. Instead, they corrupt us and enfeeble us. They make us lazy and dishonest.'

Finally, Dada-ji spoke against the condemnation of missionaries by Hindu political parties. 'We criticize them for spreading their religion among our tribals and scheduled castes, but what have we done for these neglected and backward brethren of ours? We don't go to them, work among them, but are quick to criticize others who do so. The way to stop proselytization is to give them all the riches of their own culture and heritage. Svadhyaya has taken the Vedas, the Upanishads, the Gita and the works of Shankaracharya to some of these people; now I challenge any missionary to put a cross around their necks.' According to Dada-ji, it's no use bemoaning the decline of Hinduism if we are willing to do nothing to stop it. Make yourself strong; why blame your adversary for taking advantage of your weakness? This seems to be the gist of Dada-ji's message.

Dada-ji was also critical of those who mixed religion with politics. 'We don't allow any politics to enter into Svadhyaya. No politics is permitted on the Svadhyaya platform. Those who wish to capture power should be honest about it; why pretend that they are working for Dharma?'

All this leads me to conclude that Dada-ji is a religious genius. He is a specially endowed human being who has shown us a new way to renew and reactivate our inner strength. The Templeton Prize, the richest award on earth, was conferred upon him precisely for this. His special gift was acknowledged wherever we went. Repeatedly, we were told how lives were changed after people had received 'Dada-ji's thought'.

Yet I am convinced that there is nothing fundamentally *new* in Dada-ji's thought. The newness is basically in the method of realizing the thoughts. Yet the thoughts themselves have a strange, almost mystical power, like the guru-mantra. When someone else utters it, it loses its power, but when given by the guru it ignites the spirit.

Behind the entire locomotion of Svadhyaya is the engine that is Dada-ji. Dada-ji, to use Buddhist terminology, is a Bodhisattva, a self-realized being who takes birth to alleviate the sorrows of others. Even if one does not believe in such divinely ordained births, simple facts of heredity and environment bear this out. Dada-ji's father, too, was a religious teacher, a *pravachan-kar*. It was he who had started the Gita Pathashala in Madhav Bagh in the year 1928. What was Dada-ji's contribution? He really lived up to the ideals of a *pravachan-kar's* life. He idealized his own vocation, thereby becoming a figure of inspiration to the whole society. Similarly, each of us can idealize our lives, our professions, our various roles. If the intellectuals, warriors, merchants and farmers had all done their jobs well, India would never have fallen. To restore the glory of India, each of us must do our own job properly wherever we are. This is the most basic lesson of Dada-ji's life.

Some of the other lessons are equally important. Never give up; be patient: to bring any lasting change one has to work silently for three generations. Therefore, work to improve your inner reality, the appearance will take care of itself. Dada-ji's genius lies in giving a new meaning to *bhakti* or the ancient cult of devotion. A *bhakt* or a devotee is someone who is not *vibhakt*, that is, someone who is not separated from himself and his fellow human beings. To show gratitude to God it is not necessary to offer flowers, but it is necessary to offer your time and talent to a Godly cause. What is a Godly cause? Anything which you do not for personal gain but for the benefit of others, anything done with a pure heart, anything that has the view to one's spiritual development through the service of others is *bhakti*.

On this deceptively simple premise, the whole edifice of Svadhyaya is built. Today, over 3,00,000 volunteers are fanning outwards on their *bhakti pheri* (the devotional tour), going from village to village, town to town, bringing the message of brother and sisterhood to every home in India. This is a special kind of travel and tourism. In a world based on selfishness, any act of genuine and unconditional giving touches the heart. 'We want nothing from you, not even a cup of tea. We have not come to collect donations or to convert you. We only wish to talk to you, to make your acquaintance, to establish a human relationship with you.' This is the watchword of Svadhyaya.

All their great achievements – the experiments in community making and community wealth, in recharging wells, rebuilding tanks, alternative education and farming, social reform and social upliftment – are born out of this seemingly simple and obvious idea of the *bhakti pheri*. The author of this novel idea, Dada-ji, was a genius.

In the museum at Tatvajnana Vidyapeeth, I was arrested by a representation of a human hand restraining the Lord's *sudarshan charka* or weapon of ultimate annihilation. There was nothing else in the picture – just these two hands, almost touching. The guide explained the significance: 'Man is telling God, give me one more chance. Let me try to do my best. Please don't destroy the world. Before we invoke God, we must do what we can as human beings. Have we done enough to change ourselves and to change the world? We have made the world what it is today; we can save it or at least give our lives in the attempt. This is the positive religion that Dada-ji preaches and practices.

Manushya Gaurav Diwas

On 19 October 1996 in Mumbai – Dada-ji's birthday, also celebrated as the Manushya Gaurav Diwas – over 3,50,000 Svadhyayis from all over India came to Chaupati, the famous beach near downtown, to felicitate Dada-ji. It was also the day when the first Svadhyayi cargo ship Jayashree was to be launched. This ship had been built entirely out of voluntary labour, without the loss of a single day's wages. After a full day's work, the volunteers worked from 7:00 pm to 11:00 pm each day for months to realize this ambitious dream. In fact, the whole ship was built entirely out of *bhakti*, perhaps for the first time in human history. The ship, whose carrying capacity was about 600 tonnes, was worth more than a 100 crores or 1 billion rupees.

When we entered the city, we saw large processions of Svadhyayis moving towards Chaupati. The parking lots from Chowpatty to Nariman Point were crowded with Svadhyayi buses and vehicles. Later, from the stage, we saw a sea of humanity which almost rivalled the Arabian Sea itself. But what was remarkable was the total discipline and orderliness of the assembled people. They were divided into manageable lots, each with a leader. Each lot was identified by the special caps or clothes. The arrangements, as usual, were flawless. Different groups of Svadhyayis had assumed various responsibilities; some had erected the stage, others took care of lighting, still others, of crowd control and so on. Amazingly, as soon anyone sat down, they were offered water to drink by a group of Svadhyayi ladies. The logistics of providing drinking water to over 3,50,000 people was mind-boggling. But that was just one example of Svadhyaya in action.

There were several speakers that evening, all of whom felicitated Dada-ji. The VIP enclosure near the stage was full of various dignitaries, including the then deputy Chief Minister of Maharashtra; L. K. Advani, a national political leader; two of the Hinduja brothers; and several other important people. An unforgettable sight was Maulana Wahiduddin Khan offering his namaz while Dadaji's *pravachan* was going on. What better demonstration could one get of the communal harmony so aptly depicted in the large, all-religious symbol on stage?

In the course of the speeches delivered by notable speakers, including Rahul Dev, Rev. Samdhung Rinpoche, Maulana Wahiduddin Khan, a senior Catholic priest and Ved Prakash Vaidik, some even likened Dada-ji to an avatar or divine incarnation. The process of deification was quite obvious in the evening's proceedings. Yet, it was Dada-ji himself, who struck a different note. Turning away the attention from himself and his achievements, he spoke about human dignity. When all of us had gathered there to celebrate Human Dignity Day, surely the question arose as to what the source of human dignity was.

Dada-ji said that it was conventionally thought that human dignity came from wealth, education, social status and so on, all of which were conferred from the outside. However, he asked, if this were so, then about 80% of Indians could never hope to have any dignity. Dignity, he said, came not from wealth, education or power, but from character. Alas, no one was interested today in character building. Even the present day education system was ignoring this prime need.

Character, said Dada-ji, came from *kritagnata, namrata, tejasvita* and *asmita* – from gratitude, humility, integrity and identity. When we are no longer grateful to our Creator, how can we be grateful to anyone else? Thus, we are bound to neglect our obligations to our parents, to our friends, to our community and to the nation too. Similarly, *namrata* or humility, though a hallmark of Indian culture, is disappearing from our midst. We have become rude, aggressive and violent. Character also consists of inner effulgence which comes from integrity. Given the prevailing predominance of corruption, we tend to lose our integrity quite easily. Finally, we have forgotten who we are, what our identities are. Without these four virtues we lose our character and when character is lost, we also lose wealth, prestige, honour and independence.

Dada-ji's speech was riveting. It went into the very heart of the matter. While the other speakers, however inspiring, could only offer praise or best wishes, Dada-ji was actually pointing the way to self-transformation. Without Dada-ji's speech, the whole evening would have remained incomplete. Even the massive crowds, the impressive fireworks, the large turnout of VIPs, the cargo ship – all these would have paled into relative insignificance. After all, the latter were material achievements which could be duplicated, even bettered. But what Dada-ji offered was far greater. It was the very stuff that could connect the human with the divine. It was the only thing really worth striving for on earth.

Once again, I understood that the essential core of Svadhyaya was this tremendous, transformative energy which Dada-ji generated from within himself. Without it, it would be like any other movement, more innovative perhaps, but not fundamentally different. My original intuition was now doubly confirmed: Svadhyaya, whatever its external manifestation, implied going inwards – tapping that perennial source of spiritual power which comes to us directly from our Creator. Svadhyaya helps us activate and awaken that inner power. Without such a deep transformation and awakening, all our efforts will be wasted. In more ways than one, this great event on 19 October 1996 brought to a completion my introduction to Svadhyaya.

What Makes Svadhyaya Work?

This is a question that I have often asked myself, especially when confronted with the living proof of the tremendous transformation that it has wrought on the lives of its practitioners. What makes a rich industrialist from Bombay give up all his comforts, sacrifice so much time and money, only to visit some distant village which even lacks a flush toilet? What makes a poor *beedi* (indigenous cigarette) maker from Andhra Pradesh save for six months in order to afford the ticket to go on a *bhakti pheri* in Haryana?

People undertake hardships if they are convinced that what they are getting is greater than what they are giving up. What are these people getting? I think they get what people who have undertaken successful pilgrimages get: peace of mind, inner contentment, joy of service, and spiritual growth. Once they experience the ecstasy that comes from such self-sharing, they realize that this is the most important thing in their lives.

One can, indeed, understand why certain individuals might be attracted to Svadhyaya, but how does it succeed at the community level? What is the secret? How has the latter miracle occurred? I think the answer is that this is how the Indian villages might have been once upon a time. That is, every Indian village was conceived of as precisely such a kind of ideal sub-system. In other words, Svadhyaya does not impose anything new but merely idealizes – realizes the potential of what already is.

Similarly, Svadhyaya has succeeded in Saurashtra because Saurashtra itself is a very special region, replete with the traces of earlier such experiments, the memories of which are still fresh enough to be revived. Whether it is Dada-ji or Annasaheb Hazare,[89] what these great men are doing is already inherent in the soil of the land. The seeds of the subtle karmas of our great *bhaktas*, sages, reformers and saints have been broadcast to the farthest corners of our land. They have fertilized better in some areas than in others. Saurashtra has a history of independent, fearless people. Given that Gandhi-ji himself came from here it is natural that Svadhyaya flourishes in this soil.

Similarly, when it comes to the other programmes of Svadhyaya, the success comes from a combination of factors. There is something for everyone in Svadhyaya. There is a bit of the Rotary Club in it, a social aspect, wherein people meet, exchange ideas and get to know each other. The *bhakti pheri* is a combination of a pilgrimage and a vacation. The stress on the family means that the husband and the wife get to do things together. Children are involved in the process from an early age. There is a special programme for youth and for women. Thus, everyone is involved. What time might have been wasted in trivial socializing or gossip is now channelized for a higher cause. Everyone is constantly learning; this adds to the participant's self-esteem. The participants feel ennobled by the productive work that they are doing.

Thus, to sum up, Svadhyaya not only works because of the unique religious genius and authority of Dada-ji, the utter dedication and sincerity of its workers, the extraordinary organizational and entrepreneurial skills of its managers, innovative planning and vision, but also because it offers a holistic and total approach to the needs of its practitioners, nourishing their physical, vital, mental and spiritual being. Svadhyaya works because it is practical and pragmatic, not unrealistic and other-worldly. It does not make impossible or unreasonable demands on its adherents. The extent of the involvement is left entirely to each individual. Its structure may be hierarchical, but it is totally egalitarian in its approach to problem-solving. The changes brought about by it are gradual and self-motivated, not sudden and externally imposed. Svadhyaya provides a meaningful orientation to life, an orientation based on our own cultural patterns and resources.

Ultimately, what makes Svadhyaya work is the yearning within each of us to improve our lives and to contribute our mite to the betterment of the world. Each of us has this desire, but we do not know how to fructify it. Svadhyaya shows the way.

Critiquing Svadhyaya

Without being uncharitable, it is also important to see what defects Svadhyaya has. First of all, it seems as if Svadhyaya has much in common with evangelical movements. It offers tremendous emotional and intellectual security to its adherents. It involves a 'conversion', albeit slow and non-violent, a change of lifestyle and attitude, public confessions of previous wrong-doing, plus unlimited opportunities for further proselytizing. While Svadhyaya is not at all narrow-minded, fanatical, oppositional, cultish or even violent like many of the evangelical movements, yet one cannot get away from the fact that most of its energy is horizontal, not vertical. In other words, once a person becomes a Svadhyayi, the next thing for him to do is to spread the message amongst people who haven't heard of it. *Bhakti pheri* is thus the best possible method of broadcasting the Svadhyayi creed.

Finally, I must also admit that though what I had heard and seen during my entire experience of Svadhyaya was very inspiring and encouraging, I felt as if my soul thirsted for something more, if not something else. That is why, though I was and remain a supporter of Svadhyaya, I have not joined it officially. In a way, this realization might be taken as the culmination of Dada-ji's idea of strengthening oneself.

The ultimate point of any self-culture is moral and spiritual perfection which can only come from personal endeavour, not from any external guidance and method. I myself am the problem and I myself am the solution. The external Svadhyaya of Dada-ji cannot be a substitute for the inner Svadhyaya or self-study which I must undertake for my own upliftment. To those who are walking on the path, Svadhyaya is thus the beginning, not the end of the road.

Postscript: After Dada

After my *prayog darshan* and subsequent experiences with Svadhyaya in 1997–1998, a constant thought that came up during our trip and the subsequent discussions was, 'What after Dada-ji?' Dada-ji himself believed that whatever had to happen in the future would happen; why worry oneself about it? Why not do what our nearest task is instead? Truly, it does not matter if the movement declines – like several such movements have in the past. Something else will emerge. Society is never static. There are tendencies latent in it which can either uplift it or cause its downfall. Svadhyaya belongs to the former category, that is, it is a part of a society's will to improve itself. After Svadhyaya, something else will take on a similar responsibility.

Yet, Svadhyaya does derive its strength from the ideas and inspiration of one individual; this must be understood and acknowledged. His photograph is found in all the Svadhyayi temples along with those of Yogeshwar Krishna, Amba and Parvati, and Shiva. When I talked to Ashis Nandy, India's leading political psychologist, he said with amazing candour and insight, 'It'll all collapse after Dada.'

Dada-ji did pass away on 25 October 2003, the day that most Hindus and Indians celebrated as Diwali. I was on a flight to Bangkok. An unspeakable sadness possessed me as I saw the news flashed on the television screen. As expected, the press said little. There was no mass mourning as for national leaders or even sports stars and film personalities. It was a quiet farewell and an almost private cremation, in which only 2,000 people were present. Unlike the huge gatherings numbering into millions that Dada-ji addressed, his departure was a low-key affair.

Indeed, for months before the end, Dada-ji was isolated from the people who loved and worshipped him. His illness had severely limited his movements. In fact, tragically, one of his legs had to be amputated. Worse, the Svadhyaya *parivar* itself had been beleaguered by controversy and in-fighting. Dada-ji had wished to evolve a sort of constitution, what was called an *amnaya*, for the smooth transfer of responsibility and the efficient functioning of the huge movement. Unfortunately, this constitution was never followed. In fact, it was all but scrapped. Allegedly, a small coterie of the faithful around Didi, his adopted daughter who was at the centre of power, had cornered all the resources and authority of the movement. Several old-timers had been sidelined or silenced. Some of the most respectable and senior members of the Svadhyaya power structure had actually been beaten up, implicated in false cases or unduly harassed. There were even one or two murders in the movement. Some of these developments were as shocking as they were bewildering. A decline after the passing of a great leader might be expected, but what had happened was, to all appearance, too swift and sordid a degeneration for anyone's comfort.

The present crisis seems to suggest that the leadership of Svadhyaya is controverting if not contradicting much of what Dada-ji taught and stood for. Be that as it may, I think it is important not to be totally despondent. A movement of this magnitude and calibre certainly has the capacity to correct itself. It is this that we must hope for. Even if it fails to do so, its real achievements, which were most extraordinary, must not be forgotten.

Chapter 9

Among the Swaminarayans

'Let's Catch Water Where It Falls'

*S*everal days after the field visit to Ahmedabad and its neighbouring areas to study the development-related work of the Swaminarayans, I received a Diwali greeting card in the mail. On the front was a display of conventional piety, with a picture of Pramukh Swami, the current head, and a statue of Lord Swaminarayan, the founder of the order in traditional regalia. But the message inside the card was quite different in its emphasis: 'Let's catch water where it falls' and 'make water everybody's business.' The card was signed by P. P. Bhat, project officer at the Bochasanwasi Shri Akshar Purushottam Swaminarayan Sanstha (or BAPS) Trust (Watershed), Gadhada, and Sadhu Yagneshdas-ji, BAPS Trust, Gadhada.

This Diwali greeting card immediately suggests the larger paradox of spirituality-based development. The cover is purely religious, even theological, stressing the direct link between the present head and the founder of the order. Given that the Swaminarayans have many sub-sects, such an assertion of continuity at once serves to emphasize that Pramukh Swami is the rightful heir and humble servant of the founder Shri Swaminarayan. The opulence of the clothes of the founder, who was himself a renunciate but already worshipped as a living deity during his times, suggests that the Swaminarayans are a wealthy, rather than ascetic sect. Moreover, the message inside on saving water suggests that their notion of spirituality is based on acting in and on the world, not renouncing it. In fact, the message shows a serious commitment to conserving water which, as the key to development, must be harnessed as one of our most precious resources. Yet, this secular, modern and eco-friendly message sits snugly inside a card that has all the sacred paraphernalia of the sect on its cover.

Meeting P. P. Bhat in person only sharpened this contrast. A tall, greying, sprightly man of over 65, he had a ready smile and he introduced himself as someone who was 'retired, but not tired'. Bhatt represented a simple but noble piety in all his words and actions. Modest to the point of being self-effacing, he had nonetheless achieved much in the watershed development of the area we were studying. After serving as an engineer in the Gujarat Government, he had now devoted himself full time to various water-related projects of the Swaminarayans. And it was essentially to study their work in this area that we had organized a field trip. Bhat wore white trousers and shirts, contemporary clothes, unlike the traditional robes of the swamis of the order.

He was one of the several thousand householder disciples totally devoted to service. This dedication and sincerity was the key to the success of the sect. Unlike NGOs or government agencies, religious organizations are driven by a different quality of motivation. Neither money nor fame, but spiritual advancement spurs their actions. Spiritual advancement is always grounded in, even expressed through a transformation of the material conditions. As the website of the Bochasanwasi Shree Akshar Purushottam Swaminarayan Sanstha (BAPS) declares:

> Many ask, 'How can you mix spirituality and social service?'
> We ask, 'How can you separate the two?'
> Those who wish to sincerely serve society must be spiritually pure and only those who are spiritually pure can sincerely serve society![90]

The Swaminarayans

Before this trip, my own acquaintance with the Swaminarayans was slight. To people outside Gujarat, the group is not very well known. Apart from the enormous temples that they build, especially Akshardham outside Gandhinagar, Gujarat, and in the capital, New Delhi, and the huge Swaminarayan temple at Neasden near London, the Swaminarayans are known mostly by the practice of their monks to totally avoid women, to the extent of not even looking at them. This means that when monks travel, they are surrounded and served by men; when they visit homes, the women do not appear before them; and when they give talks, women sit separately or at the back. Some of these observances have been relaxed in recent times, but only marginally.

The Swaminarayans have also been known for maintaining caste distinctions, which most other reformist movements in India have practically done away with by now. Until some years ago, their temples were still known to practice discrimination against the former 'untouchables' in spite of the Government of India's outlawing such observances. Even today, certain distinctions of caste are observed among those initiated into asceticism among the Swaminarayans. Thus, overall the Swaminarayans give the appearance of being a rather conservative branch of modern Hinduism.

Such an impression is ironic considering how the Swaminarayans seek to portray themselves in their literature and how widely recognized their social reforms were. As Raymond Brady Williams shows in *An Introduction to Swaminarayan Hinduism*, which is the standard scholarly work on the subject, the Swaminarayans frame the narrative of the founding of their sect in terms of a time of chaos and lawlessness.[91] The Gujarat of that time is portrayed as riven by internecine conflict, lacking in norms of civilized behavior, and plagued with evil social practices such as female infanticide and *sati* (the immolation of widows).

Williams, following Swaminarayan tradition, makes much of the meeting between the British Governor of Bombay, Sir John Malcolm, and Shri Swaminarayan. The meeting, which took place in Rajkot on 26 February 1830, is also depicted prominently in the Swaminarayan literature on the founding of the sect and in their museum displays. Marking the advance of British paramountcy into Gujarat, Williams considers it a welcome event from the Swaminarayan point of view. He is at pains to point out the areas of convergence and cooperation between the two regimes of order, Pax Britannica and Pax Swaminarayana, that worked together to ensure the social and religious reform of Gujarat.[92]

It is, however, clear that in the Swaminarayan story the respect that Shri Swaminarayan received from Sir John Malcolm is chiefly another example of how the secular bowed before the spiritual, just one more sign to prove the divine and miraculous life of Shri Swaminarayan. To the Swaminarayans, the British were just tools of history, destined to play their role and then to depart, but the mission of the Swaminarayans is far from over. In fact, by a strange twist of fate, the Swaminarayan ministry is now active in the land of Sir John's descendants in Great Britain itself, where the Neasden temple is a magnificent symbol of the pride and power of the sect. In fact, the Oxford Centre for Hindu Studies has put the Shikshapatri of the Swaminarayans online,[93] an acknowledgement that many of their stake holders belong to this sect.

The Founder

The childhood name of the founder of the Swaminarayan sect was Ghanashyam. According to the Hindu calendar, he was born in Chapaiya, present day Uttar Pradesh, on Ramnavami (the birthday of Shri Rama), on Shukla Navami of the month Chaitra in Samvat 1837, which corresponds to 3 April 1781. His parents, Hariprasad and Premavati Pande, were Sarvariya Vaishnavite Brahmins. His elder brother Rampratap and younger brother Ichcharama were later to provide the lineage of the leaders of the acharya sub-sects. To this day, this tradition continues. The acharyas come from the founder's family and their wives are also from the same caste in Uttar Pradesh.

Subsequently, the parents of Ghanashyam began to be known as Dharmadeva and Bhaktimata, to allegorize their giving birth to a supernatural child who is now regarded by the followers as an incarnation of God. A whole cycle of legends has grown around the boyhood of Ghanashyam. These are meant to show him as a divine child, quite like Krishna. Such birth legends and childhood mythologies are common to numerous other sages, saints and holy men and women in India, so the Swaminarayans are not unique in this respect. There is an important story about Ghanashyam having defeated the proponents of the Advaita or the non-dualist school in a debate so as to establish the supremacy of the qualified non-dualism or Visishtadvaita of the Ramanuja school. To this day, the Swaminarayan theology can be classified as belonging to this philosophical tradition.

After his parents died, Ghanashyam, then merely 11, renounced the world. He became a wandering ascetic student, a *brahmachari*. He roamed for seven years in what Manilal C. Parekh calls 'the school of spiritual vagrancy'[94] from which some of India's greatest spiritual and social reformers graduated. During these wanderings, he took the name Neelkanth. He travelled widely all over India. From the Haridwar and Badrinath in the Himalayas, he went east to Mathura, Bengal; then south to Puri, further on to Shriperumbadur and Shrirangam, both associated with Ramanuja, then to Kanchipuram, Kumbakonam, Madurai and Rameshwaram; and finally, to western India, where he visited Dwarka. From that time, he remained in Gujarat till his death, adopting it as his home and place of work.

During this period of intense austerities, Neelkanth maintained perfect celibacy, which then became one of the main rules for the monks of his sect. In Loj, near Junagadh in Gujarat, he came into contact with Swami Ramananda, a leader of the Ramanuja tradition of sannyasis. Ramananda, who was originally from Bihar, played an important role in establishing the Shrivaishnava or the qualified non-dualistic philosophy of Ramanuja in Gujarat. Ramananda initiated Neelkanth into his monastic order, giving the latter the name 'Sahajanand'. For about two years (1800–1802), Sahajanand remained in Ramananda's ashram. At this point, Ramananda appointed Sahajanand as his successor, and died shortly thereafter.

In the Swaminarayan literature, Ramananda is considered to be Uddhava, a cousin, disciple, forerunner and announcer of Krishna, the supreme avatar, somewhat like John the Baptist was for Jesus. However, Sahajanand's leadership was not unchallenged. Some householders and ascetics left the order, alienating one of the four temples associated with Ramananda. Muktananda Swami, one of the chief disciples of Ramananda, then established an organized sect around Sahajanand which later became the Swaminarayan Movement.

Very soon, Sahajanand came to be regarded not just as the undisputed leader but as a manifestation of God. He is first described as an avatar in 1804 in a book called *Yama Danda*. He also began to be known as Swaminarayan. The name, which he also gave to his followers to be used as a mantra, came to be identified with the whole sect. Swaminarayan himself, like other 'godmen' of India, now began to perform the role of a living deity. He dressed and adopted the lifestyle of a prince because his followers lavished extravagant gifts upon him. His portraiture in the idols and pictures of sect, to this day, derives from this change of image. Though he was totally detached inwardly, he donned the appearance not of the renouncing monk that he was, but of a temporal and spiritual head of a large *sampradaya* or group. In the *Vachanamritam* (ambrosia of words), attributed to Swaminarayan, he says: 'When I meditate inwardly and think about the greatness and glory of God, I discard them (objects of wealth) as absolutely insignificant and totally devoid of any attraction . . . attachment to mundane objects fades away by the influence of this divine knowledge.'[95]

By the time Swaminarayan died in 1830, the movement had grown considerably. It was headquartered in Gadhada, in the Bhavanagar princely state, where Swaminarayan lived in the house of his ardent devotee Dada Khachar. Khachar was the feudal chief of the 12 villages that made up Gadhada. Khachar's house is still preserved as a part of a large temple complex. From Gadhada, Swaminarayan undertook several tours in Kathiawar and Kutch, thereby increasing his following considerably. According to British records, the Swaminarayans numbered at least 1,00,000 at this time. 2,87,687 were listed as followers of the movement by the year 1872, out of a total population of about 6.7 million in Gujarat.[96] The Swaminarayan literature, however, estimates the total number of followers to be around about 1.8 million by the time of the master's death. It is also believed that Swaminarayan initiated 2,000 sannyasis during his lifetime. Despite the strict segregation of the sexes, he also allowed women to be initiated into asceticism, though they had to live separately in havelis and could only preach to other women.

One of the most extraordinary aspects of the Swaminarayan ministry was his reputed ability to transport his followers into a state of samadhi or spiritual trance. This was both the proof and the source of his power, and one reason for the spread of the movement. Several of his followers are reported to have seen visions of Swaminarayan as Rama or Krishna, the most popular incarnations of Vishnu.[97] However, from the more mundane or secular viewpoint, Swaminarayan was highly respected, even during his own lifetime, as a great social reformer. Both British and Indian accounts attribute to him an enormous improvement in the morals and mores of the people of Gujarat.

Before the spread of British rule in Gujarat, Swaminarayan faced considerable opposition. His devotees and ascetics were often harassed and persecuted. The strict rules that they had to follow, including the prohibition of impure food, made it easy to pollute them. Swaminarayan therefore initiated about 500 of his sannyasis into the order of *paramahamsa* or the supreme swan, which is above all social and ritual observances of purity. Another source of strength and protection came from his Kathi followers, who were of the warrior caste. Though the Swaminarayans believe in and practise non-violence even to the exclusion of self-defense, and though they stay out of all quarrels, Swaminarayan himself travelled with a huge entourage with armed bodyguards.

In both the Swaminarayan literature and the historical accounts, Swaminarayan is hailed as a great social reformer who transformed Gujarat in the early nineteenth century. This was a period of large-scale social transformation all over India. In Bengal, there were agitations against *sati*, female infanticide and other social evils. Swaminarayan also promoted such causes in Gujarat, but from a traditional rather than modernist standpoint. The movement came to be known and respected for its strict moral and sexual purity. Swaminarayan forbade his followers from stealing, committing adultery, eating meat, drinking alcohol or other intoxicants, and from receiving food from one's social inferiors. These vows are still adhered to. The last injunction, controversial in today's age, has been somewhat reinterpreted by some.

An important element of the Swaminarayan ministry was his urging his followers to work hard. The ascetics too engaged in physical work. They dug well, cut canals, repaired reservoirs and in general performed good deeds. Swaminarayan did not want his ascetics to be considered parasites or social burdens, so he enjoined upon them to become activists. The present day social service projects of the Swaminarayans, thus, can be traced to the early days of the movement under their founder. In fact, during the famine of 1813–14, the Swaminarayans played a very important role in the relief activities.

Swaminarayan also reformed the rituals of popular Hinduism. He urged his followers to eschew animal sacrifice and one of the reasons that a large number of people in Gujarat are vegetarians may be attributed to the Swaminarayan ministry. He also condemned religious superstitions, the worshipping of spirits or 'inferior' deities. He rejected magic and other forms of tribal worship in favour of the worship of Krishna as the Supreme Godhead. His followers were also instructed to worship the five major deities of the Hindu pantheon – Vishnu, Shiva, Ganapati, Parvati and Surya – the deities also worshipped by the Smarta Brahmins. However, subsequently, most Swaminarayan temples have Swaminarayan himself as the supreme deity.

According to Williams, the Swaminarayan Movement can be seen as an example of what M. N. Shrinivas called Sanskritization. This is a process of upward mobility in which lower classes and castes adopt the rituals and ideals of an all-India tradition of Sanskritic Hinduism. Shrinivas himself indicates that the Sanskritization of the Patidars (Patels – a land owning community) was affected by the Vallabhacharya and Swaminarayan sects.[98] The Swaminarayans have also been considered the puritans of India because they preached against intoxicants and sexual license disguised as religious observances.[99]

In the last ten years of Swaminarayan's life, six large temples were constructed in Ahmedabad, Bhuj, Vadtal, Junagadh, Dholera and Gadhada. Even today, temple construction is one of the main activities of the Swaminarayans. By the time of his death, British power came to be firmly established in Gujarat. The spread of the Swaminarayans coincided with this. Though one cannot consider them collaborators with colonialism, the establishment of law and order greatly facilitated the spread of this movement. The meeting between Swami Narayan and John Malcolm suggests this mutual respect and cooperation. The movement also helped in the consolidation of a standard Gujarati script for the whole state.

According to Williams, Swaminarayan 'has been correctly identified as the last of the medieval Hindu saints and the first of the neo-Hindu reformers'. He began his career when medieval India was collapsing all around him; he died before modern India came into being. As a bridge between two worlds, one dying, the other waiting to be born, he performed an important role of providing continuity and stability. What is more, he offered a new version of an old teaching that was so timely that it found many adherents. Today, the ministry has spread all across the world, wherever Gujaratis live. The British Empire is dead, but the Swaminarayan Movement is growing.

The Sects

The Swaminarayan Movement had already spread all over Gujarat during the founder's lifetime. Though he personally supervised most of the important administrative functions and duties of the sect, it became necessary to delegate power and authority. There were also the inevitable disagreements between his followers. In 1826, Swaminarayan tried to establish a line of succession. He did this by dividing the territorial affairs of the sect into two dioceses, Ahmedabad (northern) and Vadtal (southern), appointing a spiritual head or acharya to each seat. He formally anointed the sons of his two brothers – Ayadhaprasad, the son of his elder brother Ramapratap, as the acharya of Ahmedabad, and Raghuvira, the son of his younger brother Ichcharama, as the acharya of Vadtal. In doing so, Swaminarayan was following the *parampara* or tradition of guru-shishya, or teachers and disciples, which was a well-established part of the Ramanuja lineage. In this case, however, in addition to spiritual descent, there was also family lineage to lend authority to the line of succession. Swaminarayan also laid down strict rules of conduct to control and govern the lives of each acharya, his wife, and members of family.

These two acharyas were invested with the responsibility of managing all the temples, properties and wealth, which fell under their respective dioceses. They were also to initiate monks and install images in new temples. There have been six and eight acharyas so far in the Ahmedabad and the Vadtal dioceses, respectively. During the 170 years or so since the founder's death, there have been numerous disputes and schisms – among the acharyas themselves, among the acharyas and ascetics, and among the other followers. Some of these disputes were settled according to the traditional procedures laid down by the sect, while others were adjudicated by the courts. One of the acharyas of the Vadtal line, Lakshmiprasad, was deposed in 1906.

After independence, the growth of legislation has curtailed the power and autonomy of the acharyas. There are now government officials who are the legal custodians of religious trusts and who oversee their functioning. The acharyas are assisted by managing committees and boards of trustees. Some of the larger temples in both dioceses have their own board of trustees. To further complicate matters, each diocese has further sub-divisions. For instance, the Ahmedabad diocese has the Bhuj temple and trust, and the Muli temple and trust. Both Bhuj and Muli were princely states governed by laws different from British India. After independence, these semi-autonomous entities continued their separate existence. What is more, there are several *gurukuls* or schools led by ascetics, which became independent of the acharyas. Some of these swamis formed their own educational trusts and societies, especially to establish colleges or hostels.

The more fundamental schism has to do with the line of succession passing not through householder acharyas, but through ascetics. An example of this is a separate sect formed by Muktajivandas Swami in 1941. It is called the Swaminarayan Gadi and has its headquarters in Maninagar, outside Ahmedabad. This group has about 100 sadhus, 20 sadhvis, and 1,00,000 followers, including some in Britain, USA and Africa.

But the most important of the breakaway groups is the BAPS. This break is not just institutional, but doctrinal. What is more, its following is fast growing and may overtake the 'old schools' of Ahmedabad and Vadtal. It has more than a million followers. According to Williams, this is the breakdown of the strength of male sadhus in each group in 1999:[100]

Ahmedabad	Vadtal	BAPS
765	1468	700

The split came in 1906 when Swami Yagnapurushdas (1865–1951), more popularly known as Shastri Maharaj, broke away from the Vadtal temple. He taught that Swaminarayan's true successor was Swami Gunatitanand, an ascetic, and that only ascetics had the moral and spiritual courage to guide the movement. Further, that Gunatitanand, who was the perfect devotee, was the embodiment of *akshar*, the imperishable aspect of the Godhead that would manifest again and again to lead the followers. So the true line of succession consists in perfected disciples, who are embodiments of Shri Swaminarayan himself. That is why, in the BAPS temples, images of Gunatitanand are given prominence along with those of Swaminarayan.

During his lifetime, Shastri Maharaj built several temples, installed the deities in them, initiated many sadhus and toured extensively, both in India and abroad. The doctrinal split over spiritual versus hereditary lineage solidified when in 1947, the BAPS was reorganized, with all the properties vested in it instead of individual sadhus or mahants. After Shastri Maharaj, Swami Jnanijivandas or Yogiji Maharaj (1891–1971) was appointed the successor, and after him the present head, Swami Narayanswarupdas, more popularly known as Pramukh Swami, took over. The total estimated followers of Ahmedabad and Vadtal (old school) number 3.5 million while that of BAPS (new school) number 1.5 million.[101]

There is yet another breakaway group, this time from BAPS, called the Yogi Divine Society. It was founded by Dadubhai Patel and his brother Bapabhai in 1966. This group does not recognize Pramukh Swami as the rightful successor of Yogiji Maharaj. In 1986, Hariprasad Swami became the leader of this group. It has about 175 male and 225 female ascetics.

Organization and Activities of BAPS

From its headquarters in Ahmedabad, the BAPS administers five charitable trusts under the headship of Pramukh Swami: Bochasanwasi Shree Akshar Purushottam Swaminarayan Sanstha, for general activities; Swaminarayan Askharpith, for publications; Ghahyagna Vidyapith, for educational institutions; Bochasanwasi Shree Akshar Purushottam Gaushala Trust, for animal welfare; and Bochasanwasi Shree Akshar Purushottam Public Charitable Trust, for medical clinics and hospitals. In all there are 495 BAPS mandirs worldwide, with an estimated 1,50,000 pilgrims visiting them daily. The total number of sadhus is 635, and the volunteer corps, which regularly offers its time and talent to these various activities, numbers over 3,000. Each trust has a board of national trustees, made up of sadhus and householders. There are regular meetings and programmes.

Given below is a synoptic summary of their activities in 2011:[102]

International Centres:

- 3,300 centres in India, USA, UK, Europe, Africa, Pacific, Middle East
- 7,215 weekly assemblies for men and women, youths and teenagers
- 5,400 weekly assemblies for children

Worldwide Volunteers:

- 55,000 volunteers
- 1,20,00,000 annual volunteer-hours in service

Moral & Cultural Activities:

- 6,30,000 annual satsang assemblies
- 34 million visitors to cultural festivals in India, UK, USA, Africa
- 5,54,790 students have appeared in the international cultural examinations

Medical Activities:

- 8 hospitals and healthcare clinics
- 4,15,000 patients treated annually
- 76 medico-spiritual conferences have enlightened over 20,000 doctors

Educational Activities:

- 31 permanent educational institutions annually serve 11,000 students
- Over 5,000 scholarships awarded annually
- 55 schools built in disaster-hit regions

Environmental Activities:

- Millions of trees and shrubs planted in thousands of villages
- Thousands of water conservation projects in hundreds of villages
- Thousands of tonnes of paper collected for recycling annually

Social Activities:

- 33 disaster relief operations successfully managed
- 50,000 families inspired to hold daily Family Assemblies
- Over two million people inspired to quit addictions

Tribal Activities:

- 800 permanent centres for tribal uplift
- Thousands of tribal families have quit addictions and superstitions
- 9 mobile medical clinics treat 2,50,000 tribal villagers annually

Spiritual Activities:

- Over 700 BAPS mandirs worldwide
- Thousands of pilgrims visit BAPS mandirs daily
- Over 800 sadhus

While it is impossible to verify all these claims, visiting some of their sites gave us a better idea of the Swaminarayans and their work. From the very beginning of this movement, it engaged in both social reform and developmental activities. Sahajanand asked his followers to open alms-houses, dig wells, restore water tanks, and build shelters for travellers. He abolished the practice of *sati* and female infanticide among his followers and also tried to rationalize their religious beliefs. In the process, he established a new sect, if not a religion. In most of its fundamental beliefs it follows the dualistic Vaishnava theology in which Vishnu or Krishna as God is the Supreme Person to whom devotion is due. It is only through love and devotion that the devotee can attain salvation, which in this case is proximity or union with the Supreme Godhead. Swaminarayans, like most other Vaishnava sects, are strictly vegetarian and non-violent. As opposed to certain other Vaishnava sects like the Vallabhacharyas, the Swaminarayan monks practise strict celibacy. Thus, the sect prides itself on its adherence to what it considers the highest standards of piety and purity. In course of time, the Swaminarayans became one of the largest religious groups in Gujarat. It must be emphasized here that the Swaminarayans do not proselytize or actively seek followers. Rather, the aim is to shepherd and serve those who are born and brought up in the sect and also the larger civil society of which the Swaminarayans are a part.

Field Trip: October 1999

I visited several key sites of the BAPS Swaminarayan sect (led by Pramukh Swami) to learn of their developmental activities. I was with Dr Kamla Chowdhry, chair of the Vikram Sarabhai Foundation and eminent social worker, who wanted to understand the impact of spirituality on social development. Our focus was on watershed development, and the areas chosen were the Ahmedabad and Bhavnagar districts of Gujarat. We were escorted by Janak M. Dave, the chief PRO of the Akshardham Centre for Applied Research in Social Harmony, and P. P. Bhat, the project officer of the BAPS Trust which looks after the watershed projects of the Swaminarayans.

Sarangpur

Our first visit was to Sarangpur, Ahmedabad District, which is about four hours from Ahmedabad city by road. There is a large temple here, which was built by Shastriji Maharaj about 75 years ago. Today it is a huge complex which houses a seminary for the monks, a large *goshala* or cowshed that has produced several prize-winning cattle, and guest rooms, in addition to the impressive temple.

This temple complex is situated in a drought-prone area. There are 20 NGOs already working here on water-related projects. The BAPS Trust of the Swaminarayans was actually invited by the Gujarat

Government to join in the effort to conserve water. As of the date of our visit, the Trust had undertaken a total of nine projects in which a total of 52 check dams were built in two years, 1997–1999. Behind most of this work is P. P. Bhat, who supervises these projects as an unpaid volunteer. To him, his work is a part of his worship. Ninety per cent of the funds for these projects come either from the Central or the State Government; 10 per cent is borne by the villagers either in the form of labour or cash. Besides building check dams, the Trust has also recharged several wells, repaired water tanks, and undertaken other developmental works such as famine relief. We found that most of these tasks were accomplished at less than 60% of the costs of governmental projects.

At Sarangpur we not only visited the check dam, but met the villagers, including the *sarpanch* (the headman) and the *talati* (the accountant). They told us that before the dam they had very little drinking water and had to go very far to fetch it. The worst affected were the poorest of the poor, who in this village were mostly schedule caste people. After the dam, several of these who were beneficiaries of land grants could at last get a crop out of their hard and semi-barren land.

The villagers that we met were mostly poor and illiterate. Some were Dalits, once considered untouchable. They complained that though the Government had helped them all to get land, it was of very poor quality. They could only eke out a meagre living. The dam had not helped them as much as it had the richer farmers, who had better lands adjacent to the river or with access to irrigation. The villagers told us that they could get a crop only eight years out of 15. They needed a girls' school and a dispensary too. The Dalits said that they did not have proper houses. Nonetheless, more than 3,000 people had been helped, either directly or indirectly, by the check dam.

Moreover, all the villagers said that the temple was central to their lives. 'We get so much help here,' they said. I asked, 'Like what?' 'Well,' an old lady replied, 'anything and everything. When we're hungry we get food. We get water. They help us with our personal problems. We even get buttermilk to drink on a very hot day.' She was very moved as she said this. It was also clear that the temple was an important economic centre and that it gave employment to several daily wage earners. It was an important source of water in an area which had no plumbing or regular water supply. The Swaminarayans helped all those who came to them, whether they were of the same persuasion or not. Yet, the villagers here did not seem to be a cheerful or inspiring lot. They were not properly organized, nor were they proactive in their own welfare. They looked to the government or to some other agency to help them out. They were very cautious in talking to the officials and seemed rather resigned to what was their lot.

Nigana, Bhavnagar District

Here the villagers were not only better educated and more prosperous, but well-organized too. In a meeting they told us the benefits of the already constructed check dam and said that they would build one more, with or without government support. A lot of the income in this village came from the diamond-cutting industry, which gave employment to the men and women in the village. Here the Trust trained women in cooking, canning, baking, sewing and other vocational activities, in addition to their work in watershed development.

BAPS had constructed one check dam on the Sonal, which was a tributary of river Keri. It had also helped build or repair farm ponds and plugged the gullies from which water was wasted or drained away. The village was inhabited by about 5,000 people and had 2,800 hectares of cultivable land. About 40 percent of the villagers were Patels, while the rest were distributed among various castes, including Rajputs and lower castes. The village had a *gram sabha* (village assembly) instituted about two years earlier. It is this body that had decided how best to extend their water resources. They had planned three projects to develop 1,500 hectares of land plus another project for an additional 400 hectares.

The first thing they did was to construct a two-foot wall across the river. That slowed the flow of water and helped to recharge several wells. They formed a Sangathan Mandal (unity group), consisting of six users, two members from weaker sections, and two Dalits such as shepherds or leather workers to manage their projects. There was also a managing committee, which had actually approached the BAPS to help them. The whole project would take up four years. The villagers were determined to raise funds and to work on their own, even if the government support did not come through. They also had contacts outside, in bigger cities such as Ahmedabad and Surat, because of the diamond business.

We got a sense of an awakened and self-reliant community, confident and determined to improve its living conditions. The ladies were organized too. They had a community centre where they offered cooking, canning, sewing and baking classes. A lot of the women were also working in the diamond-cutting business. These were very small, usually cottage businesses, with people working out of their own homes.

Many of the villagers were Swaminarayans. They told us that water was the key to development. They had learned from Pramukh Swami that they had to work to conserve water. Several wells had been dug or recharged in that area. The BAPS helped the villagers to plant trees, lay pipes, and also support the literacy drive. The next step was to equip homes with underground water storage tanks in which rainwater could be harvested.

The villagers told us that the BAPS had taken the initiative to transform their lives, not the government. 'The government didn't help us for 50 years. Earlier, we used to enjoy a good life as long as it rained. Then we were back to misery. Now we have learned to save water, to build check dams, to recharge wells. And look at all these benefits. We have water to drink all the year round and also some for irrigation. Earlier, we had to buy water, but now we have our own.'

Gadhada

This was the place where Shri Swaminarayan spent over 25 years of his life. The large marble temple was built to commemorate this fact. We visited several villages in this area to see the various efforts at rainwater harvesting and preservation. Nearly all the well-to-do had built underground tanks to collect and preserve rainwater. They said that the water stayed well for months and was potable.

The temple was inaugurated by Yogiji Maharaj in 1951. It has three images, all made in marble: Harikrishna Maharaj, Gopinathji and Radha in the first shrine; Dham, Dhami and Mukta in the central niche; and Sukh Shayya/Guru Parampara in the third shrine. Apparently, Shri Swaminarayan himself prophesied that a temple with three spires would be built atop the hill. This did not happen during his lifetime, but there were relentless efforts since 1923 to make the dream come true. The ruler of Bhavnagar state did not allow the Swaminarayans to acquire the land to build the temple. However, after India's independence in 1947, the new collector helped them buy the land.

The massive temple, with its marble towers, looks over the Ghelo river. Ghelo means the mad one, so the river must have been brisk and frisky once, but was only a sluggish and dirty stream when we visited. From the balcony, in the evening, one could get a sense of what pre-modern India must have been like, very much a riverine civilization. The saints and devotees would have bathed at the river and walked up to temples like this one for their worship and teaching. For the Swaminarayans, this was a place of utmost importance. Their key text, the *Vachanamrit*, had mostly been narrated here. Shri Swaminarayan made several preaching tours to spread his message while using this place as the base. Here he lived in the palace of Dada Khachar. Within those premises, he built a magnificent temple to Gopinathji Maharaj in 1828.

We visited Dada Khachar's haveli and the Gopinath temple in the evening. While the complex belongs to the southern acharya (Vadtal diocese), all devotees of Shri Swaminarayan were welcome. The temple had been built at the insistence of the two elder sisters of Dada Khachar, Jaya (Jivuba) and Lalita (Laduba). Shri Swaminarayan is said to have supervised the construction, even carrying bricks from the river to the construction site. He also consecrated the idols himself. The temple itself is built with bricks and wooden columns on a raised marble platform. It is painted with bright colours on the outside. The central shrine has Gopinath and Radha, with Dharmadev, Bhaktimata and Vasudev on the western side and Suryanarayan (the Sun God) on the east. The Gopinath idol was made to resemble Shri Swaminarayan and was exactly of the same size. We also saw the rest of the haveli, which was well maintained, with a special area for women devotees and teachers.

That night we stayed at a guest-house attached to the temple. It was a longish building with an open terrace on top. Kamla-ji and I walked up and down the terrace, overlooking the river, as the sun went down. Later, we had a delicious supper in the dining room behind the temple.

Everywhere we went, we were touched by the great warmth and courtesy of the Swaminarayan devotees. Janak-bhai, our guide, was well known and admired in the Swaminarayan circles. He had practically left his home to devote himself full-time to service.

Goradka

The village near the Goradka check dam had 2,500 people in it. We visited the home of one of the Swaminarayans and were greeted warmly. The villagers, we found, were divided along political lines. They were enthusiastic, but somewhat disunited. Several women worked in the diamond industry. They could do this from home without disturbing the social mores and gender roles too much. Of an average family monthly income of Rs 4,500 among the better off, the working woman brought in as much as Rs 1,500. Our host told us how agricultural income was erratic despite the family's owning eight acres of land. It was only after the BAPS check dams and other projects that some irrigation became possible. Several homes had underground water tanks to store rainwater. These cost at least Rs 16,000, so not everyone could afford them. But gradually, even the Dalits were building smaller tanks like the Patels.

Nearby, we saw a check dam, but found that it largely benefited the rich and privileged, though the poor also came to the nearby tube well to get drinking water. We found in general that given the inequitable social and economic structures of the villages, the Swaminarayan projects tended to benefit the already affluent and advantaged sections of society. They were not specifically targeted to the poor and landless. This check dam, for instance, helped the farms on the banks of the river. These farms belonged to the rich. The poor, who had semi-arid or rocky plots far away from the river, were not likely to gain much.

On our way back to Ahmedabad, we stopped at two more villages and met several people. We also went to a Swaminarayan temple in the village. Here the temple served as a community centre. People gathered in the evenings to discuss issues pertaining to the village and its day-to-day problems.

Shahibaug, Ahmedabad

After several tiring days in the field, we returned to Ahmedabad, to the Shahibaug headquarters of the BAPS. In the heart of the city, this large and crowded complex, honeycombed with construction, houses the headquarters of the sect. It has a large, well-equipped, multi-storied guest-house, cafeteria, an open-air auditorium and also a hospital on the premises. Here I met several lay volunteers and monks. Dhiren Jhala was serving in the dining hall. He had taken early retirement to devote his life to the cause. I asked him how that had happened. He said, 'I met Yogiji Maharaj when I was 17. My fate was sealed then. I knew I would do this sooner or later.' Ritesh Gadhia was, in contrast, a young man with an MBA from the Indian Institute of Management, Ahmedabad. He could have got one of the top jobs in business or industry. In fact, he had already worked for companies like Rasna and Cadilla but now wanted to serve the Swaminarayans. He was helping create the Akshardham website. He said, 'I work for the guru. That is the meaning and purpose of my life.'

Dr Kamla Chowdhry, being a woman, could not meet the monks, but I had detailed discussions with them. Brahmavihari Swami and Vivekjeevan Swami were both associated with the editing and production of *Swaminarayan Bliss*, the monthly journal of the BAPS in English, and its Hindi and Gujarati counterparts, *Swaminarayan Prakash*. Brahmavihari Swami was born in East Africa, but came to England as a child. In 1970 when Yogiji Maharaj visited their house in London, the former underwent a transformation. Later, in 1974, when Pramukh Swami came to London, Brahmavihari Swami decided to renounce the world to become a monk himself. I asked him if he missed the fast and free life he knew in London before he joined the Swaminarayan order. He said, 'Not at all. I'm happy and contented.' I questioned him about the rather strict vows. He replied, 'We have to set an example.' 'How about changing with the times? Is it practical to avoid seeing women?' I asked. He hesitated, 'Well, it's for the leaders to decide, but I, on my part, like the strictness. It helps us spiritually. This discipline has been designed to elevate us.' When I persisted, 'But aren't you discriminating against women?' He laughed, 'Right now, you have only one question. But if we start speaking to women, you'll have many more. It's better not to open that door. You can't compromise on certain things.' 'But who trains the ladies, who initiates them if they can't meet the Swamis?' He said, 'They're trained by elder ladies in the family or female teachers. Even without direct contact, they have greater devotion and faith. That's the miracle.' I asked Vivekjeevan Swami what attracted him most to the Swaminarayan faith. He said, 'First of all, we imbibe it from our parents or our close family. But then we realize that the whole world becomes our family. For me the most precious experience has been the grace and living example of Pramukh Swami, a realized soul. What can be more fortunate than that?'

Many of the other monks were highly educated engineers, MBAs or doctors. Some were children of overseas Indians. All of them strictly avowed the Swaminarayan code of conduct. The whole order was based on service and devotion. The quieter, spiritual or contemplative aspects were not stressed as much as practical projects and the welfare of the followers.

Akshardham, Gandhinagar

From a distance, Akshardham looks utterly unreal, as if it is straight out of the set of a Bollywood film. Unlike other great monuments from India's past, it looks disconcertingly new, but it is totally unlike any contemporary building. Like a grand architectural anachronism, it stands in magnificent and isolated splendour. The 23 acre plot was acquired in an auction for Rs 1 crore (Rs 10 million). Eight acres have been built upon, and 15 have gardens and open spaces on them. 6,000 tonnes of pink sandstone have been joined together without any iron or steel. More than 12 million man-hours of 900 skilled craftsmen were required to create this extraordinary monument of 93 sculpted pillars and 40 windows carved from both sides. Constructed in accordance with the ancient Sthaapatya Shastras of India, it has 22 ft support beams of single piece stone blocks. As the website proudly says, 'The pillars are poetry in stone, with beautiful expression from foot to crown. Every carving carries a meaning. Every statue breathes life! The intricacy, the delicacy, the austerity is breathtaking. The patterns are peaceful while the dome resonates with vibrations divine. It is because Akshardham is more than an architectural masterpiece, it is the living devotion of devotees to create Heaven on Earth.'[103] It goes on to list its various salient features, which are called architectural wonders:

- Tallest structural stone pillars in India – four delicately sculpted pillars rise to 33 ft
- Longest stone support beams in stone architecture – 22 ft long single-piece beams, each weighing 5 tons
- No iron or steel – from foundation to pinnacle – only stone has been used
- 73 richly patterned and 63 partially carved pillars
- 16 pillars with profuse *roopkam* – sculptures and figures
- 64 large traditional sculptures with spiritual meanings and 192 small figures of Gods and Goddesses adorn the pillars
- 5 types of stones used in the monument: 1. pink sandstone from Bansipahadpur; 2. yellow stone from Jaisalmer; 3. white marble from Makrana; 4. maroon granite from Jhansi; and 5. white marble from Ambaji
- 25 domes of varying sizes and depths
- Grandly ornate porch and 3 exclusively decorated porticos
- Intricately carved from both sides – 30 large windows and 24 small grills
- 220 stone beams for structural support
- 57 stone screens for controlling light and enhancing beauty
- 1,60,000 cubic feet of pink sandstone has been carved and assembled
- 108 ft high, 240 ft long and 131 ft wide, it consists of three floors

Harimandapam, the main floor, has golden idols of Shri Swaminarayan, Shri Gunatitanand Swami and of those souls that have been saved and sanctified, represented by Gopalananda Swami. The idols were installed and consecrated on 30 October 1992. The Prasadi Mandapam, with its five halls, preserves the relics of Shri Swaminarayan and recreates his life story. The Vibhuti Mandapam on the upper floor contains multimedia exhibits on the personality and philosophy of Shri Swaminarayan. Akshardham uses the latest technology audio and animatronics in its various exhibits. This is a source of great wonder to the 3 million people who visit it annually. What is more, many political leaders and celebrities, including the former US president, Bill Clinton, have visited Akshardham. It is justifiably the greatest and grandest achievement of the BAPS branch of the Swaminarayans. Like the Taj Mahal, it has become a national, even international, monument. When we visited, we saw people of every denomination, including Muslims and Christians, among the visitors. It houses a high-tech museum which tells of the life of Shri Swaminarayan. Akshardham, which means the imperishable abode, is the most potent symbol of the Swaminarayans. Though its developmental purpose is questionable, it does have a powerful educative and cultural value.

Swaminarayan Mandir, London

On 20 August 1996, Pramukh Swami inaugurated the Shri Swaminarayan Mandir in Neasden, London. This large temple has the distinction of being Europe's first traditional Hindu mandir built in stone, in accordance with ancient Hindu Shilpa Shastras. It was a huge project to bring in 2,828 tonnes of limestone from Bulgaria and 2,000 tonnes of Carrara marble from Italy. These were first shipped to India, where over 1,500 sculptors worked on them for two years. Within three years, they were shipped back to London, to be assembled and put together, like a giant jigsaw puzzle. The haveli adjacent to the building was made of wood in the traditional style of architecture. It is said that such a huge haveli has not been built outside India and anywhere in the world during the last 100 years. The temple complex also has a cultural centre, an exhibition on Hinduism, a reception hall, sports facilities for youth and an adjoining school.

I visited the temple one rainy day in October 2002, taking the underground up to Neasden and then a cab to the temple. Again, I experienced the same, unfailing hospitality of the Swaminarayans. I was invited to the home of one of the devotees for lunch, something I could not accede to because I had to catch a plane. But the sense of warmth and community were ever-present, even in London.

Conclusions

When I initially started work on the Swaminarayans, I was bewildered by the variety and number of their sub-sects. While this is not at all uncommon to any major spiritual traditions, I attributed these schisms to the usual squabbling over power and money. On closer study, I discovered that this was not entirely true. In fact, I found a remarkable absence of animosity or hostility between the groups. They neither condemned each other nor claimed to be the only true followers of Shri Swaminarayan. Instead, there seemed to be considerable sympathy and cooperation between the sub-sects.

The reason for this is the unusual doctrinal cohesion among all the Swaminarayans, a testament to the founder's tremendous and somewhat modern skills of institution-building and organization. All the followers worship Shri Swaminarayan and have reverence for the tradition of acharyas and monks. But the real difference between the sects is a sort of continuous internal reform by which the sects reshape themselves and their identity. The central thrust for this reengineering is greater spiritual energy and moral purity. In other words, the breakaway sects are usually more 'protestant' than the original line of householder acharyas.

Indeed, the most active sect of the Pramukh Swami has been successful precisely because it has managed to breathe new life into what it means to be a Swaminarayan. He has turned the sect into a sort of ever-expanding service empire, almost along the lines of a corporate system of efficient management. Over time, I expect more and more of the traditional Swaminarayans to join this or another more active order, led by monks and not lay acharyas. It is the newer, more dynamic church within the religious tradition of the Swaminarayans that will drive it forward, modernizing and revitalizing the entire sect. This ability to reform itself continuously is one of the most outstanding features of Swaminarayan Hinduism.

Temple building is a crucial part of the social reconstruction programme of the Swaminarayans. This is because a temple serves not just as a spiritual centre of a place of worship, but also as the nodal point for the entire Swaminarayan community. The swamis and administrators live in temple premises, teach, and meet devotees there.

The devotees perform *seva* or service at the temples, use it as a base for their social service activities, and meet each other there. The temples, moreover, serve as the best way to publicize the work of the sect to the people at large. They are educative and promotional projects, disseminating the Swaminarayan creed better than any other form of publicity. These temples are huge projects, costing millions of rupees. They are a testament of the faith and cooperation of the members of the sect, not to speak of their fund-raising, organizational, engineering and aesthetic skills. They make the whole Swaminarayan community feel proud and cement their sense of identity.

One main reason for the success of the Swaminarayans is their very close-knit community. The swamis are not aloof, but very much a part of society, serving their constituencies with tremendous dedication and discipline. I had several personal experiences of this. Swami Tyagavallabh Swami of the Sokhda sect of the Swaminarayans, for instance, called me up in Delhi, requesting me to get the marksheets of one of the Swaminarayan children from the Indira Gandhi National Open University. This student was feeling depressed and restless because he was unable to find out how he had done in his correspondence course. No problem was too small for the swami. He would go out of his way to help, even intervening in family problems, if necessary, offering counselling, support and advice.

When I visited Rajkot, TV Swami, as he is popularly called, made me his personal guest. Two novices were asked to look after me. One evening, after a trip to Mangrol, I returned unannounced and very hungry at 9:30 pm. I knew the dining room was shut, so I said nothing and contacted no one, but within an hour, I had a freshly cooked meal delivered to my room in a tiffin carrier. Not only had my arrival been noticed, but someone had been dispatched to one of the families to get a freshly cooked meal for me.

Earlier, I had got to know Janak Dave quite well. He was a kind and compassionate man, utterly dedicated to the cause. With his wife's permission, he had left home to do this work full-time. He received board and lodge, and minimum expenses. He was calm and poised like a sannyasi himself. Everywhere he went, he was welcomed and accorded respect. All these experiences convinced me that the Swaminarayans create close personal bonds with their love and service. They are hardworking and prosperous. What is more, they donate liberally to their sect. This is what makes them so effective. I asked Janak-bhai how the Swaminarayans were so rich. He replied, 'That's because we don't fight with anyone and don't get involved in politics.'

Most of the members offer ten percent of their income to the sect, with the result that large volumes of funds can be mobilized for the common good of the people. Not just check dams, but hospitals, schools and colleges too have been started by some of these trusts. The emotional bonding and sense of solidarity helps the sect members to have stable and satisfying relationships, both within the family and outside. The Swaminarayans came across as thrifty, hardworking, devoted people who carried on their ancestral traditions. This is possible largely because of the exemplary lives of their renunciate monks, most of whom are utterly dedicated to their vocations.

Dr Kamla Chowdhry was concerned that the Swaminarayans appeared to be a conservative, even retrogressive sect. The swamis, who ran it, weren't allowed to interact with women, which made them somewhat unattractive from a modern point of view. On issues of caste, too, they appeared more conservative than progressive. The sect seemed to be very rich. The temples, which took up much more funds than any other activity, were grand, even ostentatious. The sect was not especially concerned with the poor or the marginal sections of society. Some of these criticisms were also made by Mahatma Gandhi several years ago.

I, on the other hand, felt that development in the purely secular and worldly sense was not their primary objective. I found the whole Swaminarayan sect remarkable for its cohesion, dedication and sense of community. The swamis were not just spiritual gurus, but friends, counsellors and partners of the people. They were available to the devotees day and night, solving business and family disputes too. The spirit of volunteerism and service was as remarkable as the extraordinary philanthropy of the members of the sect.

On 24 September 2002, there was a terrorist strike on Akshardham in Gandhinagar. Two terrorists entered the complex. Before they were gunned down, they had succeeded in killing 33 and injuring 70 people. They had fired into the crowds who had come thronging to see the temple. Within three years of this attack, the Swaminarayans built another huge temple on the banks of the Yamuna in the capital city of Delhi. It is a grand monument, built according to the ancient rules of temple architecture, filled with intricate stone carvings of statues. The main deity is, once again, the guru and the founder of the sect, Lord Swaminarayan, and his chief disciple Gunatitanand Swami together constituting the Akshara-Purushottam unity in duality. All visitors are frisked and searched before they enter. But this has not deterred millions of people of every religion, race, nationality, caste and creed from visiting this temple, which is now one of Delhi's greatest and most impressive modern monuments.

Chapter 10

'The Hour of God'

The Life

Born on 15 August 1872, Aravinda Akroyd Ghose[104] was the third son of Dr Krishna Dhan Ghose, a medical practitioner, and Swarnalata Devi, the eldest daughter of Rajnarayan Bose. His father was an avowed Anglophile and 'a terrible atheist'. His wish was that Aurobindo become an Indian Civil Service officer and join the ruling classes of India. To this end, he gave his eldest three sons a British education, first sending them to Loretto Convent, Darjeeling, and in 1879, to England. From the age of seven to 12, Aurobindo was in Manchester, under the care of Rev. William H. Drewett. Later, Aurobindo and his elder brother Manomohan went to London to study at St. Paul's School.

Aurobindo was a brilliant student who excelled in classics, literature and history. In 1890, at the age of 18, he was admitted to King's College, Cambridge, with a senior classical scholarship worth Pounds 80 per annum. There he performed brilliantly, passing the Classical Tripos in the first division and winning prizes for Greek and Latin verses. In 1890, Aurobindo cleared the Indian Civil Service examination in the open competition. However, he never appeared for the riding test, as a consequence of which he failed to qualify. In 1892 he obtained an appointment with the Gaekwar of Baroda and set sail for India in January 1893.

After 14 years in England, Aurobindo set foot on Indian soil in early February 1893. He worked for the Gaekwar from 1893 to 1907, serving in various departments, eventually settling down to teaching at Baroda College. In 1901, he married Mrinalini, who was then 14 years old.

Mrinalini, it would appear, was a far more conventional person than Aurobindo, besides which there were disparities of age, education and temperament. The marriage cannot be described as a meeting of souls; in fact, little mention is made of it in Aurobindonian literature.

By the end of his stint with the Gaekwar, Aurobindo had begun to take an active role in Indian politics. He belonged to the Extremist section of the Congress and was instrumental in engineering the split between his faction and the Moderates at Surat in 1907. He began to harbour designs of freeing India through revolutionary action and was the inspiration behind a secret society formed for that purpose. He had also embarked upon an ambitious programme of self-education, learning Sanskrit and several Indian languages besides mastering Indian philosophy, history and literature. Finally, he had also begun his preliminary experiments in yoga.

From 1906 to 1908, Aurobindo was at the forefront of our freedom struggle. He wrote extensively on political issues and was one of our earliest advocate of *purna* or total Svaraj. In 1908 he was arrested for sedition and was imprisoned at Alipore, Calcutta. During his incarceration, he underwent several spiritual experiences which changed the course of his life forever. After he was released in 1909, he turned his full attention to yoga. Obeying a divine command, he went into hiding in Chandranagore, a Dutch territory, and then departed for Pondicherry on 1 April 1910. Mrinalini, naturally, was left behind. In the years to come she became lonely, undergoing terrible psychological and emotional suffering. She died of influenza in 1918, just when she was preparing to join her husband in Pondicherry.

Sri Aurobindo remained in Pondicherry until he left his body on 5 December 1950.

Sri Aurobindo's Thought

The keynote of Sri Aurobindo's thought is evolution. From his earliest writings in 1890–1892, when he was an undergraduate at King's College, Cambridge, the basic orientation of his ideas was evolutionary. A remarkable unfinished work from that period called 'The Harmony of Virtue', affords us an interesting proof of this. In this dialogue between Keshav Ganesh Desai, who clearly stands for Sri Aurobindo himself, and his English friends, Sri Aurobindo proposes a new theory of virtue, beyond and, if necessary, contrary to what is conventionally considered moral and ethical. To realize what virtue really is, a descent into the nether regions of consciousness, such as is later portrayed at great length in *Savitri*, is necessary. But the key to virtue is evolution: 'Human virtue lies in the evolution by the human being of the inborn qualities and powers native to his humanity.'[105] Here we see the germ of both involution – that which is inborn and native to our humanity, and evolution – a glimpse of the glorious future in which our total potentialities will be manifested.

No wonder, according to Sri Aurobindo, man – as he is at present – is not the end-point of evolution, but a transitional being, largely mental, but not yet evolved enough to transcend the dualities and false consciousness of daily existence. I use 'man' because that is the word which, with its variations, occurs most frequently in Sri Aurobindo's thought. It includes woman and should be read as wo(man). All the conflicts, distortions and problems which beset humanity may be traced to this flawed consciousness of man.

When we look back at the whole drama of evolution, we see life emerging from matter at first, and then life evolving to the stage of mental self-consciousness in man. This evolution is not merely biological, confined to a changing of forms, but also shows itself as an evolution of consciousness. Sri Aurobindo held that the Absolute, the self-sufficient, the one without a second, or Satchidananda Parabrahman, was itself involved in what we experience as the universe. Therefore, hidden in the heart of matter is a divine impulse seeking to manifest more and more fully through evolution until it attains its own fullest splendour. This whole process had no 'reason' as such except *ananda* or the endless, boundless joy of existence. So, evolution is the law of life, but what makes man special is that he can consciously participate in it. This is precisely what Sri Aurobindo and the Mother sought to do by inviting the divine into the mental, vital and finally into the physical planes.

Indeed, even without reference to Sri Aurobindo, when we ask the question, 'After man, what?' we find a variety of answers, depending on where we look. Nietzsche conceived of the Superman, a being with a mighty will and urge to power, who could dominate and control the rest of humanity. It was a mistaken development from this ideal, mixed with a corrupted version of social Darwinism, which possibly influenced the monstrous experiments of Hitler to produce a master race. The comic book notion of superheroes is similar. Only what is stressed is that with great power comes great responsibility, almost as a comment on how the United States sees itself. Superman, Batman, Spiderman, He-man, and all such other creatures endowed with superpowers are scarcely shown to have higher consciousness. Science fiction, similarly, has given us even more frightening and unnerving portraits of Supermen. These are cyborgs – half-men, half-machines, ruthless, programmed to wreak untold destruction, sometimes ceasing to be human altogether by turning into robots and Terminators. More recently, transhumanists like Raymond Kurzweil have predicted that Artificial Intelligence will overtake human intelligence. In addition, nanotechnology and other innovations in bio-medicine will enable human life to be extended almost indefinitely. Thus human beings will enhance themselves as never before, exceeding what is normally thought of as the limitations of our species.

Sri Aurobindo's Superman, however, is an entirely different being. Though born and embodied like normal human beings, he has a consciousness which is totally and radically different. The Superman is not ego-centric, but has a wider, higher consciousness. This makes him automatically avoid the errors, conflicts and divisiveness of human consciousness, which is the cause of wars, inequalities, environmental degradation, pollution and overpopulation. The Superman, then, is an intermediate being between man and the fully divine, Supramentalized entity of the future. In other words, eventually, because total perfection is the destiny of consciousness, an even higher being than the Superman will emerge. This will be effected when the Supramental consciousness achieves its fullest fruition upon earth. The Supramental being will be even more different from man than man is from an ape; it will be a divine being in a fully divine body. It is impossible for us, with our present level of development, to conceive of such a being. All we can do is to form some mental picture from the glimpses and illuminations which we may receive from the higher planes of consciousness.

In Sri Aurobindo's conception of the world, there is a ladder of consciousness, reaching upwards from the very depths of matter and inconscience, through life and mind, to regions above the mind, the overmind planes, finally to the full manifestation of divine perfection and glory in the Absolute Supermind. This conception is in consonance with the wisdom of the Upanishads and the yoga system of unfolding levels of consciousness. Every evolutionary leap is accomplished by the wedding of an aspiration from below and the descent of grace from above. Sri Aurobindo and the Mother offered the instrument of *purana* or integral yoga to accomplish the grand destiny of humanity.

In this yoga, the material was not to be shunned or worshipped as the ultimate truth. The aim was, instead, to transform matter itself, to divinize and spiritualize all our mundane acts and works so as to lead a divine life while on earth in a human body. Hence, this yoga neither shuns nor embraces the world, but transforms it. Another special feature is that though individuals perform it, it is collective in its action. The aim is not personal salvation but total and general amelioration. Finally, in this yoga, surrender is most important. After surrender, the divine within each individual does the yoga; the ego-bound false self, which considers itself as the doer, is no more.

The Mother's Role

Mirra Blanch Rachel Alfassa was an extraordinary person by any standards. Born in Paris on 21 February 1978 into a rationalist, atheist, thoroughly modernized and secularized family of Turkish-Egyptian-European descent, she showed early signs of spiritual precocity. At the age of 16 she began to befriend artists and to study painting. Soon she came to know most of the famous painters of her time, especially the post-impressionists. At nineteen she married a painter called Henri Morisset. A son Andre was born to them.

The marriage, however, soon broke up. Yet, all her life, she showed a highly refined and well-developed aesthetic sensibility, which extended not only to conventional arts and crafts like painting, music, singing, dance, poetry, but to embroidery, story-telling, flower arrangement, interior design, architecture, couture, physical education and sports. Mirra now turned to occultism, learning the secret arts from Max Theon and his wife Alma. Both Theon and Alma were adepts of a very high order. They wished to develop the powers latent in the human psyche through spiritualist practices. Mirra went to study under them in their retreat in Tlemcen, in the Algerian mountains in Africa. The Theons had developed several *siddhis* or occult powers, including clairvoyance, astral travel, materialization, telekinetics and so on. Many of these, Mirra learnt. And yet, she was not satisfied. After Alma's death, Theon's powers seemed to diminish. Mirra was looking for something bigger, more real, grounded in a higher spiritual truth.

This she found in Sri Aurobindo. Throughout her earlier life, Mirra had had the premonitions of great things to come. She felt she had been chosen for a special role. She had seen visions and had paranormal experiences. After her legal divorce in 1908, she met Paul Richard, whom she married in 1911. Together, they travelled to Pondicherry, then a French territory, where Richard had earlier met Sri Aurobindo in 1910. He had been impressed with 'the divine men of Asia', of whom he admired Sri Aurobindo the most: 'I have found the greatest among them, the leader, the hero of tomorrow . . . Aurobindo Ghose . . . this name signifies Asia free and one-Asia resurgent.'[106]

Mirra first met Sri Aurobindo on 29 March 1914. Earlier, she had seen his photograph, but had not 'recognized' him. But their first meeting was explosive: 'As soon as I saw Sri Aurobindo I recognized in him the well-known being whom I used to call Krishna.'[107] He stood at the top of the staircase, waiting to receive her. The next day she wrote these prophetic lines: 'It matters little that there are thousands of beings plunged in the densest ignorance, He whom we saw yesterday is on Earth; his presence is enough to prove that a day will come when darkness shall be transformed into light, and Thy reign shall be indeed established upon Earth.'[108] The three of them had started the periodical *Arya* in which, from 1914 to 1921, most of Sri Aurobindo's major writings appeared. Mirra came to live in Pondicherry permanently on 24 March 1920, leaving Richard behind.

After the Mother's permanent residence in Pondicherry, the first signs of an organized ashram began to appear. After Sri Aurobindo's Siddhi Day in 1926, the final change came. Sri Aurobindo, who used to be known as Aurobindo Ghose or AG, began to be known as Sri

Aurobindo. Mirra was called the Mother and she assumed charge not only of the day-to-day management of the ashram, but also of the sadhana or spiritual progress of the disciples. Sri Aurobindo went into seclusion so as to be able to conduct his yoga more effectively.

It is commonly said that Sri Aurobindo and the Mother had the same consciousness, though they were in two different bodies. Sri Aurobindo himself declared, 'The Mother and I are one but in two bodies.'[109] Actually they were very different people as far as their personalities were concerned. An extraordinary manager and administrator, the Mother was very practical. She built one of India's most impressive and dynamic ashrams with several departments and manufacturing units. She was also an extrovert; she loved exercise and open air activities, she used to play tennis until well past her seventies. Sri Aurobindo was shy, retiring and rarely displayed much emotion. Yet, what is remarkable is the extent to which each had surrendered to the other. The Mother's surrender was so total that Sri Aurobindo was moved to remark that he had witnessed nothing of that quality and magnitude before. What is less known or realized is that Sri Aurobindo, too, had surrendered totally to the Mother; he considered her as his regent and shakti or power. It is he who set the example in considering her the embodiment of Mahashakti, Mahasaraswati, Mahalakshmi and Mahakali. He was the first to apotheosize her and deify her as a living Goddess. Of course, the Mother was not merely Sri Aurobindo's disciple, but his associate, partner and the co-author of Integral Yoga.

Together, they created a unique spiritual community which, in fact, became the nucleus of an extraordinary experiment. After the outbreak of World War II, this community grew rapidly. Families, with children, joined it. The Mother opened a school for them which would be among the best and most innovative not just in India, but in the world. There were incredible advances in all directions – painting, poetry, weaving, handicrafts, farming, printing, building, architecture and several other fields, all under the Mother's direct gaze and supervision. The Mother was a benevolent dictator; all power and authority was centralized in her, but she ruled with love, not with force. There are innumerable testimonies to her superhuman energy, competence, perspicacity, foresight and managerial skills. She managed to keep a large group of very diverse individuals not just happy, but spiritually progressing, by remote control, as it were. Each *sadhak* had a personal relationship with her and each felt her constant attention to his or her difficulties.

The Mother declared that on 29 February 1956, the Descent of the Supermind on earth had occurred. The following year, on 10 July 1957, speaking to the *sadhaks* in the ashram playground, Mother said:

> What has happened, what is really new, is that a new world is born, born, born. It is not the old one transforming itself; it is a new world that is born. And we are now right in the middle of the period of transition in which the two are intermingling – in which the old world still persists all-powerful and entirely dominating the ordinary consciousness, but the new one is slipping in, still very modest, unnoticed – unnoticed in so far that outwardly it does not disturb anything very much, for the time being, and that in the consciousness of most people it is even altogether imperceptible. And yet it is working, growing – until it is strong enough to asset itself visibly.[110]

Over the years, many miraculous powers and potencies were applied to the Mother. These along with many dramatic pronouncements created an atmosphere of incredible expectation among the ashramites. Some even began to speculate what life in the new republic of the spirit would be like, now that global changes were going to occur. A few assigned special roles for themselves as vanguards of the new race; others believed that their physical ailments, including blindness, would be cured. Several thought that physical immortality was in the offing.

The Great Passing

Even when the Mother's health in the late 1960s was visibly declining, attempts were made to depict it as a final transformation of the cells. Pranab Kumar Bandopadhyaya, one of Mother's closest disciples and considered an *adhar* or support by the Mother, himself rebelled against such blatant falsification of facts. Towards the end, by mid 1973, it was clear that the Mother was dying; there was no gainsaying this fact. On

17 November 1973, the Mother did pass away, having crossed the age of 95. But even today, in ashram circles, the word 'death' is not used in connection either with Sri Aurobindo or the Mother. The preferred word is *mahasamadhi*, in common with the traditional Indian belief that a guru does not quite 'die', but simply passes into another dimension. Sri Aurobindo and the Mother are thus not 'dead'; they are thought to be in the earth's atmosphere, still leading evolution. Some even believe that the Mother attained a 'supramental body' before her death.

Satprem, a Frenchman called Bernard Enginger and a key disciple of the Mother, recorded many hundreds of hours of conversations with the Mother right up to her last days. These were later published in the multi-volume *L'Agenda de Mere* in French and later in an English translation called *Mother's Agenda*.[111] A few months before she died, however, the ashram authorities barred him from seeing the Mother. Several *sadhaks*, particularly those who owe allegiance to Satprem, believe that the Mother did not actually die but rather entered a 'cataleptic trance' or state of suspended animation. They think that in such a state, which has been described in yogic books, even a detectable heartbeat is absent.

Satprem's last recorded conversation with the Mother was on 19 May 1973, 182 days before she died. It is an amazing exchange in which the Mother says she can't eat, can't hear, that her body is giving way. But Satprem insists that it is on the brink of a transformation, that it must happen now:

> [Mother]: For me, you see, the question is food. More and more I find it impossible to eat. Can this body live without food?
> [Satprem]: Mother, I truly believe that you are being led to the point where something else will be FORCED to manifest.
> [Mother]: I can't hear.
> [Satprem]: I think you are led to the point – the point of helplessness or powerlessness where something ELSE will be forced to manifest.[112]

Satprem continued to believe that the Mother's attendants, especially Bandopadhyaya, prevented this final transformation from happening.

Georges Van Vrekhem says in *Beyond Man*, 'The positive or negative interpretation of the passing of the Mother creates a positive or negative evaluation of the Work of the Avatar...'[113] What this means is that much of the theology rests on the attainment of physical transformation, as evidenced by the immortality of the body. As a senior and seasoned devotee, Vrekhem strives to create as positive an interpretation as possible, negating and refuting in the process the less positive interpretations, especially the 'postponement' thesis put forth by a stalwart such as Nolini Kanta Gupta, and endorsed, either explicitly or implicitly by other senior *sadhaks* like Pranab Kumar Bandopadhyaya and K. D. Sethna. According to this thesis, the fruition of work of Sri Aurobindo and the Mother was postponed by the latter's death. This seems to make perfect sense, but Vrekhem realizes that this admission of postponement would be tantamount to that of conceding failure. He instead argues that the physical transformation and immortalization of the body were never promised by Sri Aurobindo or the Mother and, therefore, their deaths should not be taken as sings of the defeat of their work. Vrekhem concludes that 'the conviction that the Mother had to or would transform her physical body' was one of the 'ashram legends'.[114]

From the book it seems that there is a prevalent belief that the Mother was transforming her body. Obviously, such a belief could not have come out of nothing. Several statements and remarks of the Mother, for instance, actually indicate that a new body to house a new consciousness was being prepared: 'For the first time, early in the morning, I have seen myself, my body. I do not know whether it is the supramental body or – how to say – a transitional body. But I had a completely new body, in the sense that it was asexual, it was neither woman nor man. It was very white, but I think that this is because my skin is white, I don't know. It was very slender – it was beautiful.' These words were spoken on 24 March 1972, when the Mother was already old, frail and bent. Similarly, the Mother had declared, 'The change has been accomplished. It will perhaps take centuries, but it has been accomplished.'[115]

So we have a situation somewhat like what the early Christians experienced on the death of Jesus. Was he dead or not? If he was truly resurrected, he could not be dead. The resolution could only be in terms of the difference between the appearance and the reality – apparent dying versus real dying. Or, to use Vrekhem's metaphor, the 'death' of the caterpillar so that the butterfly could emerge. That is how a 'true physical' is posited in which the Mother built the 'archetype' of her supramental body, letting her physical body die in the process. When these justifications prove too difficult either to comprehend or to accept, the familiar ploy of the Aurobindonians is used: self-condemnation and guru-exaltation. We are too stupid, this argument runs, ever to understand what Sri Aurobindo and the Mother did for us. As Vrekhem puts it: 'The caterpillar in the *sadhaks* was unable to see anything but the caterpillarhood of its own world.'[116]

The Cult

In time, a whole set of beliefs and rituals began to be built up around Sri Aurobindo and, more so, around the Mother. So much so, that the death of each of them caused dismay and disappointment among large sections of the faithful. Many of the devotees had grown to believe that some miraculous transformation of the physical bodies of their gurus was in the offing. Naturally, these believers were disappointed when this did not happen in the manner they had come to expect. Beside this, a whole theology began to be developed, especially because of the extensive records of what Sri Aurobindo and the Mother had said about the impending transformation.

This theology not only asserts the avatarhood or divine incarnation of Sri Aurobindo and the Mother, but also builds around them a special cult of worship and devotion. Several miracles and special interventions in world events are attributed to them, many of which have a basis in the words of the masters themselves, yet which call into question our normal intelligence. There is a belief that the Mother, sitting in meditation in a house on Dupleix Street in Pondicherry, stopped the fall of Paris in 1914 during World War I. The Mother saw Kali entering the room: 'She executed a wild dance, a really wild dance. And she said to me: "Paris is taken! Paris will be destroyed!" . . . I turned towards her and said: "No, Paris will not be taken, Paris will be saved," quietly, without raising my voice, but with a certain emphasis.' This account from *Entretiens*[117] was narrated to the children by the Mother.

'THE HOUR OF GOD'

Similarly, it is believed that Sri Aurobindo, with his occult force, turned the tide of World War II in favour of the Allies. He saved the Allied troops at Dunkirk in May 1940 by sending a fog to shield them and enshrouding the Luftwaffe with clouds. A moment's hesitation on the part of the Germans, it would seem, allowed the British troops to cross the channel and save themselves. All this was reported to Sri Aurobindo, who was following the developments with keen interest. Sri Aurobindo remarked, 'Yes. Fog is rather unusual at this time.'[118] From this, most ashramites concluded that Sri Aurobindo wanted to hint that he had created this fog to help the Allies.

The avatarhood of Sri Aurobindo is proclaimed by quoting his own words, where he was attempting to explain his relationship to his followers:

> I was concerned with the possibility of people following the Path I had opened, as Christ, Krishna, Buddha, Chaitanya, etc. opened theirs. You were declaring that no human being could follow and that my life was perfectly useless as an example—like the lives of the Avatars.[119]

Once again, we may wonder how these words are really to be interpreted. One can either say that Sri Aurobindo's is one more path to the Divine among many others, or that it includes and supersedes all the previous paths. Most Aurobindonians would believe the latter. As regards avatarhood, in India at least, every guru has been deified and thousands of gurus have been accorded the status of avatars. In what way are the claims of the Aurobindonians any different or more worrying? What St Paul did to Christ, other disciples have done to their gurus time and again in history, constructing a theology around them. Such deification does serve to knit together a community of believers, but it is uncertain if it contributes to individual or collective evolution. To evolve, we must first be free, free to believe and to disbelieve according to the *svabhava* of the Divine within us.

Indeed, a careful reading of the masters' words shows that it was never their intention to claim such an incontrovertible and transhistorical infallibility or to encourage the formation of a cult or a sect. The Mother said, 'Truth is not a dogma that one can learn once and for all and impose as a rule. Truth is infinite like the supreme Lord himself and it manifests at every moment in those who are sincere and attentive.'[120] She warned her devotees several times to not constitute a new theology out of Sri Aurobindo's works: 'I repeat that in connection with Sri Aurobindo it is impossible to talk of a teaching or even of a revelation: his is a direct Action by the Lord, and thereon no religion can be founded... Spiritual life can only exist in its purity when it is free of all forms of mental dogma.'[121]

Perhaps, she had already observed signs of such mental dogma, even during her own lifetime. That's why she said, 'One must at any price prevent this from becoming a new religion. For as soon as it would be formulated in an elegant, impressive and somewhat forceful way, it would be finished.'[122] Perhaps, the most important statement of the Mother in this regard is this: 'Do not take my words for a teaching. Always they are a force in action, uttered for a definite purpose, and they lose their true power when separated from that purpose.'[123] This makes it abundantly clear that no theory or philosophy or system of beliefs or set of rituals can be extrapolated from the Mother's words. Now that their original contexts are no longer available to us, we need to exercise the utmost circumspection in taking them literally.

In issuing these admonitions, the Mother was reinforcing what Sri Aurobindo himself had declared: 'I must say that it is far from my purpose to propagate any religion, new or old, for humanity in the future.'[124] But, unfortunately, this is precisely what has happened, with his followers indulging in an unthinking hero-worship and deification, or worse, turning his ideas into an esoteric cult, like a new religion. There is also a tendency of what we might call 'the master-saving' mechanism which post facto justifies whatever was said by the masters. The most common explanation, for instance, as to why the transformation has not occurred as planned or predicted is that we, the disciples, failed the masters; they sacrificed their lives for us, but we couldn't live up to their dreams.

Though a certain narrowness of outlook persists among several ashramites and followers, the saving grace is that there is no official hierarchy, no order of designated successors and no spiritual authority in charge of the teaching. Pondicherry, consequently, is one of the most decentralized and pluralistic of spiritual communities, with each *sadhak* pursuing his or her own path, without the supervision of any official power centre. While this has sometimes led to indiscipline or even the exploitation of the ashram by unscrupulous elements, it has also ensured a high degree of spiritual responsibility on the part of each individual member. All the same, this remains a modern movement, one in which we move (or progress) from the traditional polytheism (or henotheism) of Sanatan Dharma, to a sort of mono- (or bi-) theism, in which only Sri Aurobindo and the Mother are worshipped. Usually, one does not see any other image, icon or representation of any other God, Goddess, saint, sage or sacred object in the ashram. Not just that, the entire course of human evolution is seen as resting on the efforts of two individuals, Sri Aurobindo and the Mother. In effect, we see the creation of a master narrative which shuts out or co-opts all other narratives to a single grand purpose.

Luckily, among the devotees, *sadhaks* and admirers of Sri Aurobindo and the Mother, there is still a great diversity of view and opinions. Like elsewhere, there are factions and schisms, which are evidenced in the removal of someone from the ashram. While there is no attempt to enforce one unified theology on everyone, there are subtle means of pressure and coercion. Sadly, a lot of Aurobindonians have stopped reading or thinking. It is a classic case of the closing of the mind of a once vibrant and progressive community. Ironically, some do not even read Sri Aurobindo himself.

Sri Aurobindo himself said that freedom was the highest goals of the human spirit and also a precondition to its true flowering. Yet, it is doubtful if this is actually recognized or practised by the community. If there is a single drawback in the whole movement, it is this lack of plurality and openness. Surely, the course of evolution can neither be fully predicted, nor restricted to any pre-fabricated template that the custodians of a particular sect or ideology possess. As Sri Aurobindo himself wrote, 'All is possible, but all is not licit – except by a recognizable process; the Divine Power itself imposes on its action limits, processes, obstacles, vicissitudes.'[125]

'Beyond Man'

The real achievement of the great work of the masters can be gauged only when one is somewhat familiar with the vast archive of Sri Aurobindo and the Mother, not to speak of an even larger body of secondary and interpretative material on them. Sri Aurobindo's own works extend into 35 volumes; those of the mother are more than half as bulky; besides these original sources, there is a vast amount of correspondence, records of talks and that fascinating multi-volume opus of Satprem's, *Mother's Agenda*. Theirs was no doubt a great and noble endeavour, whose ultimate goal was the perfection of the human race and the establishment of divine life on earth.

This is an exciting, even thrilling adventure of consciousness in which many would like to participate and add their own humble efforts. The message of Sri Aurobindo and the Mother also fills one with great hope and promise. It assures us that we are on the brink of a new era. As the Mother put it, 'Humanity has been waiting for centuries for this moment. It has come.' And, as Sri Aurobindo said earlier, 'It is a step for which the whole of evolution has been a preparation.'[126] In this new age, all the old religions are insufficient. Science and philosophy, too, are inadequate. Only a total transformation in human consciousness will do. Such a transformation is already underway. According to Vrekhem, 'The vision of Sri Aurobindo and the Mother is probably the only platform that is high enough'[127] to help us climb to the next peak of evolution.

Yet, really to move ahead, we shall need the humility and the integrity to admit that all was not right in Camelot, that the utopia that Sri Aurobindo and the Mother projected was dangerous for less mature or stable minds, resulting in severe trauma and insecurity among the believers. Instead, the right direction might be to stress the basic steps of the yoga of Sri Aurobindo and the Mother: self-purification, surrender, *tapasya*, overcoming of the ego, conquest of the physical, vital, mental, the opening of the psyche to the divine, the transformation of all levels of consciousness, and so on. It is often said that Sri Aurobindo's yoga begins where the conventional yogas end. True, but how many of Sri Aurobindo's followers have achieved the end, the acme, the final fruit even of the conventional yogas?

'The Hour of God'

The spiritual community at Pondicherry may well be the nucleus of a new race. It may even be the vanguard of our next evolutionary jump from the human to the superhuman. On the other hand, the experiment may be more widespread, with many centres and alternative paths, and happen in ways which are totally unpredictable and unexpected. While the ashram in Pondicherry will always remain special, it does not have an exclusive claim or privilege over integral yoga. The divine cannot be circumscribed; no limitation can be placed upon it. Even Sri Aurobindo's thought and work do not exhaust the potencies of the divine, whose scope of action is infinite. Therefore, the thought of Sri Aurobindo may be seen as another opening, another descent of gnosis or grace, not as a final consummation or culmination. History shows us that wherever great ideas exist, distortions and confusions are bound to creep in over time. Attempts at closure or control of thought have not only resulted in untold suffering, but have ultimately failed. That is why utmost care ought to be exercised to ensure that integral yoga continues to be a method of spiritual evolution, and is not turned into another form of idolatry.

Chapter 11

Ten Meditations on the Guru

Introduction

As an Indian, a Hindu and a Sanatani, the idea that Gods can be confined to temples, churches or mosques is rather strange to me. The temple is a place of concentration, no doubt, which reminds us of the deity, but the divinity that the Gods represent is everywhere. As the Isa Upanishad says, all these worlds and whatever is contained in them are imbued with the divine presence. God(s) can be found wherever you look for them. If we wish to discover them outside temples, we shall as soon find them there as we will inside temples.

But this chapter is about a special kind of God, a living, walking, talking form of the divine – God as guru. Living in our midst out of compassion for us, the guru helps us discover our true selves, our identity with the absolute.

Throughout I refer to the guru as 'he', but the guru is neither male nor female, even if he or she has a male or female body. The body is not the guru, though it seems to be so to the extent that it 'supports' the state of consciousness that is the guru.

After the guru leaves his body, or even when he is embodied, he may dwell in or be interred in a temple, but a guru is always beyond his habit, habitat or habitation. The guru is thus always beyond the temple even though it may be the temple of his own body.

The guru, like God, is both within and beyond at the same time, whether it is a body or the temple that he inhabits. To see beyond the body, then, is to seek beyond the body too – it is, ultimately, to seek the *real*, whether as guru, God or self.

Ten Meditations on the Guru

To that extent, what I wish to say cannot be contained in this chapter. The chapter is the body, but it gestures beyond itself to something that can only be hinted at, but never fully grasped. Or even when fully grasped, its bounty is not exhausted. It invites decoding again and again.

So, who can speak of the glory of the guru, he whom words cannot touch? Words go to sleep at the feet of guru. The seeker and sought are annihilated. The guru alone remains in his splendid isolation – sole, absolute, complete – one without a second.

Who can know the guru? The one who speaks does not know. The one who knows does not speak. Those who know *and* speak cannot tell all they know or know all they speak.

Out of his infinite compassion, the guru reveals a fraction of himself to/through whomsoever he chooses. This fraction of his self, his majesty, is like an invitation to the limitless treasures of his being which he will share with those he deems fit. The imperfections of that fraction cast no shadow on the perfection of the guru. They merely show up the inadequacies of the instrument.

These meditations on the guru are likewise fragments that show the inadequacy of the instrument. My limitations are native to me as is the guru's limitlessness native to him. We must each play our role. Mine is to meditate on the splendour of the guru, on his mercy, grace and goodness. I can only do so in my partial and restricted way. This partiality and restriction serve only one purpose: to point to the boundlessness and vastness of the consciousness that is the guru's.

The guru's work is so wonderful because it begins here, in this world, the world of humans, the world of confusion, suffering and delusion. In that sense he is one of us. He is the symbol of what anyone of us can be, the heights of mastery that we can also aspire to attain. But though his action begins here, it does not end here. He takes us from here to eternity, from the imperfect to the perfect, from the relative to the absolute, from the dual to the non-dual, from the *jiva* state to the Shiva state. That is why the guru is worthy of our highest respect and devotion.

1. The Guru Is a Really 'Heavy' Dude

The word 'guru' is used as both adjective and noun in Sanskrit. As an adjective it means a variety of things including weighty, heavy, long, extended, immense, formidable, great, momentous, important, arduous, difficult, excellent, venerable, best, intense, excessive, violent, and so on. These senses of the guru do get transferred to the sense of guru as a father, teacher, preceptor, spiritual guide, head of an order, master, lord, which are more commonly associated with it.

But the reason I consider the etymological meaning 'heavy' valuable is that the guru is someone who is calm, steadfast and unflappable. He is unmoved in both adversity and prosperity. Though the distress of others may move him to display compassion, he is not unnerved by it. Unlike the rest of us whose consciousness fluctuates so much, the guru's mind is like a still, smokeless flame – straight, clear and luminous.

Many of us do have glimpses of higher consciousness or do experience exalted states of mind now and then. What is missing, however, is the steady abidance in the higher reality and truth which is the hallmark of the guru.

The guru's acts are deliberate and unhurried. While we tend to be anxious, absentminded or thoughtless, the guru is most solidly here, established in the moment as firmly as a mountain. Even though he does not move much, the guru makes a lot of things happen around him.

What is more, he is not blown away by the vicissitudes of life. We, on the other hand, are toys of fortune, which winds us up to dance or cry as it wills. Some small piece of good news drives us to ecstasy while an equally trivial misfortune is enough to make us miserable. The guru, on the other hand, shows the dignity of those who rooted in the deeper substratum of reality. He refuses to let the daily, oh-so-messy business of living dislodge him from himself.

2. The Guru Is Not a Person

Because we are persons, because we think our being is bound by the confines of our bodies, we think that the guru is also a person. That is why we make the mistake of trying to establish a human relationship with him. But the guru is surely not limited to his body, even if he seems embodied just like us. The guru far exceeds his body in ways we cannot even begin to imagine.

The body is in the guru rather than the guru is in the body. The body is just a thought that the guru has to project to perform his role in our lives. To put it differently, the guru has taken on the body just for us, out of compassion. That is because we are convinced by truth only if it comes in our own likeness, in the shape or form that we can recognize, in a body like ours.

The guru is not a person but a function, a process, a principle. Whoever takes us closer to God, to the higher consciousness, to our reality, is the guru. Whoever takes us away from it cannot be a guru.

Since the guru is not a person, his action is limitless. It neither begins with our assumption of this body, nor will it end with its demise. The action of the guru is infinite, transcending all notions of time, space and understanding.

That the guru is not a person is indicated in the concept of the *akhandagurutatva* or the undivided guru principle. Among Vaishnavites, there is the belief that this principle is manifested in the *siksa guru* (the one who teaches), the *diksa guru* (the one who initiates) and the *caitya guru* (the indwelling guru, which is the self).

According to the Advayataraka Upanishad, 'gu' means darkness and 'ru' means dispeller. Anyone or anything that dispels our inner darkness bears the sign of the guru. The guru is a non-person who seems to be a person. Raja Rao, the famous novelist, sometimes used the word '*abhuman*' to describe such a person or principle.

3. The Guru Is None Other than 'God'

Ramana Maharshi says that God himself takes the form of the guru to help the devotee in his upward spiritual path. When the longing for God intensifies to the point that ordinary life becomes intolerable, God out of compassion manifests as the guru. If anything, guru is 'greater' than God – one cannot see God, but one can see one's guru. The latter's proximity allows one to serve, follow, obey or worship him, all of which leads to one's own liberation.

Otherwise, God who is everywhere would be hard to identify. Sri Ramakrishna said that rainwater is hard to collect unless it passes through the spout of the drain on the roof. When it so reaches the ground, it has the force and concentration of coming through one channel. The guru, likewise, is the channel which funnels the infinite, ever-present grace of God for us to receive.

Those who consider God and the guru to be separate have not understood the way. As the Guru Mantra says:

Gurur Brahma Gurur Vishnu Gurur Devo Maheshwarah
Gurursakshat Para Brahma Tasmai Sri Gurave Namah

Meaning, the guru is indeed Brahma, Vishnu and Shiva; I salute that all-auspicious guru who is verily the transcendent Brahma.

There are many other beautiful celebrations of the guru in our tradition, for instance, the Guru Stotra:

Brahmanandam Parama Sukhadam
Kevalam Jnana-Murtim
Dvandvateetam Gagana Sadrisham
Tattwamasyadi Lakshyam
Ekam Nityam Vimalam Achalam
Sarvadhi Sakshi Bhootam
Bhava Teetam Triguna Rahitam
Sadgurum Tan Namami

I bow to that *sadguru*, who embodies the bliss of Brahman, who is the giver of supreme happiness, who is sheer knowledge, who is beyond the pair of opposites, who is as extensive as space, who is characterized by signs of realization like '*Tat Twam Asi*' (That Thou Art), who is one, eternal, pure and changeless, who is the witness of all beings, who transcends all modifications, and who is devoid of the three modes (of Prakriti – satva, rajas and tamas).

This is indeed a grand and glorious conception of the guru, probably unmatched in any other tradition or civilization.

4. The Guru Is None Other than the Self

When we worship the guru or God, we are actually worshipping none other than the self. The guru is only the best of what we are or can be. The guru is that entity who has made the transition from the earthly to the divine. This he does by discarding his own lower nature and identifying himself completely with the divinity within. The guru thus represents what each of us can be and are in potential.

To say that the guru is none other than the self also means that the self is always realized. But because we don't know it, because of false identification, we think that we have to move towards self-realization. As long as the self thinks it is not realized, it needs a guru. As soon as its ignorance ends, it understands that the guru was none other than the self.

The guru as the 'self' pulls us to the truth from within; the guru as the 'guide' points to the truth outside. Thus from both within and without we are urged towards the goal. Within and without are, after all, purely relative. Actually, God, guru and self are identical.

5. The Guru Is One (But Not All Gurus Are the Same)

In the veritable market place of gurus today, there seems to be too much of a good thing. So many godmen, saints, mahatmas, yogis, mahants, sufis, healers, avatars, *jnanis* and so on – almost a surfeit of spirituality. Market watchers have actually begun to talk about brand equity, market shares, profit lines, export potential and so on. In the West, the commoditization of spirituality is an accepted fact. It is only in India that we are still somewhat suspicious when there is a price tag on truth.

But the crucial question is how to decide which the right one is? Who can set about listing the qualifications of a genuine guru? This is certainly not a matter of external measurement (maya, incidentally, means that which can be measured), but of inner experience. What you experience in the presence of the guru will tell you what to think of him.

Sri Ramakrishna once said that there are three kinds of teachers. A good teacher is like a doctor who tells the patient what to take for the latter's illness. A better doctor actually brings him the tablet with a glass of water, urging the patient to take it. But the best doctor is one who 'forces' the medicine down the patient's throat by pinching his nostrils, forcing him to open his mouth and swallow the medicine.

Like the best doctor, the best guru is one who takes you to the destination or who shows you how you are already at the destination. All those who help you get there, no matter how many or how varied, are just forms of the same emancipatory principle.

When we reflect on this a little more deeply, we understand that what we experience has to be a peace that passeth understanding. We must feel this peace, this joy, this stilling of thoughts and sensations, a movement towards our own higher nature. All this is natural because the guru shows us what is already in us. He does not bring something from the outside or give us anything that is alien to us.

Ramana Maharshi went to the extent of saying that anyone who asks you to do something to achieve your own state is either Brahma (who wants to create a new world) or Yama (being anything other that yourself is akin to death), but not the guru. The guru, instead, says, 'Look no further. You have arrived. You are already home.'

6. The Guru Is the Hunter not the Hunted

How do I find my guru, is the question many ask. They hear or read that a guru is essential for their salvation, but then how to find one? How to know who is the right one? The fact of the matter is that it is not just us who are looking for the guru, the guru is looking for us too. The guru stands for the knowledge that preys on egoism. What we think is the quarry, is actually the predator.

Sri Ramakrishna once likened himself to a king cobra, whose venom was sure even if it wasn't swift. A rat so bitten may die at once or may go back to its hole to die, but die it must. This is the rat of the ego which the guru destroys either instantly or after a certain period of time. There is no escape. Similarly, Ramana Maharshi likened the guru to the tiger who has the deer by its throat; the death of the deer is certain. The guru destroys egoism, which arises from ignorance. He is merciless in performing this task.

We think that we're searching for the guru, but guru stalks us in the most unlikely places. We may encounter him within us as our inner voice, giving us hope and direction, telling us what to avoid and what to accept. Or he me be a stranger who suddenly tells you something about yourself without prompting.

For instance, I was once going to a meeting where I was about to commit myself to something both dangerous and potentially damaging. While I was turning into the gate of the colony, a man came up to me and said, totally unprovoked, 'Are you blind? Can't you see where you're going?' It was so extraordinary that I said nothing at all, but silently drove on. Needless to say, the deal didn't go through; I simply couldn't commit myself to it. Perhaps, the guru's warning, delivered through a most unlikely courier, saved me.

To give another example, when I was still a child, one evening I began to kill some insects. The table lamp, which had a metal shade, had grown quite hot. Some tiny creatures, which came to perch near the light, would be singed to death if they were held down by a pin. I was fascinated to see the happy insects soon become uncomfortable, then sizzle, until they went up in smoke. Even as I killed one or two, I felt somehow that I shouldn't continue my sport. I felt it would be wrong to take life just for the heck of it. But then I thought, this is surely an irrational thought. If it's really wrong to kill these insects, 'God' will tell me so. Within seconds of the killing of a few more insects, my mother suddenly walked into the room and asked with unexpected sharpness, 'What *are* you doing?' Then, before I could give her a clear answer, she smiled strangely at me, and left the room.

I stopped my stupidity immediately, realizing that some force had answered my prayer or responded.

7. Only the Guru Really Loves You

All earthly love is tainted by expectation of some return. This love is usually self-centred. The person loved is seen in relation to oneself, one's joys or sorrows. She is seldom seen or regarded as an end in herself.

The guru's love, on the other hand, is impersonal, not related to his 'needs', but to our welfare. The guru loves us for our own benefit. This is the purest, most elevating kind of love, without a particle of selfishness in it. The guru, out of compassion for our suffering, urges us towards our own liberation. This love of our welfare for the sake of our welfare is impossible in worldly relationships.

Wherever we encounter such pure love, untarnished by expectation or return, it is nothing but a form of the guru. The guru binds us to himself through this power of love. We bask in its presence, feeling an inner transformation. No words or actions are necessary. The power of love is self-evident. But what is so amazing is that this impersonal, non-selfish love is experienced in the most personal way.

The guru loves each of us, no matter how different and unlovable we might be. He does this with an amazing ease and capacity to contain contradictions. This confuses many who think they have a special relation or claim on the guru's affections. They do, but everyone else also does. Brinkmanship, jealousy and possessiveness can only harm or delude us in our approach to the guru.

I experienced such a love the first time I visited the Sri Aurobindo Ashram in Pondicherry. When I went to the dining hall, I felt a wave of love pouring out of Mother's framed photograph on the wall. I felt a surge of emotion in me, as if I was being welcomed home. I understood something that had eluded me for years despite the thousands of pages of writings I'd read on Sri Aurobindo and the Mother. The Mother's force was love; that was her real action. This was a vast and dynamic force, stronger than words. This force was alive, still active in our world, urging us on to the golden dawn of the supramental. What I couldn't learn from tomes of philosophy, I realized in that one instant of deep experience.

After years of such experiences, howsoever ephemeral and intermittent, one understands that they are not figments of one's imagination, but actual facts. We may forget everything else, but we cannot forget the guru's love and compassion.

8. You May Forget Him, but the Guru Does Not Forget You

The guru's action is real and continues way beyond the shedding of his body. Time and space are no constraint to this. The guru-shishya *parampara* or the master-disciple tradition is unbroken and never-ending. From the 'first' guru, Shiva himself, who took the form of Dakshinamurti – a young man of 16 – to enlighten through silence the aged sages, to one's 'present' guru, there is a sure and direct line of the transmission of knowledge.

Suddenly, from being one among the 'ignorant' masses, one discovers that one is also a part of this great tradition. From birth to birth, the guru has been watching over one's spiritual growth, coming to one's aid in crucial times. Manifest or unmanifest, the guru's grace and direction have been guiding the course of our lives. Again and again, we meet our guru; even though we may forget him again and again, he does not forget or neglect us.

If it is our nature to forget, the guru's nature is to remind. Having taken responsibility of your spiritual progress, he never abandons you. He shows you how to turn a disadvantage into an advantage. You are not the body, he tells you; why have you forgotten that? You 'borrowed' the body. Be prepared to return it. The body isn't yours, nor are you the body's. You are deathless, immortal and forever free. Live that. As Kabir put it, likening his body to a *chadar* (sheet) which he returned the way it was, '*Jyon ki tyon dhar dini chadarya*.' He did not, like the rest of us, soil or spoil that bed sheet of a body, but gave it back in its pristine state. But how can that be? Only a self-realized soul could do that because no karma touches or taints him. Such a one was Kabir.

The shishya, understanding this, himself becomes the guru. He folds his hands in gratitude and says, 'Lord, you have made me like yourself, just as the touchstone turns base metal to gold. But you have done more than that because you've turned base metal not just into gold, but into a touchstone.'

In his gratitude, the shishya worships the guru as the liberator, the slayer of ignorance, the luminous, inspiring being, who is above all other beings. The guru ever raises his hand and says, 'My Father blesses you.' His gaze of compassion rests on your face, boring into your consciousness, stilling the waves of thought.

From deep within, the ties of karma are loosened. The hold of desire weakens. The mantra given by the guru beings the process of inner cleansing. The cleansed mind begins to perceive the reality.

Thus the mere thought of the guru elevates. He has the power to grant *shaktipat*, the awakening of the inner being. We begin to glimpse the perfection which is already within each of us.

9. Guru and Grace Are Inseparable

Who is the author of this essay? Who made it possible? How and where did these ideas come from? For whom are they written? Which random reader will grasp its full import? All these questions may have various plausible and logical answers. But there is a mystery to the workings of grace. The action is subtle, often internal. We may not gauge it by its external results.

Thinking of the guru is grace, remembering the guru is grace, writing about the guru is grace – none of this would be possible without that grace which is identical with the guru. Whatever strengthens our faith, whatever shows us our own higher nature, whatever prompts us to live in higher consciousness is grace. Grace happens because the guru wants to reinforce our inner aspirations. Little acts of grace remind us that he has not forgotten or abandoned us. Bigger acts of grace occur when we remember who we really are and live as that. But the biggest act of grace is when the guru draws us within and leaves us no other support or comfort but himself.

Even those who say that no guru is necessary are able to say so only because of the grace of the guru. The very act of denial becomes an act of affirmation. Like a great chessmaster, the guru moves the pieces over the chequered board of life.

He fine-tunes our receivers so that the signals suddenly become clear. With a gentle push, he sets our rocking chair in motion.

Ultimately, all attempts to describe the greatness of the guru must be acknowledged to fail; no matter how bright your candle is, it loses its light in the brilliance of the sun.

10. The Guru Is an Embodiment of Non-duality

The guru is how non-duality presents itself to duality. We function in the latter most of the time, but long for the former. The guru reminds us that 'I', 'you', 'he', 'she', 'this', 'that' and so on are not the ultimate reality, however convincing they may seem. All these are one, indivisible and integral. Only the guru can show us our non-separation from all that is, from the humblest particle of dust to the distant stars.

From the very beginning of time, we have been here, in one form or another, and we will continue to 'be' till the very end of things.

Time and space are convenient partitions of reality which is really indivisible and whole. Yet, time suggests eternity as space – the emptiness that contains all.

That is why though we may have many gurus or guides, the real guru is only one. That is the *sadguru* or the true guru. All the others are what are called *upagurus* or subsidiary gurus. The 'one guru' may come to us in many forms or guises, but we recognize his action despite all these disguises and masks.

Beguiled by forms, we think of the gurus as many, different or even as contradictory. One says this, the other says that. Superficially, this may be true. They may appear to be many, but are they really different? The teachings are many, but their underlying action and purpose are one.

The contradictions exist in our minds, not in the actions of the gurus. We might think we're 'ditching' one in favour of the other, but the gurus are not in competition. Their sole interest is your real welfare, which is your spiritual advancement.

'All life is yoga,' Sri Aurobindo said. This means that every little thing that happens is leading us to realizing the truths that are latent within.

Modern biology shows us that all life is one, just as modern physics that all matter and energy are indivisible.

It is only when we begin to understand the interrelatedness of everything that we ourselves merge with the guru and become a part of his greater action.

At that point, there is no 'I' or 'Thou', but only 'That' – the guru principle, acting and operating everywhere, through all things.

Even life and death cease to be opposites, because to live as an individual means to die as the whole and to die as an individual means to be reborn as the whole.

As Nisargadatta Maharaj said, 'Give attention and you will find that birth and death are one, that life pulsates between being and non-being, and that each needs the other for completeness. You are born to die and you die to be reborn.'[128]

Epilogue
Love Matters

This last piece of the book is, of course, about love. Love is the most powerful force in the universe. If we cannot love, our lives are wasted; we are as nothing, having amounted to nothing. It is not that we must be something great or grand to love. Even if lower than dust, we are capable or receiving and giving love. That anyone would be incapable of love would be impossible because this world was birthed in love, and it is love that permeates every atom of it. Even the dead respond to love, as do animals, trees and stones. Everything is informed by consciousness, which is nothing but a form of love. Love quickens us and pushes us towards life. Love also draws the final gasp from us and snuffs out our lives.

It is impossible to place a limit on love's action. It can be as cruel as kind. Life constantly teaches us lessons in love and loving. We cannot be spiritual if we are blind and deaf to such lessons.

Events, small and big, catastrophes, great and little also reveal love's capacity to help and heal in the most precarious of circumstances. Love means letting go of possessiveness, possessions, emptying the self – that is the prelude to being filled up again.

Loss

When I first wrote these words, the palm computer on which they were composed and saved, suddenly went into a hang mode. It was Christmas Day, 2004. I was in Pondicherry with my wife Sarina, feeling most blessed and fortunate. After a concentrated period at the samadhi in the morning, I met an old friend and ashramite at Sabda, the ashram bookstore.

Epilogue

She said, 'You must try to attend the ashram Christmas celebrations at the theatre. But for that a pass would be required, always difficult to get for non-ashramites and particularly so since it is already Christmas Day.'

I thought there was no harm trying. We went to the Bureau Central, where the passes were being distributed. The person at the reception said that they had stopped giving them since yesterday and that in any case we were unlikely to have been given a pass because we were not directly connected with the ashram. But, he said, 'Since you've come, you may as well ask the man sitting over there, who is responsible for their distribution.'

I crossed over to the indicated individual. He was actually a pleasant young man who asked me how he might help me. I explained my purpose, adding that we were staying at the International Guest House run by the ashram, and that I was closely associated with the Sri Aurobindo Ashram – Delhi Branch. He seemed to pause for a moment, then smiled at me and said, 'Ok.' That was it; we were soon in possession of a pass for two. He also suggested that we take the sea view road skirting the beach to reach the theatre.

The ashram Christmas celebration is a special event which the Mother initiated upon the urging of Udar Pinto, an important ashramite. Signifying the descent of light, Christmas is a festival not just of joy and gift-sharing but also of the intervention of the divine in human affairs and the corresponding upliftment of our consciousness. At the ashram, preparations are made as much as a year in advance. Several thousand gifts are packed, many of them lovingly sent from various corners of the world by devotees and well-wishers.

There is a large Christmas tree in the middle of the theatre. The compound is bustling with ashramites and invitees. Over 3,000 people participate. It is also one of the few occasions when ashramites congregate for any festival in the year, dressing up in their best clothes. Students of the ashram school, their parents, children from other Aurobindonian institutions, families and friends of the ashram, devotees from around the world, all meet here on this special day.

Groups are called out and the gift distribution goes on tirelessly till everyone on the premises gets a gift, no matter how simple or modest.

Epilogue

Actually, it is the children who get the best presents, while adults have to make do with a few eatables or knick-knacks. But it is the joy of sharing that is universal. With carols playing in the background and an international group of participants from all religious backgrounds, this is perhaps the most unique Christmas celebration of its kind in India.

Sarina and I met several old friends, many of them from Delhi, who are now settled here. Pondicherry, like a magnet, draws in talent from all parts of the world. Where else is there such a large national and international settlement, with people from all states of India and most countries of the world, all united in the common pursuit of self-transformation?

In the middle of the gift giving, however, Sarina lost her patience. 'There's no point waiting for hours to get a little gift,' she said, 'we've already seen what it's like so we can go now." We had already been there for a couple of hours; she had had enough. As outsiders, our turn would come right at the end, after the children, the ashramites, the former ashramites and so on. We left, after excusing ourselves from our friends.

When we returned to our room, as if by instinct, I picked up my palm to write the last few paragraphs of an essay that I had had been working on for days. The page which I was composing earlier opened all right, but neither was I able to key in anything nor turn the little machine off. I had the premonition of something terrible. It was as if before my eyes what I had worked on for days, an essay on lessons in loving, was being destroyed. Along with it dozens of pages of entries over the last three weeks or so since I had left Delhi, not to speak of much other material, were also at stake.

As I feared, I lost all my data on the palm, including phone numbers, addresses and my whole years' schedule of tasks and appointments. The palm had to be reformatted; I felt a hollow ache and sense of utter helplessness. It was like watching someone you really cared for bleed to death.

Dying Slowly

Actually, the simile of a slow dying was not inapt for what I had been going through for over a year. I was in the middle of what seemed like a slow and painful emotional bleeding. Everything that I held precious

Epilogue

and dear – everything that I had worked to build over the last 25 years, the sum and substance of my entire life – was lying in ruins about me. What had happened during the ashram Christmas celebration was only the prelude to something worse. It was like the typical Christmas story being played out in reverse. Instead of a time of joy and union, it was going to be one of sorrow and parting.

Tall, gaunt and impeccably accoutred in his signature *kurta-pyjamas*, my friend and gifted novelist said rather wryly, 'If you think it'll be over soon and that you'll recover, you're wrong. You'll continue dying for a very long time.' Even as I pondered over what seemed like a prolonged term on death row, he added, 'If your significant other were a trashy bitch, it would be all too easy to part ways. The real problem occurs when she's a high-quality person. Then, you're in deep trouble.' As if putting the final nail in the coffin, he added, 'And if you're anything like the person I know you to be, consumed by guilt, you'll blame yourself for years to come.'

We were walking from Colaba to Churchgate, in the still genteel parts of old Bombay. Silently, we crossed the Oval. My friend himself had had a difficult year, with a host of medical problems and painfully intermittent writing spells. Yet he had found the time to be with me without in fact having a clue of what I had been going through. Now it was as if he knew more than I wanted or he had bargained for.

At Churchgate, he got into a cab and disappeared into the Bombay traffic.

I turned towards Eros, the old movie theatre, to find another dear friend, one of my guru-bhais, waiting for me along with his girlfriend. He looked excited and waved something at me from across the road. Turned out, it was tickets to the refurbished, Technicolor *Mughal-E-Azam*. Originally released in 1960, this film was reputed to be one of the biggest grossers in the history of Bombay cinema. How could I resist the tear-jerker?

Bollywood was all kitsch, but sometimes so uplifting. Inside the once magnificent, now shabby movie theatre, there was a huge replica of a prison cell, complete with plaster of Paris chains. It was draped in muslin curtains. The contraption extended from the roof down to the ground in the foyer. Undoubtedly, it must have been used in the relaunch of the blockbuster just after Eid, the octogenarian thespian, Yusuf Bhai, aka Dilip Kumar, doing the honours with a Madhubala-substitute trapped inside, the proverbial prisoner of love.

Both Dilip and Madhubala looked pretty awful in the film. Madhubala was fat and pimply. Perhaps, my taste had been spoilt by the much better-maintained stars of today. In the re-tinted film, with gaudy colours in place of the original black and white, Madhubala often looked even more garish if not downright hideous. Dilip Kumar, with his weak upper lip slightly protruding over his thicker lower one, was in a perpetual pout. Instead of the great champion of love, he looked more like a spoiled, petulant brat. The scene-stealer was undoubtedly old Prithviraj Kapoor playing an unpopular and severe Akbar, the emperor who stamps out his young son's love to maintain imperial power.

Full of ridiculous and contrived scenes, including the totally implausible and historically untrue climax in which Salim or Dilip Kumar is about to be blown up by a cannon for not renouncing his love interest, Anarkali, the film dragged on and on to a ridiculous conclusion in which Akbar, in a face-saving twist, only pretends to brick Anarkali alive, but actually lets her go in exchange of her wish to obtain one night with her lover as the princess of Hindustan. After the briefest of honeymoons, she drugs him with the juice of the pomegranate blossom, hence her name, Anarkali, pomegranate bud, to disappear from the pages of history. Salim goes on to be Emperor Jahangir and the doting husband of Mumtaz Mahal.

Despite all these irritants, there were saving graces, like the superb music and also the manner in which the passion between Salim and Anarkali was slowly stoked. It was a deliberate and smouldering ardour, very delicately developed, until the audience itself was throbbing in its spell. And when Anarkali lifts up her eyes to stare the emperor in his face for the first time, raising her hand in a gesture of defiant questioning, 'Jab pyar kiya to darna kya?' I felt a shiver run down my spine, down the row in which I was sitting, down to the front of the theatre, where the hoi polloi sat spell-bound. Who could remain unmoved by that dramatic declaration of the power of love to overcome not just the fear of death but the dread and soul-killing laws of state and society?

Epilogue

That this story, like *Devdas*, had touched a chord in Indian audiences was obvious. There were at least three other cinematic versions, the first as early as 1928. But the Anarkali revival had been triggered by the popular 1953 romance, with Beena Rai and Pradip Kumar in the lead roles. In addition Nur Jehan, who played a supporting role in this film, was Anarkali in the Pakistani version of 1958.

Anarkali, pomegranate bud, was said to be a dancing girl in Lahore for whose charms the spoiled prince Saleem is said to have fallen. With little or no evidence to support it, this romance did not make it into history books but lived on in the hearts of the people as a legend to love. There is a tomb in Lahore supposedly built by the besotted prince to his dead sweetheart which gives the area, Anarkali Bazaar, its name. Whether the bones interred there are actually Anarkali's is not clear, but the Persian inscription definitely bemoans thwarted love:

tā qiyāmat shukr gūyam kardigāre khīsh rā
āh! gar man bāz bīnam rūī yār-e khīsh rā.
(Unto the Day of Judgement would I give thanks to my God
Ah! Could I but behold the face of my beloved once more.)

What a sad end to a beautiful love story. A mere dancing girl had dared to love a prince; the only outcome of such effrontery could be death.

I thought the earlier Bina Rai–Pradip Kumar version of 1953, though tackier, was at least a little less far-fetched. Here, Anarkali is whipped into displaying herself and her talents, auctioned and sold, of course, to none other than Salim in disguise, imprisoned and, in the end, bricked alive. Salim, played by Pradip Kumar, is not only weak, but juvenile and revolting by turns. The only redeeming feature is the music, the 14 or so memorable melodies composed by C. Ramchandra. What is common to both movies, however, is the portrayal of love or *mohabbat* as a force higher than kingly or temporal power. Yet, its only redemption is in self-sacrifice and death. The solution to the earthly crucifixion of love is the promise of its resurrection in the eternal afterlife. Here on earth, however, the Anarkalis of the world are doomed; the punishment for breaking the love laws is, of course, death.

Epilogue

It was to Bina Rai's credit that despite such on-screen degradation, she never looked cheap nor lost her look of innocence. Pradip Kumar played the weak and irresolute prince who is crushed by his powerful father in the reversal of a classic Oedipal finish. (Indeed, some versions of the legend have it that Anarkali was actually Akbar's wife or mistress.) No wonder, for in India, powerful fathers usually triumph over sons. An unconvincingly hackneyed story nevertheless makes one think of not only the fragility of human love, but also its glory: *ye zindagi usi ki hai* – this life is hers who can give herself to someone and lose herself in love. Surely, says the heart-broken Anarkali, there must be a realm other than this where lovers will be united and our dreams come true:

Do dil yahaan na mila sake, milenge us jahaan mein
Khilenge hasaraton ke phul, maut ke aasmaan mein
Ye zindagii chali gai jo pyar mein to kya huaa
Ye zindagi . . .
(Two hearts unable to meet here, will in that other world unite
The flowers of our anguish will bloom in the heavens of the dead.
So what if this life was lost for love?
This life . . .)

Sunaa rahii hai daastaan, shamaa mere mazaar kii
Fizaa mein bhi khil rahi, ye kali anaara ki
Ise mazaar mata kaho, ye mahal hai pyaara ka
Ye zindagii . . .
(The flame at my grave is sounding my tale
And the air still blossoms with the pomegranate bud.
Don't call this a mere grave, it is the mansion of love.
This life . . .)

As I walked out of the theatre with my friend, I thought of his situation, so sad and yet so hopeful. For several years, he had been separated from his wife, but she was not willing to let him go. Though they lived in different cities, he still was not free – legally or mentally. His lovely girlfriend was waiting for a resolution but under pressure from her own parents to settle down. How long would she wait? They were both from conservative families and maintained a certain decorum in their relationship. They were so close to each other, yet so far. I found myself praying for their happiness. So much love, so much sorrow.

I thought about my own suffering over the past years, the sense of hopeless confusion and distress, the dull ache of a man once clear-sighted, but suddenly blinded by a dense fog, groping about without a stick, not knowing where he was or where to go. When would the fog lift? When would I be able to see again? Like the protagonists in Tolstoy's novels, I was experiencing a mid-life dying, slow and painful, like an internal haemorrhage.

As in a flash of lightening on a moonless night, I had seen once again, the beloved's face of immaculate beauty and purity, but instead of pulling me towards her in a swift embrace, she was pushing me into the ceaseless storm, her back turned to me.

Amor or *Caritas?*

For months before this trip to the south, I had been grappling with the problematic of love. Just before the release of my fourth collection of poems, *Partial Disclosure*, my PhD student who had read the manuscript said, 'The three sections of the book do signify some movement in the concept of love, don't they?'

'Yes, I suppose they do,' I replied.

'There's experience, memory and debate in them.'

'Yes, sort of like *anubhav*, *achar* and *vichar* (experience, conduct and thought).'

'But,' she asked, 'don't you think there's not just a forward movement, but a backward movement too?'

'What do you mean?'

'Well, in the third section, the poems make a definite shift from the physical to the metaphysical, the carnal to the spiritual, but . . . ?'

'Do you mean that the shift is not convincing?'

'Not exactly. You see, the claims on behalf of the "higher" sort of love are of course valid, but they don't seem to erase the unresolved tensions of the more ordinary kind of love that was expressed in the earlier sections.'

'Ah!'

Epilogue

'I mean just because the speaker has glimpsed the "higher", the lower does not disappear, nor are its demands stilled.'

'That's a very astute observation,' I admitted.

'Come to think of it,' she continued, 'this is the key thematic twist in the collection. The book seems to progress from a certain place in a certain direction, but there is simultaneously a reverse movement.'

The more I reflected on this, the more I saw how true her observations were. The longing for fulfilment in the lower planes neither contradicts the higher perfection nor indeed is that longing obliterated because of the elevated planes of realization. The unhappy yearnings in the physical and the vital cast their long shadows on whatever spiritual conquests the soul makes in its quest for perfection. This was the paradox of love: the higher was not necessarily the answer or antidote to the lower. Both needed attention and fulfilment.

Human love, with its anxieties and needs, is no doubt imperfect, but how grand and ennobling it can be. It is love that makes ordinary people rise to extraordinary heights of courage, sacrifice or kindness, even if briefly. To belong to someone and know that that person belongs to you seems like the only antidote to the radical alienation that each of us feels when we are born into this world. And yet, how messy such a love is, how devastating. Like a cyclone it sweeps through our lives, leaving in its wake a trail of destruction and suffering.

Does this mean that human relationships themselves, built as they are on illusions of permanence and reciprocity, are futile? Neither to give oneself to another, nor to receive another's exclusive attention: is that the inevitable course of self-transformation? *Mere to Giridhara Gopala, doosaro na koyi*, as Meera put it – only Giridhara Gopal is mine, nobody else. To love only God and none other as Rabia of Basra did: is that the predestined end of all love's journeys?

Which was the truer kind of love: the exclusive or the non-exclusive, the possessive or the non-possessive, matrimony or friendship, fidelity or promiscuity? I actually asked this question to a friend. She replied, 'Possessive love is so passionate and fulfilling, but it is also so messy. Non-possessive love, on the other hand, though it is cleaner and less-damaging, also seems to lack the passion and the pain that makes love so memorable.'

The love of the saint, the sage, the self-realized soul is indeed perfect, but it nevertheless lacks something of the warmth and vulnerability of the human. That is why Gandhi's sons, especially Harilal, found in him such an inadequate father. Harilal wanted to be loved as a son is entitled to be loved by a father, but Gandhi belonged equally to everyone. All those who came to him were like his sons and daughters. How could he give that singular attention or caring to his son?

Mira Behn or Madeleine Slade, too, could only love as a woman loves a man. Such love Gandhi did not accept, sending her away. Later, she turned to Prithvi Singh, the handsome terrorist converted to nonviolence. Unfortunately, even he could only respect her from a distance, not reciprocate her desire for him. Her burning passion remained unrequited. She had sacrificed everything for India but was unable to find her true love in this country. Oh the sorrows of unrequited love! Even the pain, loss, rejection and sense of betrayal of the jilted lover do not compare with this trauma!

Life without love is meaningless, but can human love be elevating and liberating, rather than painful and destructive?

Love Matters

As if in answer, I heard a voice telling me, *Live as if love matters*. Why 'as if'? Because in reality love may or may not matter. It would be impossible to determine the truth empirically. But when we live *as if* love matters, it really begins to.

If love *really* mattered, how would we live? Wouldn't we strive to be in accordance with our highest and purest intentions, secretly hopeful in the belief that somewhere, somehow our love was going to count and that everything would work itself out? *Eventually* even if not immediately? Wouldn't we live burning with the knowledge that we held deep within our hearts the greatest force in the universe, the power that was responsible for creation itself?

If this world was nothing but the manifestation of love, why should we despair? How else could it have come into being? What else could be its function? Because loving is also a way of knowing, the divine manifested itself thus only to know itself better. God is pure light; the world is His reflection, his Maya, his shakti or power.

Epilogue

Love or Eros is that power of attraction. It is the magnetism that holds the whirling electrons in their orbits around the denser nucleus; it is what binds one atom to another to form molecules and compounds. It is the spark that flies across pure space to connect two wires that are at crackling distance from one another. It is what gives colour and form to objects. It is the *rasa* or the relish that we all derive even from the most elementary of living functions. It is the *ananda*, the jouissance, which bubbles forth in every breath and in every particle. It is the deepest urge in the dullest matter, the consciousness implicate in the most inconscient substance. It is the force that moves the stars, prompting their magnificent births, propelling them all the way to their spectacular deaths aeons later. It is the throb of subatomic particles, the dance of Shiva.

So, *live as if love matters.*

What does *not* matter is whether we are alone or with someone, single or married, separated or together, divorced or wedded. In all circumstances and situations, we must live as if love matters. Love must be the constant, not the nature or the type of relationship.

In Tiruvannamalai, at the ashram of Yogi Ramsuratkumar, Devaki Ma, who had served the master with such attention, said that when love directs your actions the other person spontaneously feels loved. You have to make no declarations or speeches. Words are unnecessary because love informs every gesture.

Love ever gives, asking for no recompense. There is no dignity, no self-esteem in love. Go down on your knees a thousand times if you love someone. What does it matter who is at fault? Own up even to mistakes you did not commit. When you do so, the other person will come to your rescue and say, 'Oh no, it's really my fault.' But if you try to defend yourself, you are bound to end up quarrelling.

Forget the past, what did or did not happen, what you did or did not do. Remove all rancour and resentment from your heart. Don't cling to your grief. Open your spirit to kindness. Just see, isn't there an outpouring of grace at all times? Why are you unable to receive it? Why have you closed up your soul?

When you stand on the seashore of eternity, why have you brought only a thimble to carry back the waters of immortality? 'Strike, strike at

Epilogue

the root penury in my heart,' Tagore cried. So must you too, so that love expands your being and allows you to open yourself to receive and give it. It is in this exchange that you will be ennobled and blessed. This is how you will find yourself, no matter how broken or defeated you may be.

Don't be anxious when someone tells you he or she loves you. Why are you so *afraid* of love? Why have you become so suspicious of life's bounties? Why do you doubt so much, as if your questions will save you from pain? Why do you cavil so much, as if your complaints are justified? Where is your innocence? Why have you forgotten to be simple?

Why are you so preoccupied, harassed and frantic? Why are you always rushing about from place to place, task to task, and thought to thought? Why have you not stopped to look at the flowers at your feet? Why did you not pause to admire the moon tonight, as it hangs low in the grey sky, reddish yellow?

If no one cares for you, you care for others; nurture and embrace everyone. Assume responsibility. Carry your share of the burden. Learn to love. Make love your sadhana. Try to practise love.

Love yourself. Admit to who you are. Own up your body. Treat it well. Eat well, sleep adequately. Dress up occasionally. Radiate health. Dive deep within. Smile. Be content. Cherish your gifts. Show gratitude. Enjoy life.

Then, try to love those around you; start with your family. Charity, as they say, begins at home. Make those around you happy. Your own interest lies in making others happy. Learn to enjoy their joys; grieve with them in their sorrows.

Merge with the source. Become one with life. Accept that you don't exist, except in relation to others. Why attach so much importance to your own troubles? What is the salience of your individual existence in the larger scheme of things? As a fragment, you are nothing, but as the whole, the universe is yours.

Yogi Ramsuratkumar taught us how to love. Even when people spurned him, he did not stop blessing them. 'My father blesses you,' he would say, raising both hands. How he was mocked and reviled, jeered at, and even stoned. But his compassion was boundless.

He had no home. For years he lived in the open, sleeping under a tree or on the bench of a closed shop. When he was hounded by urchins, he took shelter in the Big Temple. When he thought that his touch would help someone, he touched their feet even when they kicked him in his teeth. Quoting Tulisdas, he would say that a saint is like a mango tree; when you throw stones at it, it only gives you back fruit.

Tsunami

On the morning of 26 December 2004, I woke up early, around 4:00 am. I had had disturbing dreams. I went to the samadhi at 5:00 am, in the bustle of the *sadhaks* cleaning and decorating. Everything seemed quiet. Then to the beautiful Ganesh temple nearby to enjoy the 5:45 am puja, complete with *nadaswaram* and *mridangam*.

Little did anyone know that a huge calamity was about to engulf the entire region from south-east Asia to India. A massive earthquake in Sumatra would divide islands, shift the tectonic plates, compress the earth, tilt the axis by an inch, even accelerate our planet's rotation by a microsecond. The quake, measuring 9 on the Richter scale, would cause massive upheavals in the Indian Ocean, unleashing tsunami waves several hundred metres high.

More than 45,000 people in Indonesia would be killed. In Sri Lanka, the losses would exceed 12,000 lives. India too would mourn more than 10,000 dead and several thousands more missing. Half the population of the 20,000 residents of Car Nicobar would be washed away. All over coastal south India, from Nagapattanam to Kanyakumari, there would be heaps of dead bodies washed back to the shore. In Pondicherry itself, there would be close to 900 dead or missing.

That morning, when we were buying presents and souvenirs at Splendour, the outlet of the Sri Aurobindo Society right on the sea front, we saw huge crowds at the embankment. They were watching the strange and scary tidal waves. For 40 years the beaches in town were receding, but now, when the sea pulled back, large stretches of sand were once again visible. But at the next moment, an equally large wave came crashing back into the coastline. The Pondy police, in their quaint red French-style caps, were busy pushing the people back. But the look on their faces said it all: something was terribly amiss.

Not fully aware of the extent of the tragedy, we got into the taxi that

Epilogue

would take us to the Madras Airport. The coastal highway was closed. There was an eerie quiet as we neared Chennai. We didn't know of the damage to the Marina Beach or the massive loss of lives. We not only reached the airport on time, but found that our flight back to Delhi was also to depart as scheduled.

The seventeenth to land on the fog congested airport in Delhi, we were still unaware of the extent of the disaster. It was only when we reached home that we realized that our only child had been frantically calling helpline numbers to find out our whereabouts or that my mother in Bangalore had called my mobile all afternoon, unable to get through.

The tsunami claimed many victims. I got away unscathed, not except for the crash of my palm computer which was simultaneous but unrelated. But my marriage was over – so I too felt the helplessness of someone watching a loved one die before his eyes.

I rewrote my lost essay on love. I did it because I felt it is something I owe not just to myself but to all the victims of the storm. Similarly, people whose lives were devastated by this calamity also found the strength to live again, to rebuild what they had lost. What is lost will also be restored to us in one form or another. Sri Aurobindo once said that it is providence that saves one when a thousand others are killed; it is also providence which chooses the one when a thousand others are saved.

The circumstances that govern our lives are not in our control. Anything may happen at any time. There are no guarantees in the here or the hereafter. The placid rhythm of life, so reassuring and predictable, may be jolted out of kilter in one sudden wrench. We may have unfinished business to execute when our time comes. Without forewarning, leaving everything in the middle, totally unprepared for departure, we may find that we have to make an immediate and unceremonious exit, suddenly to embark on a long journey – destination unknown. All this that we cherish and nurture may be taken away from us without the least prior warning.

What then is the use of love? How does love matter?

Live as if love matters. The nostrum that I had received in response to my prayers and sorrows also hid another meaning in its womb. To live as if love matters also means *to die* as if love matters. Love may or may not actually matter, but if we believe that it does, if we live as if it does, then it *will* matter. Similarly, if we can *die* as if love matters, then we will know how to live and love.

To die as if love matters is to die nobly, purely, simply and easily. It is to embrace death with open arms, to regard it as a friend, a liberator, a servitor of the divine – the door to immortality. It is to love death too, as we have loved life. It is to empty ourselves and offer everything up to cosmos.

To die as if love matters means not to cling to life, not to hold on tenaciously, not to be so possessive about our borrowed bodies. To have the grace to return what was not ours in the first place, to return the body benevolently, to smile as we exhale our last breath, to be calm in mind, to cultivate *Bodhichitta*, to gift ourselves away gently and quietly – that is the way of love. To die as if love matters is to be at peace – with oneself, with one's near and dear ones, and with the world. It is to make our concord with the here and the hereafter.

To die does not mean only to do so physically; it means to let go, give up clinging, and cease to crave. It means to let bygones be bygones. It means to move on, to rebuild your life, to end sorrowing over the past. A clean, pure, painless break with what has already ended. That is the lesson of death.

It's not as hard as it seems, actually. It's easy if you try.

Notes and References

1. Gupta, Mahendranath, *The Gospel of Sri Ramakrishna*, tr. Swami Nikhilananda, Ramakrishna-Vivekananda Center, New York, 1977
2. The famous lines from the Bhagavad Gita: *na jayate mriyate va kadacin nayam bhutva bhavita va na bhuyah/ajo nityah sasvato 'yam purano/na hanyate hanyamane sarire* (2.20) may be translated as: There is neither birth nor death at any time [for it]; it has not been born, does not take birth, nor will it do so [in the future]; it is eternal, ever-existing and primeval, and not slain with the killing of the body. Similar lines with similar meaning are also found in the Kathopanishad: *na jayate mriyate va vipascin/nayam kutascin na babhuva kascit/ajo nityah sasvato 'yam purano/na hanyate hanyamane sarire* (1.2.18).
3. Dostoyevsky, Fyodor, *The Brothers Karamazov*, tr. David Magarshack, Penguin, Harmondsworth, 1958
4. Ibid., p. 400
5. Ibid., pp. xix–xx
6. Hawthorne, Nathaniel, *Young Goodman Brown and Other Tales*, ed. Brian Harding, Oxford University Press, New York, 2009
7. Anantha Murthy, U. R., *Samskara: A Rite for a Dead Man*, tr. A. K. Ramanujan, Oxford University Press, New Delhi, 1977
8. Aurobindo, Sri, *The Foundations of Indian Culture*, Sri Aurobindo Ashram, Pondicherry (now Puducherry), 1985, p. 110
9. Prabhavananda, Swami, *Spiritual Heritage of India*, Doubleday, New York, 1963, p. 18
10. Ibid., p. 25
11. Prabhavananda, Swami, *Vedic Religion and Philosophy*, Sri Ramakrishna Math, Chennai, 1968, p. 8
12. Ibid., p. 20

13. Rao, Raja, *The Meaning of India*, Vision Books, New Delhi, 1996
14. Gambhirananda, Swami, *Eight Upanishads*, Advaita Ashrama, Kolkata, [1957], 1996
15. Chattopadhyaya, Bankim Chandra, *Anandmath*, tr. and adapted Basanta Koomar Roy, Vision Books, New Delhi, 1992; tr. Julius Lipner, Oxford University Press, New Delhi, 2005
16. See *Home and the World*, tr. Surendranath Tagore, Penguin Classics, New Delhi, 2005, and *Gora*, tr. Radha Chakravarty, Penguin, New Delhi, 2010
17. Paranjape, Makarand, *Mysticism in Indian English Poetry*, B. R. Publishers, Delhi, 1988, p. 221
18. Paranjape, Makarand, *Decolonization and Development: Hind Svaraj Revisioned*, Sage Publication, New Delhi, 1993, p. 69
19. O'Flaherty, Wendy Doninger, *The Rig Veda: An Anthology*, Penguin, New York, 1981, p. 10
20. Basham, A. L., *The Wonder That Was India: A Survey of the History and Culture of the Indian Sub-Continent before the Coming of the Muslims*, Grove Press, New York, 1959, p. 328
21. Krishnamurti, J., *Tradition and Revolution*, Orient Longman, New Delhi, 1972, p. 64
22. Aurobindo, Sri, *The Foundations of Indian Culture*, pp. 2, 4–6, 11, 14
23. Krishna, Daya, *Indian Philosophy: A Counter Perspective*, Oxford University Press, 1991, p. 4
24. Ibid., p. 6
25. Aurobindo, Sri, *The Foundations of Indian Culture*, p. 20
26. Ibid., p. 97
27. Nehru, Jawaharlal, *The Discovery of India*, Oxford University Press, New Delhi, 1994
28. Gandhi, M. K., *Hind Swaraj*, Navjivan, Ahmedabad, [1909], 1984, p. 30. Gandhi spells the word as 'Swaraj', but I prefer '*svaraj*', which is closer to Sanskrit, but also a way of distinguishing my use of it from Gandhi's. Ultimately, each of us must find our own understanding of this grand idea.
29. Gandhi, M. K., ed., *Young India*, 12 January 1928, p. 65
30. Gandhi, M. K., *Epigrams from Gandhiji*, comp. S. R. Tikekar, Publications Division, New Delhi, 1971, p. 156
31. Gandhi, M. K., *A Gandhi Reader*, ed. K. Swaminathan and C. N.

Patel, Orient Longman, Chennai, 1988, p. 134
32. This phrase has been used to describe Hinduism itself, but it actually means 'the perennial way'. I use it more in the latter sense.
33. Devin, Christine, *Shakuntala, or the Ring of Remembrance*, tr. Roger Harris, Editions Auroville Press International, Pondicherry (now Puducherry), 2000
34. Gandhi, M. K., *The Collected Works of Mahatma Gandhi*, Publications Division, New Delhi, vol 32, pp. 247–248
35. Aurobindo, Sri, *Uttarpara Speech*, Sri Aurobindo Ashram, Pondicherry, 1983; also available online: http://intyoga.online.fr/uttaspch.htm
36. Rao, Raja, *The Meaning of India*, Vision Books, New Delhi, 1998
37. Forster, E. M., *A Passage to India*, Penguin Classics, London, [1924], 2000
38. Kipling, Rudyard, *Kim*, Penguin Classics, London, [1901], 2011
39. Gandhi, Ramachandra, *I Am Thou: Meditations on the Truth of India*, Indian Philosophical Quarterly, Pune, 1984
40. Gandhi, M. K., *Hind Swaraj or Indian Home Rule*, Navjivan, Ahmedabad, [1909], 1984
41. Gandhi, M. K., *Collected Works of Mahatma Gandhi*, Publications Division, New Delhi, 1998, vol. 91, p. 326
42. Brunton, Paul, *A Search in Secret India*, [1934]; reprint B. I. Publications, New Delhi, 1982
43. Housden, Roger, *Travels through Sacred India*, HarperCollins, New Delhi, 1996
44. Rushdie, Salman, *Imaginary Homelands*, Granta, London, 1991, p. 224
45. Holland, Patrick, 'Travel Literature (Overview)', *Encyclopedia of Postcolonial Literatures*, ed. R. D. Killam, et al., Routledge, London and New York, 1996, pp. 1586–1589
46. Adams, Percy G., *Travel Literature and the Evolution of the Novel*, Kentucky Universit Press, Lexington, Kentucky, 1983; Porter, Dennis, *Haunted Journeys: Desire and Transgression in European Travel Writing*, Princeton Universit Press, Princeton, 1991; Pratt, Mary Louise, *Imperial Eyes: Travel Writing and Transculturation*, Routledge, London, 1992; Spurr, David, *The Rhetoric of Empire:*

Colonial Discourse in Journalism, Travel Writing, and Imperial Administration, Duke University Press, Durham, 1993
47. Rushdie, Salman, *Imaginary Homelands*, Granta, London, 1991
48. Yogananda, Paramahansa, *Autobiography of a Yogi*, Jaico, Bombay (now Mumbai), [1946], 1985
49. Brunton, Paul, *A Search in Secret India*, pp. 175–177
50. Ibid., p. 14
51. Ibid., p. 130
52. Ibid., p. 118
53. Ibid., p. 64
54. Ibid., p. 141
55. Ibid., p. 146
56. Ibid., p. 152
57. Ibid., p. 159
58. Ibid., p. 162
59. Ibid., p. 163
60. Ibid., p. 271
61. Ibid., p. 275
62. Ibid., p. 276
63. Ibid., p. 277
64. Ibid., pp. 277–278
65. Ibid., p. 281
66. Ibid., p. 301
67. Ibid., p. 304
68. Ibid., p. 311
69. http://rogerhousden.com/about/
70. Housden, Roger, *Travels through Sacred India*, p. xii
71. Ibid., p. xiii
72. Ibid., p. 7
73. Ibid., p. 15
74. Ibid
75. Ibid., p. 16
76. Ibid., p. 17
77. Ibid.
78. Ibid., p. 18
79. Ibid.

80. Ibid., p. 19
81. Ibid., p. 219
82. Ibid.
83. Ibid.
84. Ibid.
85. Ibid.
86. Ibid., p. xiv
87. But, amazingly, the story did not end there. Several years later, I had occasion to spend time with Illiyaraja's wife and daughter, in the company of Yogi Ramsuratkumar. They had come to seek his blessings in a new E-Class Merc. The daughter sang for the Yogi in a slightly high-pitched voice. The whole family was musical. Iliyaraja had helped with the building of the Yogi's ashram, but because of some misunderstanding, had stopped visiting his guru. Now his family had come to make amends.
88. *Harijan*, 9 January 1937
89. The success of Anna Hazare's experiments in Ralegaon Siddhi in Maharashtra is well-known. More recently, his campaign and fast against corruption drew the attention and support of a vast majority of Indian people.
90. http://www.swaminarayan.org/introduction/index.htm Our field trip and the subsequent study were precisely to explore this link – so vital to an understanding of the success of the Swaminarayans as a social and spiritual movement.
91. Williams, Raymond Brady, *An Introduction to Swaminarayan Hinduism*, Cambridge University Press, Cambridge, 2001, pp. 5–32
92. Ibid., p. 12
93. http://www.swaminarayan.org/scriptures/shikshapatri/index.htm
94. Parekh, Manilal C, *Shri Swami Narayana: A Gospel of Bhagavata-Dharma or God in Redemptive Action*, [1936], 3rd edition Bharatiya Vidya Bhavan, Bombay, 1980, p. 5
95. Williams, op. cit., 111.39 H. T. Dave's trans. as qtd., p 19
96. Ibid., p. 20
97. Parekh, op. cit., pp. 40–42
98. Williams, op. cit., p. 25

99. Ibid., p. 26
100. Ibid., pp. 64, 108
101. Ibid., p. 68
102. http://www.swaminarayan.org/introduction/index.htm
103. http://www.akshardham.com/gujarat/
104. This was the name chosen by his father. The middle name came from Annette Akroyd, an Englishwoman and a friend of his father's, who was probably present at the naming ceremony. The first record of the name is a school document of 1884 in English; there the name is spelt 'Ackroyd'. At St. Paul's and at Cambridge the name was registered as Aravinda Ackroyd Ghose. Until 1906, he signed his name in two or three different ways; the Bengali spelling was adopted when he moved to Bengal. After 1926, he became known as Sri Aurobindo.

Portions of this chapter have appeared in earlier versions in the introduction to The Penguin Sri Aurobindo Reader, ed. Makarand Paranjape, Penguin Books, New Delhi, 1999
105. Aurobindo, Sri, Sri Aurobindo Birth Centenary Library (SABCL), 30 volumes, Sri Aurobindo Ashram, Pondicherry, 1972, vol. 3, p. 47
106. Richard, Paul, The Dawn over Asia, Ganesan and Co., Madras, 1920, pp. 81–82
107. Aurobindo, Sri, The Complete Works of Sri Aurobindo (CWSA), 35 volumes, Sri Aurobindo, Ashram, Pondicherry, 1997, vol. 13, p. 39
108. Ibid., vol. 13, p. 3
109. Aurobindo, Sri, SABCL, vol. 26, p. 457
110. http://www.auroville.org/journals&media/avtoday/avt_feb_3.htm
111. Satprem, Mother's Agenda, Institute for Evolutionary Research, New York, 1979
112. The Mother's Agenda, vol. 13, p. 258
113. Vrekhem, Georges Van, Beyond Man: Life and Work of Sri Aurobindo and the Mother, HaperCollins, New Delhi, 1997, p. 490
114. Ibid., p. 487

115. Ibid., p. 472
116. Ibid., p. 495
117. Kumar, Udhaya, Mira to Mother: A Journey of Mind to Dioine, Sura Books, Chennai, 2006, p. 44
118. Nirodbaran, Twelve Years with Sri Aurobindo, 2nd edition, Sri Aurobindo Ashram, Pondicherry, 1988, p. 17
119. Nirodbaran, Correspondence with Sri Aurobindo, 2nd complete edition, Sri AurobindoAshram, Pondicherry, 1995, p. 172
120. Satprem, op. cit., vil. 8, p. 84
121. Ibid.
122. Satprem, op. cit., vol. 9, p. 336
123. Aurobindo, Sri, CWSA, vol. 13, p.1
124. Aurobindo, Sri, SABCL, vol. 16, p. 125
125. Nirodbaran, Correspondence with Sri Aurobindo, p. 133
126. Vrekhem, op. cit., p. 513
127. Ibid., p. 517
128. Maharaj, Nisargadatta, I Am That: Talks with Sri Nisargadatta Maharaj, tr. Maurice Frydman, ed. and rev. Sukhakar S. Dikshit, Chetana, Bombay, 1973, p. 444

HAY HOUSE
TITLES OF RELATED INTEREST

Being Ultimately Perfect
The 12th Chamgon Kenting Tai Situpa

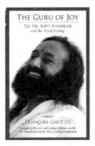

The Guru of Joy
Sri Sri Ravi Shankar & The Art of Living
François Gautier

The Mind of the Guru
Conversations with Spiritual Masters
Rajiv Mehrotra

Notes

Notes